Urban Maximilian Richter

AF287591

**Controlled Self-Organisation
Using Learning Classifier Systems**

Controlled Self-Organisation Using Learning Classifier Systems

by
Urban Maximilian Richter

Dissertation, Universität Karlsruhe (TH)
Fakultät für Wirtschaftswissenschaften, 2009
Tag der mündlichen Prüfung: 30. Juli 2009
Referent: Prof. Dr. Hartmut Schmeck
Korreferent: Prof. Dr. Karl-Heinz Waldmann

Impressum

Karlsruher Institut für Technologie (KIT)
KIT Scientific Publishing
Straße am Forum 2
D-76131 Karlsruhe
www.uvka.de

KIT – Universität des Landes Baden-Württemberg und nationales
Forschungszentrum in der Helmholtz-Gemeinschaft

KIT Scientific Publishing 2009
Print on Demand

ISBN: 978-3-86644-431-7

Controlled Self-Organisation Using Learning Classifier Systems

Zur Erlangung des akademischen Grades eines
Doktors der Wirtschaftswissenschaften

(Dr. rer. pol.)

von der Fakultät für Wirtschaftswissenschaften
der Universität Karlsruhe (TH)

genehmigte

DISSERTATION

von

Dipl.-Wi.-Ing. Urban Maximilian Richter

Tag der mündlichen Prüfung: 30. Juli 2009
Referent: Prof. Dr. Hartmut Schmeck
Korreferent: Prof. Dr. Karl-Heinz Waldmann

2009 Karlsruhe

I am not amused about killing so many chickens.

Abstract

The complexity of technical systems increases continuously. Breakdowns and fatal errors occur quite often, respectively. Therefore, the mission of *organic computing* is to tame these challenges in technical systems by providing appropriate degrees of freedom for self-organised behaviour. Technical systems should adapt to changing requirements of their execution environment, in particular with respect to human needs. According to this vision an organic computer system should be aware of its own capabilities, the requirements of the environment, and it should be equipped with a number of so-called *self-x-properties*. These self-x-properties provide the anticipated adaptiveness and allow reducing the complexity of system management. To name a few characteristics, organic systems should self-organise, self-adapt, self-configure, self-optimise, self-heal, self-protect, or self-explain.

To achieve these ambitious goals of designing and controlling complex systems, adequate methods, techniques, and system architectures have to be developed, since no general approach exists to build complex systems. Therefore, a regulatory feedback mechanism is proposed, the so-called *generic observer/controller architecture*, which constitutes one way to achieve *controlled self-organisation* in technical systems.

To improve the design of organic computing systems, the observer/controller architecture is applied to (generic) multi-agent scenarios from the predator/prey domain. These simple test scenarios serve as testbeds for evaluation. Furthermore, the aspect of *(on-line) learning* as part of the controller is specially described and the question is investigated, how technical systems can adapt to dynamically changing environments using *learning classifier systems* as a machine learning technique.

Particularly, learning classifier systems are at the focus of many organic computing projects, because they are a family of genetic- and rule-based machine learning methods that fit well into the observer/controller framework. One of their great advantages is that classifier systems aim at the autonomous generation of potentially human-readable results, because they provide a compact generalised representation whilst also maintaining high predictive accuracy. But, learning classifier systems also have drawbacks. The number of reinforcement learning cycles a classifier system requires for learning largely depends on the complexity of the learning task. Thus, different approaches to reduce this complexity and to speed up the learning process are investigated and compared.

A straightforward way to reduce this complexity is to decompose the task into smaller sub-problems and learn the sub-problems in parallel. It is shown that speeding up the learning process largely depends on the designer's decision, how to decompose a problem into smaller and modular sub-problems. Thus, different *single-agent learning approaches* are investigated, which use learning classifier systems that learn in parallel.

Furthermore, these parallel learning classifier systems are compared with the organic approach of the *two-levelled learning architecture* as part of the organic controller. At the on-line level (level 1) the proposed architecture learns about the environment, and about the performance of its control strategies. It does so on-line. Level 2 implements a planning capability based on a simulated model of the environment. At this level the agent can test and compare different alternative strategies off-line, and thus plan its next action without actually acting in the environment.

Finally, the potential and relevance of the different learning approaches is evaluated in the case of simple predator/prey test scenarios with respect to more demanding application scenarios.

Acknowledgements

Writing scientific publications, especially this thesis, is and has mostly been a lonely business. At the end, only my name will occur on the title. All mistakes and all achievements will be linked to me. However, research does not take place in an evacuated place. There have always been people, supporting my way. Thus, I would like to thank all those people, who have accompanied my way during the last years, months, and weeks and who have given me advice in many kinds so that I have finally accomplished this thesis.

Foremost, I would like to thank Prof. Dr. Hartmut Schmeck, my doctoral adviser, for supporting me and my research during the last years. I have greatly benefited from his long experience and his way of leading his research group. He has offered me many degrees of freedom to settle down on research topics that became of my personal interest. I am also extremely thankful for his commitment to timely review this thesis despite his busy timetable.

I would also like to thank Prof. Dr. Karl-Heinz Waldmann, from Universität Karlsruhe (TH), who, without hesitation, accepted the request to serve as second reviewer on the examination committee. Furthermore, many thanks to Prof. Dr. Andreas Oberweis and Prof. Dr. Hagen Lindstädt, both from Universität Karlsruhe (TH), who served as examiner and chairman respectively on the examination committee.

I am grateful to my friends and colleagues of the research group *Efficient Algorithms* for the excellent and lively working atmosphere within the team. Special thanks to Jürgen Branke for mentoring my research project and Matthias Bonn for supporting my research by *JoSchKa*, a really helpful tool to distribute computational intensive simulation tasks among free workstations and servers. Also, many thanks to Andreas Kamper and Holger Prothmann for productive, interesting, and encouraging discussions and reviewing parts of this thesis. Thanks to all others of *LS1* for – not only – having funny discussions on lunchtime.

Similarly, I am grateful to all external collaborators and project partners. In this context, special thanks to Prof. Dr.-Ing. Christian Müller-Schloer and Moez Mnif, both from Leibniz Universität Hannover. Various parts of this thesis are based on a creative collaboration with them. I have often benefited from common project meetings, their experiences, and their opinion. Moreover, thanks to Emre Çakar, Jörg Hähner, Fabian Rochner, and Sven Tomforde for making travel to Hannover, several workshops, and conferences a lovely and regular experience.

Last but not least, I would like to thank my family and friends for their permanent support and being there even in stressful and chaotic times. Special thanks to my parents and my sister, who always believed in me and supported my way in every respect. Thanks to my mother, my sister Helene, and Jan-Dirk for reviewing this thesis concerning language and grammar. Moreover, I am grateful to Niklas, Ana, and mostly Jule for their constant encouragement and for making my Karlsruhe years wonderful and unforgettable.

Karlsruhe, October 2009 *Urban Maximilian Richter*

Contents

List of Tables

List of Figures

List of Abbreviations

$\#kc$ – The number of killed chickens

2PXCS – Two parallel instances of the extended classifier system

3PXCS – Three parallel instances of the extended classifier system

d, d_j – The duration of a noise signal

e_x, e_y, e_h – The relative emergence indicators

HXCS – The hierarchical organised extended classifier system

i, i_j – The intensity of a noise signal

LCS – A learning classifier system

L2 – Learning (or planning) on level 2 of the generic observer/controller architecture

OC – Organic computing

SuOC – The system under observation and control

t_x, t_y, t_h – Predefined thresholds of critical emergence values

XCS – The extended classifier system, as introduced in [Wil95]

Chapter 1

Introduction

In the Nevada desert, an experiment has gone horribly wrong. A cloud of nanoparticles – micro-robots – has escaped from the laboratory. This cloud is self-sustaining and self-reproducing. It is intelligent and learns from experience. For all practical purposes, it is alive. It has been programmed as a predator. It is evolving swiftly, becoming more deadly with each passing hour. Every attempt to destroy it has failed. And we are the prey.

As fresh as today's headlines, Michael Crichton's most compelling novel yet tells the story of a mechanical plague and the desperate efforts of a handful of scientists to stop it. Drawing on up-to-the-minute scientific fact, Prey *takes us into the emerging realms of nanotechnology and artificial distributed intelligence – in a story of breathtaking suspense.* Prey *is a novel you can't put down. Because time is running out. [Cri02]*

These words cited above are written on the hardcover version of the techno-thriller novel *Prey* by Michael Crichton. Of course, the book is science fiction and human beings fighting against a swarm of micro-robots seems to be not realistic so far, but an interesting story is told that features relatively new advances in computer science, such as artificial life, swarm intelligence, self-organisation, genetic algorithms, or multi-agent-based computing. Major themes of the book deal with the threat of intelligent micro-robots escaping from human control and becoming autonomous, self-replicating, and, by that, dangerous. Many aspects of the story, such as the cloud-like nature of the nanoparticles and their nature-inspired process of evolution closely follow research done by computer scientists in the past (few) years, see e. g., the fields of evolutionary computation [FOW66, Gol89, Hol75], computational intelligence [Eng02, PMG98], or artificial life[1].

---

[1] http://www.alife.org

As short-sighted decision-making at the corporate level can lead to a disaster when the companies involved control dangerous new technology, the book is about the potential consequences, if suitable controls are not placed on biotechnology, before it will develop to such an extent that it can threaten the survival of life on earth. Of course, this is an important discussion and scientists doing research in informatics or biologically inspired informatics have to cope with it.

Hence, this thesis will focus on the challenge of designing technical systems, which are inspired by swarm intelligence, multi-agent systems, or self-organisation and enable controllability of these systems at the same time. The research on these different domains has intensified. A growing number of conferences[2], workshops[3], and journals[4] supports this trend.

Paradigms of computing are emerging based on modelling and developing computer-based systems exploiting ideas that are observed in nature. The human body's autonomic nervous system inspires the design of self-organising computer systems, as proposed in IBM's *autonomic computing* initiative[5]. Some evolutionary systems are modelled in analogy to colonies of ants or other insects. Highly-efficient and highly-complex distributed systems are developed to perform certain functions or tasks using the behaviour of insects as inspiration, e. g., swarms of bees, flocks of birds, schools of fish, or herds of animals.

Self-organising systems are not science fiction any more, but problems with increasing complexity and controllability of technical systems call for new system architectures, as postulated in the field of *organic computing (OC)* and explicitly investigated in this thesis.

1.1 Motivation

As mentioned in [BMMS+06], the impressive progress in computing technology over the past decades has not only led to an exponential increase in available computing power, but also to a shrinking of computer chips to a miniature format. While only twenty years ago, the predominant computing platform was a company mainframe shared by many users, today, a multitude of embedded computing devices surrounds us, including PDA, cell phone, digital camera, navigation system, MP3-player, etc. in everyday life. An additional trend during recent years has been that these devices are equipped with (often wireless) communication interfaces, allowing them to interact and exchange information.

---

[2]E. g., the International Joint Conference on Autonomous Agents and Multi-agent Systems (AAMAS) or the Genetic and Evolutionary Computation Conference (GECCO)

[3]E. g., the International Workshop on Learning and Adaptation in Multi-agent Systems (LAMAS) or the International Workshop on Learning Classifier Systems (IWLCS)

[4]E. g., Artificial Life (MIT Press Journals) or ACM Transactions on Autonomous and Adaptive Systems (TAAS)

[5]http://www.research.ibm.com/autonomic or see Section 4.5.1

Amongst others this outlook towards smaller, more intelligent, and more numerous devices surrounding everybody in his everyday life is given by the paradigm of *ubiquitous computing*, which was first introduced by Mark Weiser in [Wei91]. Future information processing will be integrated into a broad range of everyday and everywhere objects making these objects intelligent. These devices will be interconnected and they will communicate over various communication channels. Thus, networks of intelligent systems will grow, and their behaviour will no longer be predictable with certainty due to interaction effects, see [Sch05a].

In addition, other large technical systems consist of more and more interconnected electronic devices. For example, in cars, numerous processors and embedded systems keep the vehicle on the road, control the engine with respect to combustion and pollution, assist the driver, provide security with air bags and seat belt systems, provide functions such as air conditioning, navigation, parking assistant, information services, and entertain the passengers. All these controllers are connected to a complex communication network. And this development has not stopped yet.

Technical innovations are only a stone's throw away from scenarios like smart factory, with flexible robots self-organising to satisfy the needs at hand [Gui08], or smart cars that adapt to different drivers and road conditions, communicate with other cars on special events, or integrate personal devices (PDA, mobile telephone, or notebook) into their network.

While this development is exciting, the resulting systems become increasingly complex, up to the point where they can no longer be designed or used easily. Even today, in the automotive sector, it is estimated that about half of all car break-downs are caused by electric and electronic components. E. g., in 2005 weak car batteries head the table of causes for break-downs listed by the ACE Auto Club Europa with 25% [ACE06], while electronic components are listed on third position (currently) with 13%, still increasing their percentage.

Thus, the questions arise, how to design such complex distributed and highly interconnected systems, and how to make them reliable and usable. Clearly, the designer is not able to foresee all possible system configurations, and to prescribe proper behaviours for all cases. Additionally, the user is relieved from having control in detail over all parameters of the system, allowing him or her to influence the system on a higher level, e. g., by setting goals.

OC has the vision to meet this challenge of coping with increasing complexity by making technical systems more life-like, and endowing them with properties such as self-organisation, self-configuration, self-repair, or adaptation [Sch05b]. Future systems will possess certain degrees of freedom to handle unforeseen situations and act in a robust, flexible, and independent way. Thus, these systems will exhibit self-organised behaviour, which makes them able to adapt to a changing surrounding. That is why, in the field of OC, these systems are called *organic*. Hence, an OC system is a system, which dynamically adapts to the current situation of its environment, but still obeys goals set by humans. In addition to this environmental awareness, systems

3

providing services for humans will adjust themselves to the users' requirements (and not *vice versa*). Based on these trends, the question, also addressed in this thesis, is not, whether complexity increases or informatics is confronted with emergent behaviour, but how new technical systems will be designed that have the possibility to cope with the emerging global behaviour of self-organising systems by adequate control actions.

1.2 Objectives and Approach

As outlined before and motivated in Chapter 2, OC has a major research interest in new system architectures that self-organise and adapt exploiting certain degrees of freedom. To achieve these ambitious goals of designing and controlling self-organising systems, adequate methods and system architectures have to be developed, since no general approach exists to build OC systems. Therefore, OC proposes a regulatory feedback mechanism, the so-called *generic observer/controller architecture* [MS04], which constitutes one way to achieve *controlled self-organisation* in technical systems.

Using this control loop, an organic system will adapt over time to its changing environment. It is obvious that this architecture could benefit from learning capabilities to tackle these challenges. Therefore and as described in detail in Chapter 4, the controller has been refined by a *two-levelled learning approach*. At the on-line level (level 1) the proposed architecture learns about the environment, and about the performance of its control strategies. Level 2 implements a planning capability based on a simulated model of the environment. At this level an agent can test and compare different alternative strategies off-line, and plan its next action without actually acting in the environment. Thus, the two research questions addressed in this thesis are defined in the following in more detail.

1. What does it mean to establish and utilise controlled self-organisation in the context of technical OC scenarios specially focussing on *learning classifier systems (LCSs)* as machine learning technique on level 1 of the proposed two-levelled learning architecture?

2. How is the (on-line) learning process speeded up?

In other words, the observer/controller architecture is refined into a form that can serve as a generic template containing a range of components, which should be necessary in a range of OC application scenarios. It enables a regulatory feedback mechanism and the use of machine learning techniques to improve a single-agent's or a multi-agent system's behaviour in technical domains with the following characteristics.

- There exists a need for on-line decision-making,

- decisions are based on (aggregated) sensor information,

- decisions are influenced by and based on decisions that have been taken by other agents, and

- several agents act with a cooperative/competitive, well-defined, and high-level goal.

Thus, the agents are assumed to have the following characteristics.

- The ability to process, aggregate, and quantify sensor information,

- the ability to use this information to update and control their (local) behaviour, and

- the ability to cope with limited communication capabilities, e. g., caused by local neighbourhoods, low bandwidth, power restrictions, etc.

In the following, scenarios are mainly investigated, where a collection of (non-adaptive) agents is observed and controlled by a centralised observer/controller architecture. In these scenarios, learning takes place on a higher level of abstraction.

The general approach to answering the thesis questions has been to investigate selected ideas of the generic observer/controller architecture within different multi-agent scenarios, which serve as representative OC test scenarios. Since the main goal of any testbed is to facilitate the trial and evaluation of ideas that show great promise for real world applications, e. g., smart production cells, smart factories, logistics, traffic, automotive industry, or information technology, the chosen test scenarios are assumed to have the following properties.

- To allow for generalisation of the results, each test scenario should exhibit a different emergent phenomenon, which could be observed and controlled, hence justifying the utility of the observer/controller architecture.

- On the other hand, the test scenarios should be rather simple to implement and easy to understand.

Therefore, all of the thesis contributions have originally been developed in simulated scenarios of the *predator/prey domain*, which has served as demonstrating and evaluating scenario for manifold research ideas for a long time.

An initial assumption was that in domains with the above characteristics agents should map their sensor information to control actions. LCSs could provide such a mapping. Therefore, their suitability had to be investigated. The use of LCSs is specially focussed on level 1 of the proposed two-levelled learning architecture and methods are successfully contributed, which equip such multi-agent scenarios, as mentioned above, with OC ideas.

5

While LCSs have drawbacks in learning speed, which seem to be critical in combination with technical applications, mechanisms have been investigated, which speed up the learning process of LCSs. These approaches are compared with the proposed two-levelled learning architecture that learns on-line (level 1) about the environment and about the performance of its control strategies, while on level 2 a planning capability is used, based on a simulation model of the environment, where an agent can test and compare different alternative strategies off-line, and thus plan its next action without actually acting in the environment.

1.3 Major Contributions

In brief, this thesis makes three main contributions related to the research fields of OC. First, OC research is summarised that has been done over the last five years and specially focusses on the design of the generic observer/controller architecture, which serves as a framework for building OC systems. This architecture allows for self-organisation, but at the same time enables adequate reactions to control the – sometimes completely unexpected – emerging global behaviour of these self-organised technical systems. The proposed architecture can be used in a centralised, distributed, or multi-levelled and hierarchically structured way to achieve controlled self-organisation as a new design paradigm. Thus, Chapters 3 and 4 address related work in the field of architectures for controlled self-organisation. Some contents have been published in [ÇMMS+07, SMSÇ+07, SMS08]. Chapter 4 mainly bases on [BMMS+06, RMB+06].

Secondly, the idea of a two-level learning approach is introduced as part of the controller. Since a learning capability is an essential feature of OC systems, the generic architecture and, in particular, the controller, has to include adequate components for learning. The work, presented in this thesis, focusses on on-line learning and specially on the investigation of LCSs as an adequate machine learning technique.

Thirdly, several distributed variants of LCSs are investigated with the objective of improving learning speed and effectiveness. While conventional LCSs have drawbacks in learning speed, this thesis investigates possible modifications by decomposing a problem into smaller sub-problems and by learning these subtasks independently. Furthermore, the performance of these variants of on-line LCSs are compared to the combination of on-line learning and off-line planning capabilities, as suggested by the observer/controller architecture.

Since the second and the third contributions are inherently domain-specific, the following chapters provide a general specification as well as an implementation within multi-agent test scenarios. The used multi-agent test scenarios are selected from the predator/prey domain and can therefore be generalised to other domains. Also, work, which has been done in [RRS08], is shortly summarised in Chapter 6. Chapters 5, 6, and 8 present results that have been published in [MRB+07, RM08, RPS08].

In Chapter 9, an extended review of the empirical results validating the major contributions of this theses is given.

1.4 Reader's Guide to this Thesis

To enjoy oneself reading this thesis and to identify the most relevant chapters from a personal point of view, a general description of the contents of each chapter should guide the reader. The presented work is structured as follows.

- Chapter 2 summarises the vision of OC, since this thesis is mainly based on OC research topics and copes with an interdisciplinary view, unknown in literature before, which connects different research fields, e. g., control theory, machine learning, or multi-agent theory.

- In Chapter 3 related work concerning the topic of controlled self-organisation is reviewed. Self-organisation and emergent phenomena have been research topics in several areas. The most relevant ideas are summed up with regard to this thesis.

- In Chapter 4 the generic observer/controller architecture is introduced, which serves as a framework to build OC systems. The presented work is focussed on the centralised variant of this design paradigm and every module of this architecture is explained in detail. To compare the organic approach to other regulatory feedback mechanisms, the two-level learning approach as part of the controller is specially described.

- Since the capability to adapt to dynamically changing environments is in the main focus of OC systems, the aspect of learning is investigated in detail. Thus, LCSs are presented in Chapter 5. This chapter reviews the state of the art from LCS's literature and defines the idea of parallel classifier systems to speed up the learning process.

- Chapter 6 introduces the domains used as test scenarios within the thesis. A nature-inspired scenario has been implemented and serves as a testbed to validate the learning cycle of a centralised observer/controller architecture.

- General design decisions concerning the implemented learning architectures with respect to the nature-inspired test scenario are outlined in Chapter 7. The actual analysis of the results is given in Chapter 8.

- Chapter 9 summarises the contributions of this thesis and outlines the most promising directions for future work. Since several chapters of this thesis contain their own related work sections describing the research most relevant to their contents, this chapter is used for a survey about OC from an LCS's perspective.

1.5 How this Thesis Was Written

This thesis is the outcome of several years of research with financial support by the German Research Foundation (Deutsche Forschungsgemeinschaft, DFG) within the priority programme 1183 OC. Several papers have been published with different colleagues in a close cooperation between the research group of my doctoral adviser, Prof. Dr. Hartmut Schmeck, and the group of Prof. Dr.-Ing. Christian Müller-Schloer from Leibniz Universität Hannover and were taken as the basis for the following chapters. For reasons of presentation, the chronological order, in which the articles appeared, does not coincide with the presented order within the following chapters.

Chapter 2

Organic Computing (OC)

It is not the question, whether *adaptive and self-organising systems will emerge, but* how *they will be designed and controlled.* [Sch05b, SMSÇ+07]

Since the work presented here is mainly based on OC research topics, this chapter summarises the vision of OC. Motivation and challenges of this young research field are explained in short, before the contributions of this thesis are described in the following chapters.

As outlined in Section 1.1, the increasing complexity of technical systems calls for research into new design principles. It is impossible for a designer to foresee all possible configurations and to explicitly specify the entire behaviour of a complex system on a detailed level. In particular, if the system consists of many interacting components, it may exhibit new, emergent properties that are very difficult to anticipate. Emergent phenomena are often identified, when the global behaviour of a system appears more coherent and directed than the behaviour of individual parts of the system (the whole is more than the sum of its parts). More generally, such phenomena arise in the study of complex systems, where many parts interact with each other and where the study of the behaviour of individual parts reveals little about system-wide behaviour. Especially, in the area of multi-agent systems emergence and self-organisation have been studied extensively, see [DFH+04, DGK06] for two recent surveys.

Despite their complexity, living creatures are very robust and have the natural ability to learn and adapt to an uncertain and dynamic environment. The idea of OC is therefore to address complexity by making technical systems more life-like and to develop an alternative to the explicit total *a priori* specification of a system. Instead, organic systems should adapt and self-organise with respect to some degrees of freedom. But, OC systems should be designed with respect to human needs, and have to be trustworthy, robust, adaptive, and flexible. They will show the so-called *self-x-properties*: Self-configuration, self-optimisation, self-healing, self-explanation, and self-protection. Such systems are expected to learn about their environment during life time, will survive attacks and other unexpected breakdowns, will adapt to their users, and will react sensibly, even if they encounter a new situation, for which they have not been programmed explicitly. In other words, an OC system should behave more life-like (organic).

This can only be achieved by adding some kind of awareness of their current situation to the system elements and the ability to provide appropriate responses to dynamically changing environmental conditions. The principles of OC are strongly related to the objectives of IBM's *autonomic computing* initiative, see Section 4.5.1. But, while autonomic computing is directed towards maintaining server architectures, which should be managed without active interaction between man and machine [KC03, Ste05], OC's focus is more general in its approach and addresses large collections of intelligent devices, providing services to humans, adapted to the requirements of their execution environment [Sch05b]. Thus, besides showing the self-x-properties, interaction between man and machine is an essential part of OC systems.

The term *organic computing* was formed in 2002 as a result of a workshop aiming at future technologies in the field of computer engineering. The outlines of the workshop and the OC vision were first formulated in the joint position paper [ACE+03] of the section of computer engineering *(Technische Informatik)* of the *Gesellschaft für Informatik (German Association for Informatics, GI)* and the *Informationstechnische Gesellschaft (German Association for Information Technology)*. In 2005, the German Research Foundation (Deutsche Forschungsgemeinschaft, DFG) approved a priority research programme on OC for six years (2005–2011). This research programme addresses fundamental challenges in the design of OC systems; its goal is a deeper understanding of emergent global behaviour in self-organising systems and the design of specific concepts and tools to construct and control OC systems for technical applications. Topics, such as adaptivity, reconfigurability, emergence of new properties, and self-organisation, play a major role. Currently, the research programme provides funding for 18 research projects with a total volume of around EUR 2 million per year. The topics of these projects range from traffic control over robot coordination to chip design. Information on the different projects can be found via the OC website[1].

Self-organising systems bear several advantages compared to classical, centrally controlled systems. Amongst others, the failure of a single component should not cause a global malfunction of the whole system. Such a system will be able to adapt to changing circumstances. As a result, self-organisation could be described as a method of reducing the *complexity* of computer systems.

In such self-organising systems the local interaction of the system elements *may* result in an emergent global behaviour, which can have positive (desired) as well as

---

[1]http://www.organic-computing.de/spp

negative (undesired) effects. Self-organisation and emergent phenomena also initiate new problems unknown in the engineering of classical technical systems. A global emergent behaviour usually is a nonlinear combination of local behaviours. Its design process with both potential design directions (top-down vs. bottom-up design) turns out to be a highly non-trivial task: For a top-down approach it is hard to deduce adequate local rules from a desired global behaviour, and in the bottom-up direction it quite often remains unclear how local rules go together with global behaviour, see [KC03].

In this context and in order to assess the behaviour of the technical system and – if necessary – for a regulatory feedback to control its dynamics, the so-called *observer/controller architecture* has become widespread in the OC community as a design paradigm to assure the fulfilment of system goals (given by the developer or user), see Chapter 4. The observer/controller uses a set of sensors and actuators to measure system variables and to influence the system. Together with the *system under observation and control (SuOC)*, the observer/controller forms the so-called *organic system*. An observer/controller loop enables adequate reactions to control the – sometimes completely unexpected – undesired emerging global behaviour resulting from local agents' behaviour.

However, besides this fascinating outlook, the *materialisation* of the OC vision depends on several crucial factors, which are summarised in [Sch05b].

- Designers of OC systems have to guarantee that self-organising systems, based on OC principles, do not show unwanted (emergent) behaviour. This is particularly important, when malfunction can have disastrous consequences, e. g., in safety critical applications. The generic observer/controller architecture, as described in Chapter 4, seems to be a promising approach in asserting certain functionality and additionally in keeping the system at an effective state of operation. OC systems will only become accepted, if users can trust them. Therefore, trust/reliability could turn out to be the most important prerequisite for acceptance.

- Closely related is the need for the user to monitor and influence the system: It has to be guaranteed that it is still the user, who guides the overall system. Therefore, the system developer has to design user interfaces, which can be used to control the system – which means that there has to be a possibility to take corrective actions from outside the system. The generic observer/controller architecture considers this requirement.

- Developers of OC systems have to determine appropriate rules and patterns for local behaviour in large networks of smart devices in order to provide some requested higher functionality. Important topics in the design of self-organising systems are the utilisation of arising emergent phenomena and controlling the local level in such a way that the system shows the desired behaviour at global

11

level. Therefore, the task is to derive a set of behavioural and interaction rules that, if embedded in individual autonomous elements, will induce a certain global characteristic. The inverse direction of anticipating the global system behaviour based on known local decision rules is also very important in this regard.

- On interacting with humans an OC system has to show context sensitive characteristics and has to filter information and services according to the current situation or user's needs. In general, an OC system has to be aware of its environment and should act accordingly.

- Building OC systems, one has to think carefully about how to design the necessary degrees of freedom for the intended adaptive behaviour. Certain degrees of freedom are needed to enable self-organisation, but it is easily imaginable that allowing the different parts of a system a broad range of possible (re-)actions in a specific situation could result in uncontrollable chaos.

- The implementation of learning abilities as part of OC systems provides great chances, but also bears several problems. Learning systems often learn from mistakes. In fact, they will make mistakes, if no countermeasures are taken. Additionally, developers can guide the learning process of a learning system and they can assure that the system does not develop itself in an unwanted (emergent) manner. This aspect of learning is focussed on in detail in Chapter 5.

This list could be considerably expanded, but it already represents the most important topics. The following chapter will concentrate on the organic vision of *controlled self-organisation.*

Chapter 3

Controlled Self-Organisation

> *Technological systems become organised by commands from outside, as when human intentions lead to the building of structures or machines. But, many natural systems become structured by their own internal processes: These are self-organising systems, and the emergence of order within them is a complex phenomenon that intrigues scientists from all disciplines.* *[YGWY88]*

Self-organising systems are well known from nature and have been studied in domains like physics, chemistry, and biology. In recent years research interest has succeeded to apply concepts of self-organisation to technical systems. The reason is a paradigm shift from monolithic systems to large networked systems driven by the technological change of integrating more information processing into the everyday life, objects, and activities. The necessity to find new approaches to cope with upcoming problems of increasing complexity attracts awareness to the principle of self-organisation.

OC systems should use self-organisation to achieve a certain *externally provided* goal. Furthermore, the system has to adapt to changing environmental requirements and to be capable to deal with (unanticipated) undesired emergent behaviour. Therefore, OC systems are assumed to support *controlled self-organisation*. Whenever necessary, this requires a range of methods for monitoring and analysing the system performance and for providing appropriate control actions. The generic observer/controller architecture – this architecture is introduced in detail in Chapter 4 – promises to provide the necessary components for satisfying all these demands, see Figure 3.1.

Similar to the MAPE cycle (monitor, analyse, plan, and execute) of IBM's autonomic computing initiative, see Section 4.5.1, a closed control loop is defined to keep the properties of the self-organising SuOC within preferred boundaries. The observer observes certain (raw) attributes of the system and aggregates them to situation parameters, which concisely characterise the observed situation from a

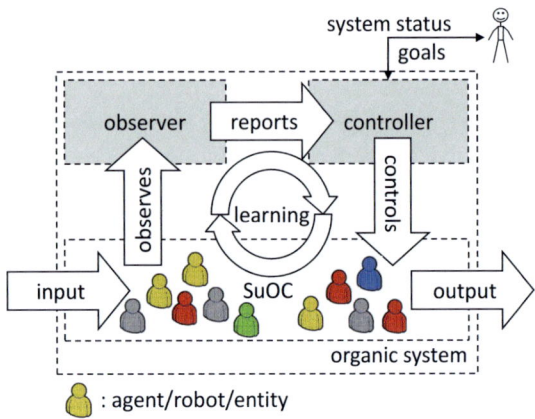

Figure 3.1: *Simplified view of the generic observer/controller architecture*

global point of view, and passes them to the controller. The controller acts according to an evaluation of the observation (which might include the prediction of future behaviour). If the current situation does not satisfy the requirements, it will take action(s) to direct the system back into its desired range, will observe the effect of the intervention(s), and will take further actions, if necessary. Using this control loop an organic system will adapt over time to its changing environment. It is obvious that the controller could benefit from learning capabilities to tackle these challenges. Although the observing and controlling process is executed in a continuous loop, and the SuOC is assumed to run autonomously, even if the observer/controller architecture is not present – even though in a suboptimal way. Furthermore, *emergence* plays a central role in OC systems. Emergent and self-organising behaviour has been observed in nature, demonstrated in a variety of computer simulated systems in artificial life research, and it has also occurred in highly complex technical systems, where it has quite often led to unexpected global functionality [BDT99]. Despite the importance of a rigorous description of these phenomena, the quantitative analysis of technical self-organising systems is still a rather unexplored area. Therefore, this chapter describes the understanding of the basic mechanisms of self-organisation and emergent behaviour in complex (organic) ensembles, summarises related work, and provides appropriate (metrics and) tools for utilising *controlled self-organisation.*

In Section 3.1 research is summarised that has been done in the area of self-organisation and in Section 3.2 about the related concept of emergence. There may be instances of self-organisation without emergence and emergence without self-organisation, and there is evidence in literature that the phenomena are not the same.

However, future research is needed to clarify the relation between these two terms. Finally, in Section 3.3 an architectural-based approach for the design and engineering of technical systems is proposed that makes use of controlled self-organisation, before describing the OC approach in Chapter 4.

3.1 Self-Organisation

The dynamics of a system can tend by themselves to increase the inherent order of a system. This idea has a long history, being first introduced by the French philosopher René Descartes. In 1947, the term *self-organisation* was introduced by the psychiatrist and engineer William Ross Ashby [Ash47]. Cyberneticans, like Heinz von Foerster, Stafford Beer, Gordon Pask, and Norbert Wiener, took up this concept and associated it with *general systems theory* in the 1960ies. In the 1970ies and 1980ies physicists adopted self-organisation to the field of *complex systems* and established the topic in scientific literature. Even if the concept of self-organisation is very promising to solve complex problems, as explained in [Ger07], the notion of self-organisation will remain somewhat vague, and discussion has been widespread. The extensive FAQ-list[1] is a good link to research that has been done so far.

The term self-organisation is used frequently, but a generally accepted meaning has not emerged. As the list grows, it becomes increasingly difficult to decide whether these phenomena are all based on the same process, or whether the same label has been applied to several different processes. Despite its intuitive simplicity as a concept, self-organisation has proven notoriously difficult to describe and define formally or mathematically. Thus, it is entirely possible that any precise definition might not include all the phenomena, to which the term of self-organisation has been applied. In the following, it will not be attempted to give a new definition facing the philosophical problem of defining *self*, the cybernetic problem of defining *system*, or the universal problem of defining *organisation*. Instead, research is summarised that has been done so far to characterise the conditions necessary to call a system self-organising. Answers will be given to the following questions: What is a self-organising system? What is it not? And what are possible approaches to engineer self-organising technical systems?

3.1.1 Understanding Self-Organisation from the Viewpoint of Different Sciences

As pointed out by Carlos Gershenson in [Ger07], the term self-organisation has been used with different meanings, e.g., in computer science [HG03, MMTZ06], biology [CDF+03, FCG06], mathematics [Len64], cybernetics [Ash62, von60], synergetics

---

[1]http://www.calresco.org/sos/sosfaq.htm

[Hak81], thermodynamics [NP77], complexity [Sch03], information theory [Sha01], and evolution of language [de 99]. Selected ideas, which specially contribute to the idea of OC, are summarised from the viewpoint of different sciences.

Self-Organisation in Nature

According to [CDF$^+$03], self-organisation in biological systems is often described as

> *a process, in which a pattern at the global level of a system solely emerges from numerous interactions among the lower level components of the system. Moreover, the rules specifying interactions among the system's components are executed using only local information, without reference to the global pattern [YGWY88].*

A self-organising system in nature acts without centralised control and operates according to local contextual information. Thus, spontaneous behaviour without external control produces a new organisation reacting to environmental changes/disturbances. Natural systems often show a robust behaviour, they adapt to changes, and they are able to ensure their own survivability. There are quite a few examples of natural systems, which are not at all robust (in particular at the individual level) and which cannot adapt to changes. Robustness often is a property of a population/swarm, not of an individual. In some cases, self-organisation is linked to emergent behaviour, as described later in Section 3.2. Individual components carry out a simple task, and as a whole these components are able to carry out a complex task emerging in a coherent way through the local interactions of various components. Typical examples from nature are found in the following.

- Social insects, like ants, termites, or honey bees, where communication occurs through *stigmergy* by placing chemical substances, pheromones, into the environment. In 1959 the theory of stigmergy has been defined as *the work excites the workers* by [Gra59]. Direct interactions between the individuals are not necessary to coordinate a group. Indirect communications between the individuals and the environment are enough to create structures. Thus, coordination or regulation tasks are achieved without centralised control.

- Flocks of birds or schools of fish, where collective behaviour is defined by simple rules, like getting close to a similar bird (or fish) – but not too much – and getting away from dissimilar birds (or fishes) to collectively avoid predators.

- Social behaviours of humans, where emergent complex global societies arise by working with local information and local direct or indirect interactions.

- The immune system of mammalians, where cells regenerate self-organised.

From a very general point of view, the notion of *autopoiesis* is often associated with the term of self-organisation. In the 1970ies biological studies established autopoiesis (meaning self-production) [MV91, Var79], which describes the process of a living system as an organisation to produce itself. An autopoietic system is autonomous and operationally closed, in the sense that every process within it directly helps maintaining the whole. For example, cells or organisms self-maintain the system through generating system's components. The cell is made of various biochemical components such as nucleic acids and proteins, and is organised into bounded structures such as the cell nucleus, various organelles, a cell membrane, and cytoskeleton. These structures, based on an external flow of molecules and energy, produce the components, which, in turn, continue to maintain the organised bounded structure that gives rise to these components.

In computing, an analogous concept is called *bootstrapping*, which refers to techniques that allow a simple system to activate a more complicated system, e. g., when starting a computer a small programme, the *built in operating system (BIOS)*, initialises and tests the hardware (peripherals or memory), loads another programme, and passes control to this programme (an operating system).

Self-Organisation in Chemistry

Self-organisation is also relevant in chemistry, where it has often been taken as being synonymous with self-assembly. To name a few, this includes research in *molecular self-assembly*, which is the process, by which molecules adopt a defined arrangement without guidance or management from an outside source [Leh88, Leh90]. Additionally, self-organisation is used in the context of *reaction diffusion systems*, which are mathematical models that describe, how the concentration of one or more substances is distributed in space changes. This occurs under the influence of two processes that are local chemical reactions, in which the substances are converted into each other, and diffusion, which causes the substances to spread out in space [Fif79]. Other examples are *autocatalytic networks*, or *liquid crystals*.

Through thermodynamics studies [GP71] the term self-organisation itself has been established in the domain of chemistry in the 1970ies. When an external energy source is applied to an open system, this system decreases its entropy (where order comes out of disorder, see Section 4.1.5). In other words, a system reaches a new system state, where entropy is decreased, when external pressure is added. Compared to the stigmergy concept, mentioned in Section 3.1.1, where self-organisation results from a behaviour occurring *inside* the system (from the social insects themselves placing pheromones in the environment), this is a fundamental difference from the understanding in chemistry. In the latter case, self-organisation seems to be a result of an external pressure applied from the *outside*.

Self-Organisation in Mathematics and Computer Science

Self-organisation has also been observed in mathematical systems such as cellular automata [TGD04]. In computer science, some instances of evolutionary computation and artificial life exhibit features of self-organisation.

Research in artificial systems has been oriented towards introducing self-organisation mechanisms specifically for software applications, see [BDHZ06, BDKN05, BHJY07, DKRZ04]. These applications have been inspired by already mentioned nature-inspired concepts like stigmergy, autopoiesis, or the holon concept introduced by Artúr Kösztler in [Kös90]. The term *holon* describes systems, which represent whole systems and parts of larger systems at the same time. Then, *holarchies* describe hierarchies of such holons. Typical examples of self-organising artificial systems are swarm-inspired techniques for routing [BDT99] or load-balancing [MMB02].

Furthermore in multi-agent systems, (software) agents play the role of self-organising autonomous entities. Frequently, multi-agent systems are used for simulating self-organising systems, in order to get a better understanding of the dependencies in such systems or to establish models of the simulated systems. As mentioned in [DGK06], the tendency of initiatives like OC or autonomic computing is now to shift the role of agents from simulation to the development of distributed systems. Components (e. g., software agents) that once deployed self-organise in a predefined environment and work in a distributed manner towards the realisation of a given (global) possibly emergent functionality.

3.1.2 Properties of Self-Organisation

In general, the understanding of self-organisation seems to be widespread. According to [DGK06] self-organisation essentially refers to a spontaneous and dynamically produced (re-)organisation. Several, more qualitative, properties/issues should be extracted from the different viewpoints mentioned above in the following section to end up in a possible definition in Section 3.1.3.

Properties of Self-Organisation in Nature

According to swarm intelligence [BDT99], self-organising processes are characterised by four properties.

1. Multiple interactions among the individuals,

2. retroactive positive feedback (e. g., increase of pheromone, when food is detected),

3. retroactive negative feedback (e. g., pheromone evaporation), and

4. increase of behaviour modification (e. g., increase of pheromone, when new path is found).

From the more biologically-inspired viewpoint of autopoiesis, a self-organising system could be characterised as an autopoietic machine, which is a machine that is

organised (defined as a unity) as a network of processes of production (transformation and destruction) of components, which

1. *through their interactions and transformations continuously regenerate and realise the network of processes (relations) that produced them; and*

2. *constitute it (the machine) as a concrete unity in space, in which they (the components) exist by specifying the topological domain of its realisation as such a network [MV91].*

Properties of Self-Organisation in Chemistry

Under external pressure, self-organising behaviour is characterised by a decrease of entropy and satisfies the following requirements, as stated in [GP71].

1. *Mutual causality: At least two components of the system have a circular relationship, each influencing the other.*

2. *Autocatalysis: At least one of the components is causally influenced by another component, resulting in its own increase.*

3. *Far from equilibrium condition: The system imports a large amount of energy from outside the system, uses the energy to help renew its own structures (autopoiesis), and dissipates rather than accumulates, the accruing disorder (entropy) back into the environment.*

4. *Morphogenetic changes: At least one of the components of the system [has to] be open to external random variations from outside the system. A system exhibits morphogenetic change when the components of the system are changed themselves.*

Properties of Self-Organisation in Artificial Systems

In [DGK04], two definitions of self-organisation in artificial systems have been established. Self-organisation implies organisation, which in turn implies some ordered structure as a result of component behaviour. A new distinct organisation is self-produced, since the process of self-organisation changes the respective structure and behaviour of a system.

- Strongly self-organising systems *are systems that change their organisation without any explicit, internal or external, central control.*
- Weakly self-organising systems *are systems where reorganisation occurs as a result of internal central control or planning.*

3.1.3 Definition of Self-Organisation

The previous sections have shown that it is not trivial to give a precise definition of self-organisation. However, a practical notion, as given in [Ger07], will suffice for the purposes of this thesis.

> *A system described as self-organising is one, in which elements interact in order to dynamically achieve a global function or behaviour.*

Furthermore, this self-organising behaviour is autonomously achieved through distributed interactions between the system components, which produce feedbacks that regulate the system. Instead of answering the question, *which* are the necessary conditions for a self-organising system, another question can be formulated: *When is it useful to describe a system as self-organising?* In [Ger07], it is argued that self-organising systems (in the sense of distributed systems) will have advantages in dynamic and unpredictable environments, where problems have to be solved that are not known beforehand and/or the addressed problem changes constantly. Then, a solution dynamically arises by local interactions and adaptation to unforeseen disturbances quickly appears. In theory, a centralised approach is also able to solve the problem, but in practice such an approach may require too much computation time to cope with the unpredictable disturbances in the system and its environment, e. g., when a system or its environment changes in less time than the system requires to compute a solution.

In [Ed08], another brief sentence has been worked out to explain the main idea of self-organisation, being similar to the definition given by Carlos Gershenson in [Ger07].

> *A self-organising system consists of a set of entities that obtains an emerging global system behaviour via local interactions without centralised control.*

3.1.4 Summary

The investigation of self-organisation in many different disciplines of science has advantages and disadvantages at the same time. Many definitions from different domains have blurred the whole idea, which definitely is a disadvantage in terms of definition and terminology. On the other hand, the many disciplines keep the potential for many ideas and new approaches for creating (controlled) self-organising systems. This possibility will be even more attractive, if the research on self-organising systems converges towards a more standardised nomenclature, probably even forming a new field of science some day.

Several positive effects from the interdisciplinarity of self-organisation became apparent when discussing possible ways to design the behaviour of the particular entities that form a self-organising system. The local behaviour is an integral part of a self-organising system, since the whole behaviour of the system emerges from the local interactions of the entities. In [Ed08], three basic approaches have been identified for finding a suitable set of local rules: Nature-inspired design, trial and error, and learning from an omniscient solution.

In the case of dynamic self-organising systems, with distributed control and local interactions, emergence appears to be some kind of structure on a higher level. Since literature investigating self-organisation is also linked to the term of *emergence*, this phenomenon is addressed in the next section.

3.2 Emergence

The phenomenon of emergence has been a fascinating topic for scientists such as John Stuart Mill [Mil43], George Henry Lewes [Lew75], and Conwy Lloyd Morgan [Llo23] for a long time, and the philosophical discussion of this topic is more than 150 years old. These so-called *proto-emergentists* consider the emergent process as a black box, where only the inputs and the outputs at the lowest level can be discerned without any knowledge about how the inputs are transformed into outputs.

However, in the case of designing technical OC systems more recently characterised aspects of emergence need to be considered. A different perspective, referred to as *neo-emergentism*, summarises approaches of Jochen Fromm [Fro04, Fro05], John H. Holland [Hol98], Stuart Kauffman [Kau93], Aleš Kubík [Kub03], and others, where the root of emergence bases on the dynamics of a system, where investigations focus on reproducing the process, which leads to emergence, and where emergent phenomena are less miraculous than in the black box view.

Emergence is the phenomenon occurring when a population of interconnected relatively simple entities self-organises to form more ordered higher level behaviour [Joh01]. Emergence can be referred to as the effect that *the whole is greater than the sum of its parts*. Emergent phenomena are defined by

1. the interaction of mostly large numbers of individuals

2. without centralised control with the result of

3. a global system behaviour, which has not explicitly been *programmed* into the individuals [Bea03].

The journal *Emergence*[2], a journal of complexity issues in organisation and management, provides the following characterisation of emergent behaviour.

> *The idea of emergence is used to indicate the developing of patterns, structures, or properties that do not adequately seem explained by referring only to the system's pre-existing components and their interaction. Emergence becomes of increasing importance, when the system is characterised by the following features.*
>
> - *When the organisation of the the system, i. e., its global order, appears to be more salient and of a different kind than the components alone;*
>
> - *when the components can be replaced without an accompanying decommissioning of the whole system;*
>
> - *when the new global patterns or properties are radically novel with respect to the pre-existing components; thus, the emergent patterns seem to be unpredictable and non-deducible from the components as well as irreducible to those components.*

Good examples for emergence originate from the observation of ants and other insects. The social insect metaphor for solving problems has become a diverse topic during the last years [BDT99]. For example, foraging behaviour in ants is characterised by the distribution of pheromones, thereby encouraging (but not forcing) other ants to follow the paths. This behaviour, despite its simplicity and distributedness, results in a very robust and efficient emergent phenomenon, i. e., that ants collectively find the shortest path between nest and food source. This observation has resulted in powerful metaheuristics for solving complex problems, called *ant colony optimisation*.

Another example for emergent behaviour is the (human) brain. Although the exact function and interrelation of the different brain sub-systems is not really understood, scientists assume underlying emergent effects, as explained in [Rot05].

> *Today's neurobiology is able to investigate those processes in human and animal brains in detail, which are responsible for the higher level cognitive functions like object recognition, attention, memorising, thinking, problem solving, action planning, empathy, and self-reflection, i. e., processes usually related to consciousness. It shows that these functions can uniquely be mapped to certain brain regions, and vice versa. This does not mean a violation of known physical/chemical/physiological laws. Neither are there any unexplainable gaps. Therefore, it seems necessary to view these brain functions as emergent states of a physical system. This is not in*

---

[2]http://www.emergence.org

contradiction with the fact that the specific conditions for the occurrence of consciousness are not yet exactly known.

Emergence and the effects of self-organisation have been looked at in various sciences, e. g., philosophy, as mentioned above, biology, chemistry [SMR$^+$04], physics, or mathematics [Jet89]. But so far, only few research fields, as summarised in [Mni09], seemed to be interested in using emergence in a systematic (quantitative) way. This topic is again addressed in Section 4.1, when metrics are described to quantify emergent behaviour as part of the generic observer/controller architecture.

3.3 Architectures for Controlled Self-Organisation

From the viewpoint of this thesis and OC, respectively, the main question is how to *design* single components in such a way that they self-organise to achieve global goals. The interest and the difficulty lies in having both, self-organisation and emergent properties, being caused by low level interactions between the components. Defining global goals and designing local behaviour so that global behaviour emerges is the gap to bridge, since it seems to be unpredictable, how the local goals match to a global goal. By definition, emergence is a *bottom-up* process whereas design and engineering tasks typically follow *top-down* constraints. The combination of both approaches results in the requirement of what is called *controlled self-organisation* (which might be a contradiction by itself).

As mentioned in [SMS05], the classical top-down design process is strictly organised hierarchically consisting of a sequence of modelling steps, since the developer is in principle able to predict all possible system states. The top-down design process starts with a high level specification, which is broken down through a number of refinements to a final model. This is used to control manufacturing machines or to generate executable code. However, because today's technical systems become more and more complex, it seems to be impossible to predict all system states and designing top-down is no longer feasible.

In comparison, in the bottom-up approach the design starts with specifying requirements and capabilities of individual components, and the global behaviour emerges out of interactions among constituent components and between components and the environment. As described in Section 3.1.1, examples from nature have shown, e. g., that ants follow the pheromone traits placed by other ants, that it is not possible to predict the exact positions of these traits between places of food and the nest. However, from the viewpoint of technical systems, it would be highly desirable to be able to predict the final outcome more exactly, in other words: The presented work is interested in describing the relationship between local interactions and global behaviour. Moreover, it is the question, how this relationship can be designed.

In [CGL08], the question is addressed, which design methodology (top-down vs. bottom-up) is appropriate for a given engineering problem. Furthermore, a comparative study of the two approaches in engineering a multi-agent system is analysed with a focus on the limitations and advantages of each approach. Thus, criteria for the applicability of the two approaches are established.

The bottom-up approach starts with the specification of the individual agent behaviour through a set of agent capabilities or rules of engagement, which delimit the set of obtainable group level behaviours. The top-down approach starts with global requirements as in a centralised control system and translates those into necessary agent capabilities. But, the last step implicitly assumes that the global system requirements can be delegated to individual components. In fact, in the case of complex systems this might not be straightforward.

As in many cases, the solution seems to be somewhere between pure top-down and pure bottom-up. Since the developers will not capitulate in setting the goals as known from top-down approaches and it also seems to be not very realistic that a collection of screws, metal parts, and electronic devices autonomously assemble into a car, the requirement of *controlled self-organisation* or *controlled emergent behaviour* is in the focus of today's research, see [BCD+06, Ger07, Tri06].

Moreover, when coping with the vision of OC systems and addressing the problem of increasing complexity, it is necessary to have methods and tools to enable such systems to produce the *wanted* emergent phenomena and to prohibit the *unwanted* ones. But, so far, there is no systematic analysis on how to achieve controlled self-organisation. The proposed generic observer/controller paradigm might be a possibility.

Thus, in the following, a focus on the use of an architectural-based approach is proposed, because it offers the following potential benefits, as stated in [KM07].

Generality — To address a wide range of application domains, each associated with appropriate software/hardware architectures, the underlying concepts and principles should be defined in a general way.

Level of abstraction — To describe dynamic changes in a system, such as the use of components, bindings, and composition, rather than at the algorithmic level, an architecture can provide an appropriate level of abstraction.

Scalability — OC focusses on solutions that could be used in the domain of large-scale and complex applications. Varying the level of description and the ability to build systems of systems, architectures generally support both, hierarchical composition and hiding techniques.

By achieving and demonstrating controlled self-organisation, several architectures have been investigated in a broad range of research areas — not only limited to computer science. Therefore, a short survey is given in the following chapter. All mentioned architectures are understood as conceptual or reference architectures (like a framework), which identify the necessary functionality for aspects of controlled self-organisation. They are not considered to be implementation architectures.

3.4 Summary

Based on the OC vision, this chapter has reviewed related work concerning the topic of controlled self-organisation. Concepts like self-organisation and emergent phenomena have been research topics in many sciences for a couple of years until today. The most relevant ideas have been summarised, as pointed out in Sections 3.1 and 3.2.

Then in Section 3.3, the idea of an architectural-based approach has been outlined that enables controlled self-organisation, while the organic approach, which is proposed in this thesis, is introduced in the following chapter.

Chapter 4

Observer/Controller Architecture

To reduce the complexity of tomorrow's technical systems, OC systems are endowed with self-x-properties making them flexible and adaptive. Examples motivating this goal are frequent in nature. In contrast to natural systems, which seem to have intrinsic goals, the technical context specifies the system goals explicitly and in many cases even requires the fulfilment of some constraints. Therefore, reaching the stage of endowing the system with intrinsic local goals can be seen as a long-term plan.

The design process of such an organic system will be neither a classical top-down approach, as practised in classical system engineering, nor a bottom-up approach, as suggested by the notion of self-organisation in general and as observed in nature. In OC, technical systems are endowed with an observation and control layer called *observer/controller architecture*, as proposed in [MS04]. This design paradigm is able to achieve the objectives given by the user or the developer.

As shown in Figure 4.1, the SuOC accomplishes the productive work of the system and is endowed with self-x-properties. The SuOC is similar to a multi-agent system composed of agents communicating with each other to achieve a system-wide goal based on local rules. The observer/controller layer monitors all components and aggregates the results to system-wide indicators reflecting the overall situation of the system (called *situation parameters* or *system fingerprint*). This set of situation parameters is reported to the controller, which has the task to influence the system to satisfy the objective function as specified by the system developer or user. Therefore, the controller continuously searches in its *rule base* for the best mapping of situation parameters to correspondent actions. Furthermore, it has to adapt to dynamically changing environments (changes in the SuOC or changing goals). These changes require learning capabilities, as investigated in detail in Chapter 5.

It is important to note that an organic system will continue to work, if observer and controller stop working. Thus, the main objective of this proposed architecture is to achieve *controlled self-organised system behaviour*. In comparison with classical system design, OC systems have the ability to adapt and to cope with some emergent

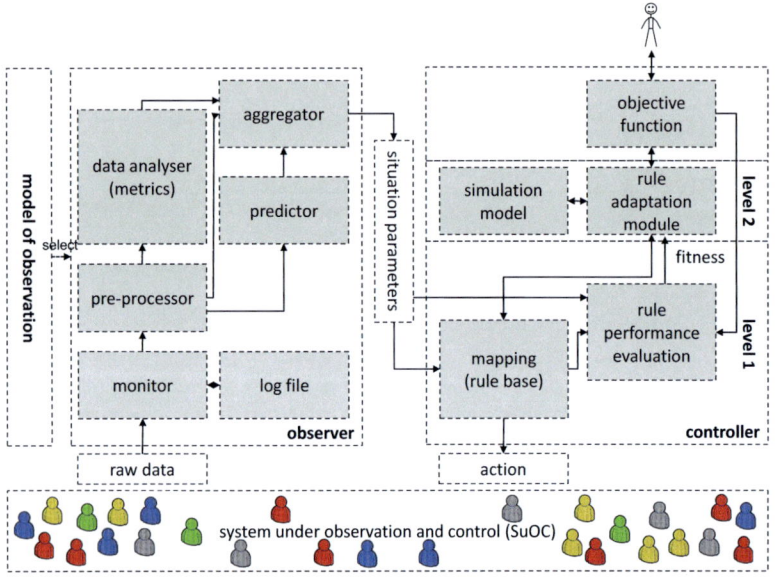

Figure 4.1: Generic observer/controller architecture with two-level learning

behaviour, for which they have not been programmed explicitly.

The development, introduction, and implementation of an observer/controller architecture is one of the main contributions of this thesis. This chapter is based on [BMMS+06, RMB+06], explains the principles of the *centralised* generic observer/controller architecture, and introduces the observer in Section 4.1 and the controller in Section 4.2, respectively. The main advantage of the controller is discussed in Section 4.3. Section 4.4 presents *hierarchical* and *distributed* variants of the generic observer/controller architecture.

4.1 Observer

It is the observer's task to measure, quantify, and predict emergent behaviour with basic metrics. Therefore, the observer collects the raw data coming from the SuOC and aggregates them to a global system-wide fingerprint. This process includes a pre-processing of the data (smoothing, extraction of derived attributes like velocity when observing x- and y-coordinates of agents, etc.), an analysis to determine system-wide indicators, and a predictor to forecast the next raw data as well as the next system wide indicators (by using specified or statistical methods like chart analysis methods). For this purpose, the observer needs metrics and methods to quantify (emergent) states of the system. Finally, the aggregator collects all this aggregated information, the so-called *situation parameters*, and passes them to the controller, which appropriately influences the SuOC.

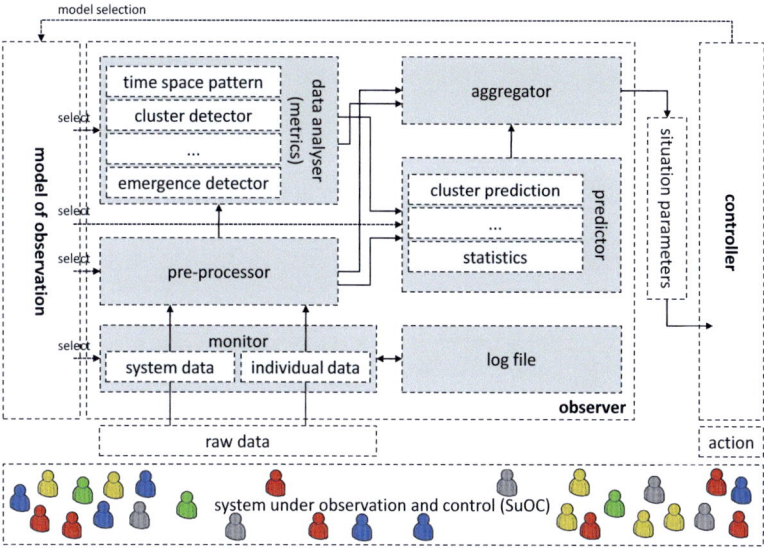

Figure 4.2: *Generic observer architecture consisting of a monitor, a pre-processor, a data analyser, a predictor, and an aggregator*

The observation behaviour itself is variable. The *model of observation* influences the observation procedure, e. g., by selecting certain detectors or certain attributes of interest. The feedback from the controller to the observer pays attention to certain observables of interest in the current context. Based on the aggregate results from the observer, the controller can benchmark the data with an objective function and either knows or learns, which actions are best to guide the SuOC in the favoured direction. The two main tasks of the observer can basically be summarised as in the following.

1. Identifying and characterising the current system status, and

2. predicting the future status of the system.

29

Figure 4.2 outlines the generic observer architecture, which is described in more detail in the following sections. As shown, the observer is guided by a *model of observation*, which is responsible for the following tasks.

1. Selection of observable attributes,

2. selection of appropriate analysis tools with regard to the purpose given by the controller, and

3. selection of appropriate prediction methods.

The whole observation process involves the following listed and explained steps and components. The *data analyser* and the *predictor* are presented in more detail in Section 4.1.5 and in Section 4.1.6, respectively.

4.1.1 Model of Observation

The *model of observation* allows to focus on the observation of system parameters with respect to requirements depending on a situation. It influences the observation procedure, e. g., by selecting certain detectors or certain attributes of interest. The feedback from the controller to the observer pays attention to certain observables of interest in the current context.

In large collections with a centralised observer/controller architecture, it seems to be impossible to observe the whole SuOC in detail. There are not enough sensors, the communication bandwidth is not sufficient, the centralised observer is not able to process so much data, the collection of data consumes too much energy, etc. In the presence of such constraints, it seems to be necessary to adjust the model of observation, either in terms of granularity (it only collects high level data rather than every detail), in terms of scope (it only focusses on some parts of the SuOC), or w. r. t. the sampling frequency. Therefore, the model of observation provides mechanisms necessary to dynamically adapt the model of observation to the current needs of the controller, in order to obtain the most relevant information needed for controlling the SuOC.

4.1.2 Monitor

The SuOC is considered as a set of elements possessing certain attributes (or agents in terms of multi-agent systems). The *monitor* samples the attributes of the SuOC according to a sampling frequency given by the model of observation. The information coming from the SuOC constitutes raw data (unprocessed) for the observer, which can be classified into *individual data* common to all elements of the system and some *global system attributes* reflecting the whole system (behaviour). From a chronological point of view, monitoring the SuOC is nothing else but the generation of a time series, reflecting the current state of the system as well as its history. The sensory equipment of the SuOC, which may also change dynamically, limits the selection of observable attributes and the resolution of the measurement.

4.1.3 Log File

All measured data are stored in a *log file* for every loop of observing and controlling the SuOC. These stored data can be used within the predictor or within the data analyser to calculate (emergent) *time space patterns*.

4.1.4 Pre-Processor

The *pre-processor* computes some derived attributes from the raw data. E. g., an attribute velocity can be derived from the attributes x-coordinate and y-coordinate taking into account the history of these two attributes. The pre-processing of the raw data also includes a selection of the relevant data, which is required to compute aggregated system-wide parameters. The pre-processed data are passed to the data analyser and the predictor components.

4.1.5 Data Analyser

The data analyser applies a set of detectors to the pre-processed data. These detectors could be a kind of computation of data clustering [Ber06, JMF99], emergence following the definition in [MMS06], or some other mathematical and statistical values. At the end of this step a system-wide description of the current state is provided that characterises the global system behaviour.

During operation, the observer ought to measure the current level of emergence among the SuOC. This raises the question of how to evaluate the *amount* of emergence. Different measurement approaches deal with this subject and several concepts addressing this question have been developed. Although, this thesis does not provide an extensive introduction to this field of science, it cannot ignore it totally, since controlling and learning to control a system behaviour is based on quantified system parameters. Without quantitative measurement it seems to be impossible to address the topics of the presented work in later chapters. Thus, the general thoughts of measurement theory are outlined to understand the observer/controller framework. For more information about this domain the interested reader is referred to have a look at [KLST06, LKST06, SKLT06], which give an extensive overview of research that has been done in the past years[1]. The following statement given by Lord Kelvin characterises the idea of the essence of measurement as well.

---

[1]A more concise outline is given by `ftp://ftp.sas.com/pub/neural/measurement.html`.

When you can measure what you are speaking about, and express it in numbers, you know something about it; but when you cannot express it in numbers, your knowledge is of a meagre and unsatisfactory kind; it may be the beginning of knowledge, but you have scarcely in your thoughts advanced to the state of science (William Thomson, 1. Baron Kelvin of Largs, (Lord Kelvin)).

The aim of the data analyser is to convert the amount of emergence *in a form of a number*. This number is used to compare different system states and the effectiveness of different control strategies or parameter variations on the controller's side. Therefore, designing metrics consists of two steps.

1. Firstly, the requirements on the emergence measure given by the intended use have to be defined.

2. Secondly, metrics, which fulfil these requirements, have to be developed.

The requirements on the metric to quantify emergence are the following.

Normalisation — The metric to quantify emergence has to be normalised to be independent of the parameters of the observed system. Therefore, the metric can be used to evaluate changes in the system, e. g., to vary the number of agents, with regard to their effect on the emergent behaviour.

Limited range — The metric must have a defined range of values to be perspicuous and self-explanatory. Therefore, the range is often set from 0.0 to 1.0, where 0.0 is equivalent to *no emergence* and 1.0 to *total emergent behaviour*. No emergence would correspond to a perfect system behaviour and total emergent behaviour would characterise a system showing no optimal behaviour depending on a specific objective function.

On-line measurement — The metric has to give an instantaneous view of the current situation of emergence. This is essential, as the controller interventions are also on-line and rely on the information about the current system state given by the observer.

Monotony — The metric takes values in such a form that the order of the numbers reflects an order relation defined on the attribute, i. e., an emergence value of 0.2 represents less emergence than a value of 0.4. However, the statement *a value of* 0.2 *represents half of the emergence than a value of* 0.4 would be meaningless when having an order relation. Statements like this are not in the focus, the order relation is sufficient for the needs of this thesis.

In general, the idea of constructing metrics to quantify emergent behaviour bases on the comparison of an ideal system behaviour in terms of ideal parameter values and actual parameter values obtained by an observation. Following this idea, the deviation of the current system state from the ideal values is calculated. This deviation is expressed as a number and indicates the current amount of emergence present in the system.

In the context of a selected system, one has to decide, which parameters could be utilised in order to evaluate emergence firstly. For this purpose it is necessary to understand the characteristic traits of emergent phenomena in order to identify the parameters that constitute these traits.

The investigation of metrics and answering the question how emergence can be quantified in technical systems are not in the focus of this thesis. Thus, the discussion is stopped about designing metrics or answering the question how difficult it is to express emergent behaviour in quantified numbers. A single metric is only summarised, which is used on the observer's side later in this thesis and is based on Claude Elwood Shannon's information theory [Sha48a, Sha48b], in particular on the information theoretical definition of entropy. For more details the interested reader is referred to [MMS06, Mni09].

How to Quantify Emergence (in a Technical Context)

In the past years various approaches and frameworks have been investigated, which have tried to understand and characterise emergence and/or self-organisation in a quantitative way, see Chapter 3. The following is a brief survey of the idea how to define emergence quantitatively, since this metric has been used within the following chapters to evaluate the proposed generic observer/controller architecture.

Quantitative Emergence

Defining emergence is a rather controversial issue [MSS06]. In literature, several definitions from different scientific fields are found. These definitions range from non-explainability, non-predictability, etc. to those, which try to give a formal mathematical definition [DGK06]. In a technical context, it is obvious that a definition has to dissociate from the former ones and has to search for a formal – and at the same time – practically usable characterisation of emergence. In the following an entropy-based definition of emergence is summed up, as presented in [MRB+07].

Entropy is a measure of order and therefore potentially interesting for the purpose of identifying emergence. Entropy is used in thermodynamics as well as in information theory. Its definition is based on the probability of the states of a system. The second fundamental theorem of thermodynamics claims that the entropy in a closed system will always increase, eventually leading to a uniform distribution. Dissipative structures, a special form of emergent systems investigated in [PS90], show that in complex systems far from the thermal equilibrium, order can increase, effectively decreasing the entropy. There are several papers, which have tried to define entropy as a metric to characterise self-organisation. In [Pol03], entropy of self-organising systems based on its information theoretic definition is introduced. In [Ray94], the information theoretic entropy is also used to determine the diversity of the *programme population* in the *tierra system* [Ray92]. This definition is specific to this scenario and not generally applicable for the purpose as used in the observer/controller architecture.

Observations made in nature and in further emergent systems have shown that certain ingredients seem to be necessary to call an observed phenomenon emergent: A *large population* of interacting elements (agents) *without (or with a minimum of) central control* leads to a *macroscopic pattern*, which is perceived as structure or order. To summarise, emergence can be characterised as *self-organised order*. Although the resulting order is a necessary pre-condition for *quantitative emergence*, it is not sufficient. Moreover, the definition calls for an order pattern developed without external intervention, i. e., in a self-organised way.

Figure 4.3: *Example of order perception: Depending on the objective of the observer the nine balls are perceived as orderly or unorderly (position on the left hand side vs. colour on the right hand side)*

The meaning of order as perceived by a human observer is not clear without ambiguity. The perception of order depends on the selection of certain attributes. Looking at the position of the nine balls in Figure 4.3, ball formation might be perceived orderly. However, looking at the colour distribution the formation on the left obviously is not in order. Because of the similarity of the colour of the balls, the formation on the right seems to be characterised by a higher degree of order.

A well known metric to quantify order is the definition of *entropy* used in thermodynamics and information theory. Low entropy is equivalent to a higher system order and the other way around. The following entropy-based method is proposed to quantify emergence. This method produces a *fingerprint* characterising the whole system as a result of a transformation of the raw data to some higher abstract metrics. Computing the fingerprint of a system S with N elements s_i is done as follows.

1. Identify a common attribute A of the elements of S with discrete, enumerable values a_j.

2. Observe all elements s_i and quantify each s_i with a value a_j.

3. Transform into a probability distribution (by estimating the probability by means of the relative frequency) over the attribute values a_j (i.e., a histogram) with p_j being the probability of occurrence of attribute a_j in the ensemble of elements s_i.

4. Compute the entropy H_A related to each attribute on the basis of Shannon's information theoretical definition of the entropy

$$H_A = \sum_{j=0}^{j=N-1} p_j \cdot \mathrm{ld}\left(\frac{1}{p_j}\right), \tag{4.1}$$

in which A represents a given attribute.

If the attribute values are equally distributed (all p_j are equal), the maximum entropy $H_{A_{max}}$ will be obtained. Any deviation from the equal distribution will result in lower entropy values (i.e., higher order). In other words: The more structure there (unequal distribution), the more order is measured, where the unit of measurement is *bit/attribute*. Thus, the entropy value can be interpreted as the information content necessary to describe the given system S with regard to attribute A. A highly ordered system requires a simpler description than a chaotic one.

However, entropy is not the same as emergence, entropy decreases with increasing order and emergence should increase with order. Thus, emergence is defined as the result of a (self-organising) process with an entropy value H_{start} at the beginning and a lower entropy value H_{end} at the end. This leads to the following definition of *quantitative emergence*, which is the difference between the entropy at the beginning of this (self-organising) process and at the end $H_{start} - H_{end}$. Finally, the degree of emergent order of each attribute is computed according to

$$E_A = H_{A_{max}} - H_A, \tag{4.2}$$

where $H_{A_{max}}$ is the maximal entropy of the attribute A in case of an equal distribution of attribute values (lowest level of order) and H_A the current entropy. Instead of the emergence E, a *relative* emergence e with ($0 \leq e \leq 1$) can also be computed according to

$$e_A = \frac{H_{A_{max}} - H_A}{H_{A_{max}}}.$$ (4.3)

The list of all E_A or e_A (A denoting an attribute) values of the SuOC constitutes a vector, which is called the *system fingerprint*. This fingerprint characterises the whole system and evolves over time.

An emergence fingerprint can be visualised as a multi-dimensional Kiviat graph with one dimension for each attribute. In Figure 4.4 an example is presented where the attributes x- and y-coordinates, direction, colour, and so on are measured and plotted at three times t_0, t_1, and t_2.

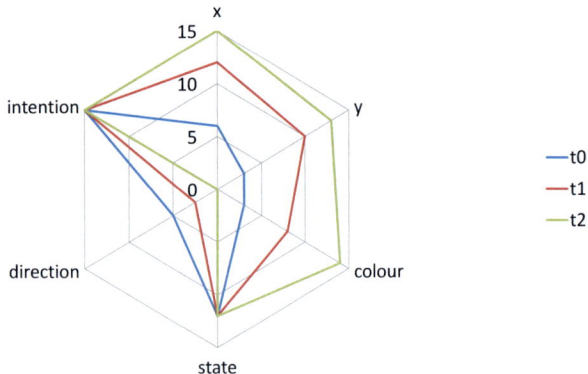

Figure 4.4: *Fingerprint with different attributes at three specific times t_0, t_1, and t_2, visualised as a six-dimensional Kiviat graph (one dimension for each attribute)*

Referring to Figure 4.3, the presented metric is summarised computing a concluding example and focussing again on the the nine coloured balls. The attribute colour is selected, the relative frequency of the colours red and green is observed, and the entropy of the selected attribute colour is computed. In the first example on the left hand side 4 red balls and 5 green balls are observed, so a frequency of $\frac{4}{9}$ is computed, respectively $\frac{5}{9}$. This is equal to

$$H_{colour} = \sum_{j=0}^{j=2-1} p_j \cdot \text{ld} \left(\frac{1}{p_j} \right)$$

$$= - \sum_{j=0}^{j=2-1} p_j \cdot \text{ld} \left(p_j \right)$$

$$= - \left(\frac{5}{9} \cdot \text{ld} \left(\frac{5}{9} \right) + \frac{4}{9} \cdot \text{ld} \left(\frac{4}{9} \right) \right)$$

$$= - \left(\frac{5}{9} \cdot \frac{\ln \left(\frac{5}{9} \right)}{\ln (2)} + \frac{4}{9} \cdot \frac{\ln \left(\frac{4}{9} \right)}{\ln (2)} \right)$$

$$= 0.471 + 0.520$$

$$= 0.991.$$

On the right hand side (where a higher order in the colour attribute can be seen) an entropy value is computed, which is equal to

$$H_{colour} = \sum_{j=0}^{j=2-1} p_j \cdot \text{ld} \left(\frac{1}{p_j} \right)$$

$$= - \sum_{j=0}^{j=2-1} p_j \cdot \text{ld} \left(p_j \right)$$

$$= - \left(\frac{8}{9} \cdot \text{ld} \left(\frac{8}{9} \right) + \frac{1}{9} \cdot \text{ld} \left(\frac{1}{9} \right) \right)$$

$$= - \left(\frac{8}{9} \cdot \frac{\ln \left(\frac{8}{9} \right)}{\ln (2)} + \frac{1}{9} \cdot \frac{\ln \left(\frac{1}{9} \right)}{\ln (2)} \right)$$

$$= 0.151 + 0.352$$

$$= 0.503.$$

These results can also be described as a curve depending on the probability of the colour, as presented in Figure 4.5 for the colour red. Obviously, emergence is defined as the difference between the maximal entropy and the current entropy value. It is shown that the maximum entropy corresponds to an emergence value of zero whereas no entropy characterises situations with maximum emergence (all balls are red or all are green).

Critical Remarks on Quantitative Emergence

In general, controlling a system correctly is based on situation parameters that are aware of the system behaviour and the real situation. Measuring and analysing the

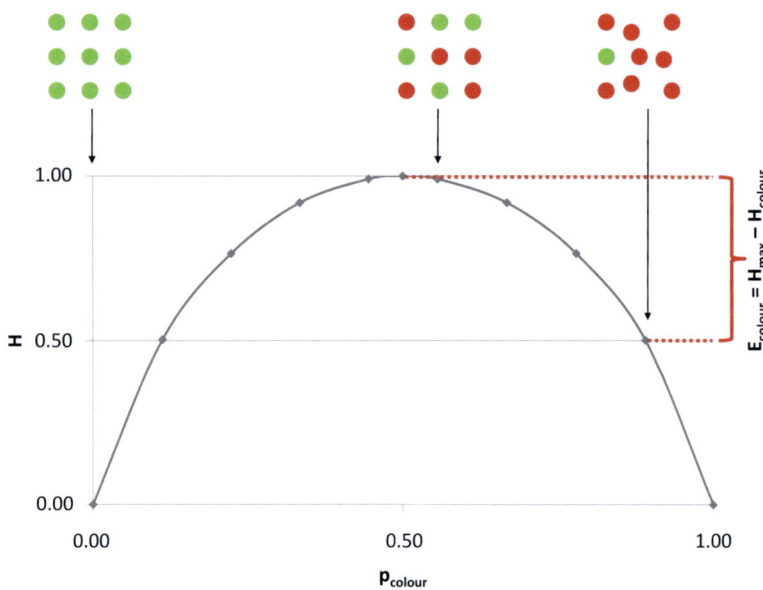

Figure 4.5: *Entropy values depending on the probability of the colour red*

system behaviour should cause clear control actions/decisions, where aggregated situation parameters are realised as definite indicators.

Now, by proposing the use of quantitative emergence the assumptions made by this metric should be discussed. It defines self-organisation as an increase of order, which in turn can be measured in terms of entropy. But as already mentioned in [Ger07], entropy depends on the level of abstraction. When different system attributes are observed with quantitative emergence, different degrees of order on entropies may exist focussing on different attributes. In other words, depending on the aspect/attribute that is focussed on, a self-organising system can be observed as emergent or not. Furthermore, the same system, described in different aspects or levels of abstraction can be modelled as self-organising/emergent in the one case, and as self-disorganising/not emergent in another. Thus, it strictly depends on the role of the observer, which decides on the granularity and aspects of the system to be observed, whether a system will be called self-organising/emergent or not. In [Bee66], this is illustrated by a simple example: When ice cream is taken from a freezer and put at room temperature, it can be argued that ice cream disorganises, since it loses its icy consistency. But, from a physical point of view, it becomes more ordered by achieving equilibrium with the room, than it had done being in the freezer. Another drawback of quantitative emergence arises in the context of the selected test scenario and is mentioned in Section 6.2.5.

Other Metrics

Nevertheless, using an entropy-based metric as part of the data analyser is not the only approach to quantify emergence. Even if the presented results in Chapter 8 are limited to this view, it should be mentioned for the sake of completeness that e. g., *clustering algorithms* or *principal component analysis* may also be possible approaches to measure and identify relevant changes in time and space patterns.

Clustering algorithms mimic the human ability to instantaneously recognise visual patterns in complex ensembles. They organise a set of objects into subsets (clusters) whose members exhibit a kind of similarity. The objects could be e. g., a set of measurements or pixels in a video sequence. Clustering algorithms have many application fields like the grouping of similar access patterns in the internet or the classification of plants and animals depending on common traits in biology. Although clustering itself is not a metric, it can serve as a pre-processing step to reveal similarities between groups of elements of the organic ensemble. Various cluster metrics have been proposed in the literature: An unambiguously defined *similarity measure* is the basic metric of all clustering algorithms, since different similarity measures may lead to totally different cluster results. In [HTTS02], a *clustering coefficient* to characterise the set of created clusters is proposed. It is defined as the ratio of the number of element connections to the number of possible connections. Thus, two elements of the ensemble have a familiarity, when they are similar to each other.

Further metrics characterising the uniformity of resulting patterns and their distribution within a certain property space are the *distance between two clusters* defined as the distance between their centroids, the *cluster compactness* specified as the average distance of all elements of a cluster to its centroid, or the *degree* of the cluster defined as the average number of nets being incident to each component in the cluster. While the cluster compactness is an intra-class metric, the *cluster separation* is an inter-class measure. The diversity of elements within a cluster is given by means of the *cluster entropy* indicating the *homogeneity* of the elements in a cluster, and by the *class entropy*, providing information how the elements of a class are represented by the various clusters created [HTTS02]. These cluster metrics assume that there is a natural classification of objects, to which the output quality of the studied algorithm can be compared. In [LRBB04], the stability of clusterings under the influence of input data variations is investigated. Some of these proposed measures are applicable in the context of the observer/controller architecture, others are not, since they represent a measure of the quality of the clustering process rather than that of the cluster patterns themselves.

Like clustering algorithms the *principal component analysis* involves a mathematical procedure that transforms a number of possibly correlated variables into a smaller number of uncorrelated variables called *principal components*. The first principal component stands for as much of the variability in the data as possible, and each succeeding component accounts for as much of the remaining variability as possible. Principal component analysis is mostly used as a tool in exploratory data analysis. Furthermore, it is focussed on for making predictive models. For more information the reader is referred to [Jol02].

4.1.6 Predictor

The *predictor* processes the data coming from the pre-processor and results coming from the data analyser with the goal of giving a prediction of the future system state. An estimation of future system behaviour is evaluated in addition to the calculation of current emergent behaviour. It allows the controller to base control decisions not only on historic data, but also on predicted situations.

The predictor can use its own methods [MMS06] or some methods of the data analyser combined with prediction methods taken e.g., from technical analysis. Prediction involves an analysis of the system history. For this purpose, the predictor is equipped with a memory to store a given time window. Special interest is based on the prediction of future behaviour in order to reduce the reaction time of the controller and – hence – to increase the probability to prevent unwanted behaviour in due time, or to perceive the success of a controller intervention at an early stage.

In order to perform the estimation, the predictor may contain a (complete) model of the system. Based on this model the predictor is able to perform a simulation of future system behaviour. The outcome of this simulation is the knowledge of future system states and especially shows the desired future emergent behaviour. How such a simulation is performed and the reasons for realising the prediction this way may depend on the scenario and the used prediction techniques.

How to Predict (Emergence)

The best way to predict the future is to invent it. (Alan Kay)

In general, a *prediction* is a statement or claim that a particular event will occur in the future in more certain terms than a forecast. In a scientific context, a prediction is a rigorous, (often quantitative), statement forecasting what will happen under specific conditions, typically expressed in the form of a rule: *If A is true, then B will also be true.* The scientific method is built on testing assertions, which are logical consequences of scientific theories. This is done by repeatable experiments or observational studies.

Methods of prediction should be better than the simplest method when the actual measured value is used as predicted value (called *no change prediction*). Moreover, the last trend, which is the difference of the last and the penultimate value, serves as predicted value (called *same change prediction*). These simple strategies are often used to validate the quality of the result of a more complex prediction method.

In general, prediction methods are divided into methods with short, middle, and long term horizon of prediction. Furthermore, qualitative and quantitative techniques are distinguished. Qualitative prediction methods are performed by experts and are based on personal knowledge. Typical methods are linear extrapolation [BZ91], opinion polls, life cycle analysis, based on market observation and market research, Delphi method [LT75], scenario planning [Rin06, Sch96], relevance tree technique [Fre83, Twi92], or historical analogies [Mac00]. Typical fields of application are stock pricing, technical trends in computer science, or long term forecasts.

More interesting in a technical context like OC are quantitative prediction methods, which are based on the use of (historical) data and result in measurable values. They are used for prediction of tax revenue, population development, or election results. The quality of prediction methods is often quantified by computing a forecasting error, e.g., mean squared error [Ful87, GH06], median absolute deviation [HMT83], or mean absolute percentage error. Quantitative prediction methods are divided into one-dimensional and multi-dimensional methods.

- *One-dimensional* quantitative prediction methods use a large amount of data and they are vague in the case of long term forecasts. But they can be applied to different scenarios and their use is easy to understand. Common methods are exponential smoothing [Sim98], where predicted values are based on historical data, trend analysis of a value series into the future, and moving averages.

- *Multi-dimensional* quantitative prediction methods are based on causation of predicted values with some other variables, e.g., the consumption of ice cream or mineral water depends on the number of sunny days per year. Common methods are regression analysis [DS98], where a causal relationship between at least two parameters is analysed, or econometric models [DM93, Gra91, PU99].

Mathematical or simulated computer models are frequently used to describe both, the behaviour of something and predict its future behaviour. In microprocessors, branch prediction [SFKS02] permits to avoid pipeline emptying due to branch instructions. An important aspect of system engineering deals with predicting failures and avoiding their negative consequences through component or system redundancy. Some fields of science are notorious for the difficulty of accurate prediction and forecasting, such as software reliability, natural disasters, pandemics, demography, population dynamics, and meteorology. To conclude, all mentioned areas of research use their own specific methods, which have exemplarily been summarised in short. The different approaches allow for a general idea how prediction methods could be used as part of an observer.

4.1.7 Aggregator

The results of data analyser, predictor, and possibly some raw data coming from the pre-processor are handed on to the *aggregator*. The aggregator also has a memory, in which current values as well as their history are stored forming a set of data vectors (one for each given result). These vectors are needed to perform filtering as e.g., a smoothing of the results to eliminate the effects of noise. The aggregator delivers a set of filtered current and previous values to the controller. This constitutes an abstract description of the current state and the dynamics of the SuOC.

4.1.8 Summary

In Section 4.1 the proposed generic observer architecture has been described. An observer measures, quantifies, and predicts emergent behaviour with basic metrics and consists of a monitor, a pre-processor, a data analyser, a predictor, and an aggregator.

To conclude, it should be emphasised that the architecture has a framework character and only puts the stress on the main components of designing an organic system. The observer needs to be customised to different scenarios by adopting the observation model (selection of observable attributes and tools) and the other components. Both, data analyser and predictor, can also be regarded as a toolbox of observation methods. The view is explicitly not limited to the metrics, prediction methods, or approaches as presented in this thesis.

4.2 Controller

By receiving a system fingerprint, the *controller* will trigger control actions and will avoid the formation of emergence states, if they are negative, and will support their formation, if they are positive (with regard to the given objective function). Controller actions should effect the system with minimal effort, since OC is interested in guiding a system showing robust and flexible behaviour and not aborting and resetting a system with hard interventions.

As depicted in Figure 4.6, the controller is mainly composed of two internal levels: Level 1 includes a *mapping*, which maps situation parameters to possible actions, and a performance *evaluation* unit that evaluates deployed mappings. This level is rather statistical, since it does not provide the possibility of adaptation of the mapping on its own. This is provided by level 2, which includes an *adaptation module*. The adaptation module takes the evaluation of the deployed mappings into account, adapts the fitness values of the mapping, and generates new mappings, e.g., using genetic operators (like crossover and mutation, see [Mit97]) or an off-line simulation driven by a given or self-generated *simulation model*.

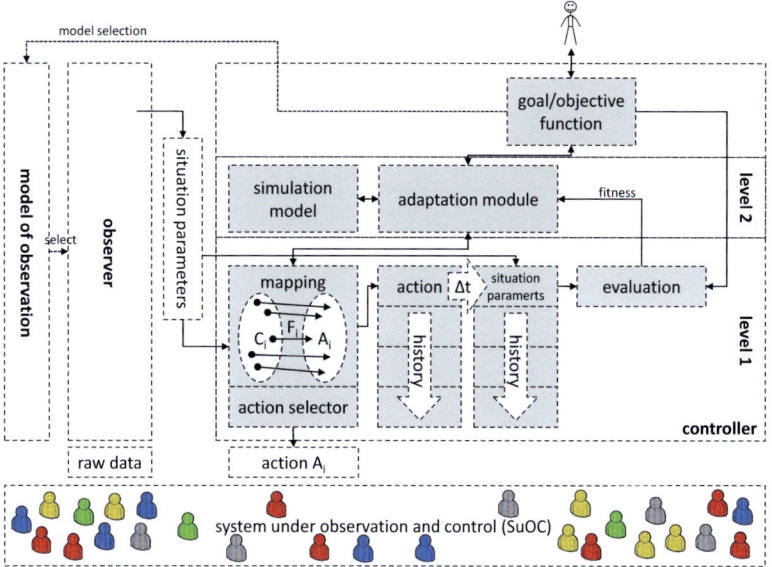

Figure 4.6: *Generic controller architecture with two-level learning*

However, the controller will only interfere when necessary, as for example when an observed situation parameter is detected to be outside of its destinated range or exceeds a certain threshold. As explained in [RMB+06], OC explores possibilities to influence the emergent behaviour of complex systems, assuming that the system consists of a large number of relatively simple, interacting elements (or agents). Then, three possible *options* exists.

1. The controller influences the system in a way that a desired (emergent) behaviour appears,

2. it disrupts an undesired (emergent) behaviour as quickly and efficiently as possible, and

3. it constructs the system so that no undesired (emergent) behaviour can develop.

It is the controller's task to guide the self-organisation process between the elements. At least three general *types of control* can be identified to generate or disrupt emergent behaviour.

43

1. Influencing the local decision rules of the simple agents modifies the local behaviour of the individual.

2. Influencing the system structure assumes that the elements base their actions on local information, where *local* is defined by a neighbourhood and an interconnecting network. The modification of this network, in particular with respect to global characteristics, will change the global behaviour of the system. Additionally, changing the absolute number of elements influences neighbourhoods and finally the behaviour of the SuOC.

3. Influencing the environment allows indirect control of the SuOC. This will only work, if system elements have sensors to measure and react to a modified environment and the controller has actuators to influence the environment. In this theoretical discussion, it is necessary to mention that the environment cannot be controlled at all. Moreover, it is not clear, where the environment of the SuOC starts and ends in fact. One possibility would be to declare some of the actuators to be part of the controller, not of the SuOC. Then the controller can actually modify the environment to change the overall behaviour of the SuOC.

There are certainly more types of control imaginable, but these three represent the most general ones.

Trying to direct the self-organising process of the SuOC, the controller periodically decides what action has to be taken regarding to the situation parameters received from the observer. In the following, a generic architecture of the controller is presented, which has to be customised to each individual scenario. As depicted in Figure 4.6, the controller has three interfaces.

1. The aggregated data are obtained from the observer.

2. The objectives are imposed on the controller by the developer using the second interface. This global objective function defines the goal of the controlled self-organising process and is also used for the evaluation routine of further actions.

3. The third interface contains all information needed for interaction and reconfiguration of the SuOC. Every controlled system provides a number of different parameters and interfaces for manipulation. This information is predetermined, depends on the scenario, and is not learned by the controller.

4.2.1 Level 1

The decision module called *action selector* and the mechanisms of machine learning are the most important components. Three main loops of planning and learning are distinguished. The *first loop* receives the observed data, selects the best weighted action A_i that is the most appropriate for the current situation C_i (a *mapping* function assigns each rule (C_i, A_i) a fitness value F_i), and the action selector forwards the chosen action to the SuOC. This loop simply applies the best action out of a given set of actions and does not involve learning. It aims at quick reaction.

The *second loop* concurrently proceeds to the first one and keeps track of *history* data. For every action at time t, the situation at $t + \Delta t$ is measured by the observer and written to a memory. These tuples of actions and resulting situation parameters are used for *evaluation* and calculation of new fitness values F_i, which are updated in the mapping. In order to avoid overcontrol a fixed time delay Δt is defined to assign results to preceding actions.

4.2.2 Level 2

Additionally to an observation based update of the fitness values F_i for a known rule (C_i, A_i), the controller can also generate completely new rules and actions by applying mechanisms of machine learning. Adaptation can occur on-line and/or by a model-based internal learning process, which is introduced by the *simulation model* in combination with the *adaptation module* in a *third control loop*. Since the generic architecture does not specify the mechanisms of machine learning in detail, methods like artificial neural networks, LCSs, reinforcement learning, or evolutionary algorithms [Mit97] are possible.

E. g., if the observer reports unknown situation parameters, no matching action will be found by the action selector in the first instance. However, by using a simulation model, the adaptation module could either evaluate a suitable action for the current situation from the set of known actions (i. e., create a new control rule) or generate a completely new action. In any case, if new rules and actions are created, a simulation model will be used to predict the possible outcome of the modification before actually applying them to the real system. OC scenarios are mostly real-time systems with hard time restrictions. Thus, pure off-line planning is often not feasible, but e. g., evolutionary algorithms could be used for generating completely new rules, and for modification of existing rules with genetic operators (mutation and crossover). Simulation would be needed to predict the success of control actions.

4.2.3 Summary

Below, the different decisions are listed, which have to be taken for every control loop. The workflow may differ with respect to the scenarios and may depend on implemented mechanisms of machine learning.

- Is there an action of the controller expected? Is there some kind of unanticipated behaviour observed? Are there some indicators exceeding their predefined thresholds? The decisions are based on local reference values for the indicators and degradation of the objective function.

- In order to avoid repeated action and overshooting control, the system has to remember recent responses to a situation. Furthermore, it has to wait some time Δt for the effect to appear.

- What is the best action for the observed situation parameters? The mapping is browsed for a best matching tupel consisting of condition (C_i) and action (A_i).

- If no suitable control rule exists in the mapping, the adaptation module will generate a new one. If the controller has access to a system model, it will rate such new control actions in a simulation model before actually applying them to the real system. If time permits, such a model will allow an internal response optimisation.

- What is the reward for the action responsible for the present situation(s)? The corresponding fitness value is changed depending on the success of the rule.

However, the presented controller architecture has a framework character. Practical implementations do not have to contain all functionalities described above. A controller only consisting of an action selector and a mapping table is possible, but very limited in its possibilities to control a system. This type of controller would not be able to adapt to changing environmental situations on its own. Moreover, it would not be able to adjust the mapping table to different system goals. Actually, it could not react to changes of system objectives at all. In Chapter 8 different types of controllers will be investigated ranging from non adaptive controllers to adaptive ones that learn both, on-line and off-line.

4.3 On-Line Learning and Off-Line Planning Capabilities

What will happen, if the organic system or only the SuOC suffer from changes in its requirements specification or changes in use, changes in resource availability, faults in the environment, or faults in the system itself? The aim of self-adaptation/learning is that the system is able to reconfigure itself in order to satisfy any situation of disorder. These dynamic changes tend to imply an off-line/planning process, in which the system evolves through a number of releases, where each release could make use of self-configuration. However, dynamic changes, which occur while the system is operational, are far more demanding and require that the system dynamically evolves, and that the adaptation occurs at runtime.

As shown before, an observer/controller architecture has been developed to enable controlled self-organisation in technical applications, which has the capability to adapt to changes on two levels: At the on-line level (level 1) the proposed architecture learns about the environment, and about the performance of its control strategies. Level 2 implements a planning capability based on a simulated model of the environment. At this level the agent can test and compare different alternative strategies off-line, and thus plan its next action without actually acting in the environment. Fixed, basic, and periodical tasks that can be learned outside the real system should be learned off-line. In fact, off-line planning is necessary for these tasks as agents do not get enough training evaluations in real situations to learn all tasks on-line.

This off-line planning capability of basic skills is similar to chunking [New94] something done by human experts in many domains. E. g., human athletes spend a lot of time acquiring basic skills so that they can automatically execute them during competition. Human tennis players learn to control and pass a ball over the net for hours and hours (for many years) of practice outside game situations.

The proposed two-level architecture (theoretically) has several important advantages.

1. The off-line planning allows to find appropriate actions without actually having to test different alternatives in the real world. The latter could be detrimental, as testing out potentially bad strategies in the real world can initiate tremendous costs and cause the system to fail permanently.

2. Level 1 acts as a kind of memory, and allows to react quickly. If a situation close to a previously encountered situation reappears, the system will respond immediately.

3. A model-based planning as on level 2 is always limited by the necessary simplifications made in the model. Thus, the best action with respect to the model is not necessarily the best action with respect to the real world. In this architecture, level 1 thus is allowed to slightly fine-tune the solutions from the planning module.

The proposed architecture has similarities with model predictive control [CB04], which only uses level 2 planning and an on-line adaptation of the level 2 simulation model, as mentioned in Section 4.5.5. It also has similarities with pure on-line learning mechanisms like LCSs or reinforcement learning, which only act on level 1. And there is the idea of *anytime learning*, presented in [GR92, RG94, SG94]. An evolutionary algorithm is equipped with a case-based memory, which can be seen as a two-level structure. However, no off-line planning takes place.

In model predictive control the model is continuously calibrated using prediction and comparing it with measurements that are received (on-line) from the process. The generic observer/controller architecture proposes a planning capability on level 2 of the two-levelled learning architecture based on a simulated model of the environment. At this level, different alternative strategies can be tested and compared off-line, and thus next actions are planned without actually acting in the environment. In other

47

words, the off-line planning allows to find appropriate actions without the need to test different alternatives in the real world. This is beneficial, since testing out potentially bad strategies in the real world can cause the system to fail permanently. But, model-based planning as on level 2 is always limited by the necessary simplifications made in the model or by incomplete model calibration due to the fact that the modelled environment changes dynamically/continuously. Thus, the best action with respect to the model is not necessarily also the best action with respect to the real world. In this case, it is argued that level 1 of the observer/controller architecture is allowed to slightly fine-tune the solutions received from the planning module. However, if fine-tuning is not sufficient, the simulation model and the reality will differ too much, then the used simulation model has to be updated.

In general, *calibration* is the process of establishing the relationship between a measuring device and the units of measure. This is done by comparing a device or the output of an instrument to a standard having known measurement characteristics. For example the length of a stick can be calibrated by comparing it to a standard one that has a known length. Once the relationship of the stick to the standard one is known the stick is calibrated and can be used to measure the length of other things.

Model calibration consists of changing values of (simulation) model parameters in an attempt to match real world conditions within some constraints. This requires real world conditions to be properly characterised. Lack of proper characterisation may result in a (simulation) model that is calibrated to a set of conditions, which are not representative of actual real world conditions.

In [BZL06], a robot is described that autonomously recovers from unexpected failures, by continuous self-modelling. This robot uses actuation-sensation relationships to indirectly infer its own structure, and it uses self-models to generate forward locomotion, e. g., if a leg is removed or not functioning properly, the robot will adapt its self-model. This leads to a generation of alternative gaits. Other fault tolerant robots are described in [GWTS05, MB06].

In [Ant07], several modified, nonlinear Kalman filter methodologies [Kál60] are used (e. g., extended Kalman filter (EKF), iterated EKF, and limiting EKF) for traffic estimation and prediction (or dynamic traffic assignment) models to contribute to the reduction of travel time delays. An on-line calibration approach that jointly estimates all model parameters is presented. The methodology imposes no restrictions on the models, the parameters or the data that can be handled, and emerging or future data can easily be incorporated. The modelling approach is applicable to any simulation model and is not restricted to the application domain of traffic.

Continuous parameter calibration of microscopic traffic models in on-line simulations is also discussed in [LW05]. An algorithm is described, which uses unscented Kalman filter. The algorithm is supplied with data of loop detectors and, of course, with a model. The model parameters are continuously adapted to the incoming data in order to keep the on-line simulation as realistic as possible.

In most cases of model calibration, the data available for calibration (usually consisting of labelled data points) are provided externally, and have to be accepted as they are. More recently, researchers have started to consider cases where the system can decide, which data points out of a large set of possible data points should be labelled, i.e., the system can actively influence the data set available for model calibration. This research field is known as *active learning* or also *optimal learning*. Since the learner chooses the examples, the number of data points needed to calibrate a model can often be much lower than in normal supervised learning. One of the first papers on active learning is [CGJ96]. Typical heuristics used are to query data points close to the decision hyperplane, e.g., [TK01], or to choose data points with the greatest reduction in estimated generalisation error probability [RM01].

In summary and with respect to the known literature, the proposed two-level learning approach as part of the observer/controller architecture is new in the field of (collaborative) multi-agent systems. The architecture has the advantage of on-line adaptation and prevents the disadvantage of testing bad solutions in the real world by using a model of the reality for validation of promising new actions.

4.4 Architectural Variants of the Observer/Controller Architecture

The generic architecture needs to be customised to different scenarios by adapting the various components of the observer (including the observation model) and the controller. As stated in [ÇMMS+07], the architecture may be realised in the following ways, see Figures 4.7 and 4.8.

The choice of the appropriate observer/controller realisation is a design decision that has to be made by the developer in the design phase of the technical system. Many distribution possibilities exist and vary from fully centralised to fully distributed. In the former case, only one observer and one controller is taken for the whole system, see Figure 4.7(a), whereas in the latter case one observer and one controller is established on each agent, see Figure 4.7(b), in the system. The fully centralised and the fully distributed architectures define the two extreme points in the design space. Other distribution possibilities like a multi-levelled architecture are sited between these two extreme points, see Figures 4.8(a) and 4.8(b).

In particular, e.g., in larger and more complex systems (where the objective space drastically increases) it will be necessary to build multi-levelled and hierarchically structured OC systems instead of trying to manage the whole system with one centralised observer/controller.

In the case of multiple observer/controller levels the SuOC at the bottom of the whole system will consist of simple elements like single software or hardware modules. However, at higher levels a SuOC will comprise sub-systems, where each of these sub-systems represents an OC system including an observer/controller on

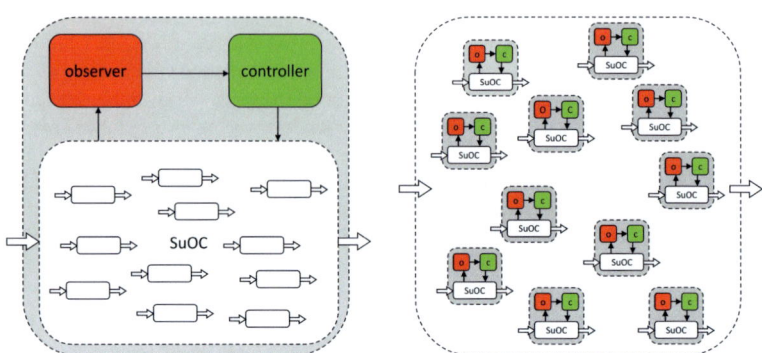

(a) Centralised: An observer/controller for the whole technical system

(b) Distributed: An observer/controller on each system element

Figure 4.7: *Centralised and distributed variants of the generic observer/controller architecture*

its own. Goals of the controller become more abstract and general on further steps up in the hierarchy. As described in [Rib07], this corresponds to the management of a company, where high level administration units are not bothered by low level decisions. In the business world, it is necessary to separate low level from high level management tasks to handle the complexity of management tasks in the way mentioned above. This paradigm can be transferred to the field of OC systems: Regarding to [ÇMMS+07] the need for *multi-levelled* observer/controller architectures is based on complexity in terms of variability. Variability is the number of possible, by an observer detectable configurations of a SuOC, and will be apparently larger, if an SuOC contains more elements. Implementing multi-levelled observer/controller architectures is a mean of greatly reducing variability and by that complexity. E.g., the investigation of *hierarchical* structured observer/controller architectures is in the focus of [LS06, LTS08, TLS07], where OC principles are integrated into *service-oriented architectures*.

In [ÇHMS08b, ÇHMS08a], a *resource sharing problem* [IK98] as a common bench-mark problem in multi-agent scenarios is implemented, which is used to evaluate assets and drawbacks between a *centralised* and a *distributed* observer/controller architecture, coping with this problem domain. To provide a more quantitative comparison of the two selected architectures, four different test scenarios with in-creasing conflict levels are developed. As comparison criteria the system performance is measured. The centralised observer/controller architecture should work at least as well as the distributed one in all scenarios. However, the experimental results show instead that the system endowed with the distributed observer/controller is

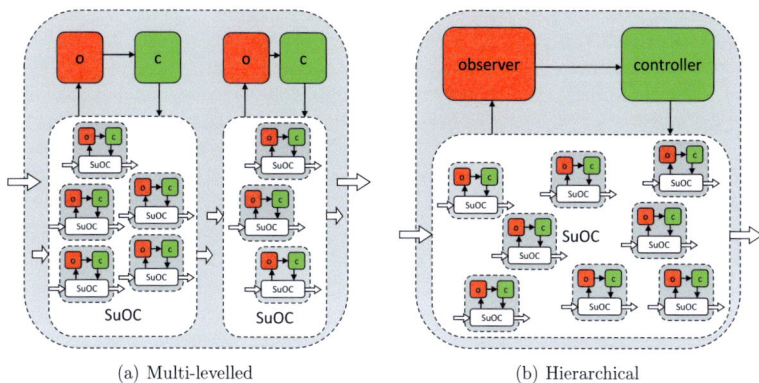

(a) Multi-levelled   (b) Hierarchical

Figure 4.8: *Multi-levelled or hierarchical variant: An observer/controller on each system element as well as one for the whole technical system*

more efficient than the centralised observer/controller in scenarios with increasing conflict level in spite of its limited view. Thus, the centralised observer/controller architecture provides a better system performance than the fully distributed one in the low-conflict scenario only. Since the optimal strategy can neither be implemented on the centralised nor on the fully distributed level, the results suggest an adaptive architecture. This architecture incorporates both architectures in the system simultaneously and allows to switch between the centralised and the distributed architectures. Thus, it benefits from the advantages of both architectures depending on the current conflict level in the system.

In general, systems with a *centralised* observer/controller instance, where the controller influences the behaviour of each component of the SuOC explicitly, cannot scale with the increasing number of components. If the controller has limited resources, e. g., a limited central processing unit (CPU) or a limited memory that cannot be expanded accordingly, these limitations will prevent the controller from influencing the system as necessary. The overall system could produce unwanted (emergent) system behaviour. Thus, in such large scale multi-component systems the behaviour of each component cannot explicitly be determined by a centralised instance. Therefore, a system developer can either implement a distributed control mechanism or modify the centralised controller in such a way that it performs its control functionality on a higher abstraction level determining (or influencing) the behaviour of groups of components instead of the behaviour of every single component. Thus, the controller can save resources like CPU or memory and is able to work with a large number of components.

Moreover, a *distributed* observer/controller architecture has been adapted to a scenario of *organic traffic control* within another research project [PRT⁺08, TPR⁺08]. Organic traffic control has served both, as a provider of requirements and as an additional experimentation platform. In particular, the need for a two-levelled learning architecture is originated in this project. In close cooperation the advances in the development of a generic observer/controller architecture have been incorporated into the organic traffic control architecture, and insights gained by adapting the architecture to traffic control have in return helped to extend the generic architecture. As a result, both architectures map nicely, a detailed description can be found in [BMMS⁺06].

While these are the general design options, it is emphasised that OC systems will always need some external high level control, possibly by the user. It is not intended to build fully autonomous systems because the system developer must always be able to guarantee the ultimate human control, which might be necessary in case of unanticipated emerging behaviour. Therefore, the centralised observer/controller architecture is investigated and the other variants are disregarded in the following chapters.

4.5 Related Architectures

Since OC is by no means the first domain, where regulatory feedback mechanisms are introduced to achieve controlled self-organisation, other architectures are summed up and compared to the organic approach in short.

4.5.1 Autonomic Computing

One of the most famous exponents is IBM's MAPE (monitor, analyse, plan, and execute) cycle [KC03, Ste05], designed as an architectural paradigm for the autonomic computing initiative, where the equipment and software of IT-infrastructures is endowed with self-managing capabilities. This architecture has also served as a great source of inspiration for developing the observer/controller architecture. Autonomic computing aims at facilitating and automating system management tasks currently performed by humans. An autonomic computing system is supposed to be self-healing, self-optimising, self-protecting, and self-adapting. It has the ability of self-configuration and reconfiguration. In this respect, the complexity of the system is hidden from the user.

Designing local and global architectures in a manner that allows self-organisation and at the same time robust, controlled, and predictable system behaviour is a key challenge not only in current OC, but also in autonomic computing research. An autonomic computing architecture [IBM06] consists of one or more MAPE closed loops. This loop is associated to system knowledge, including information about

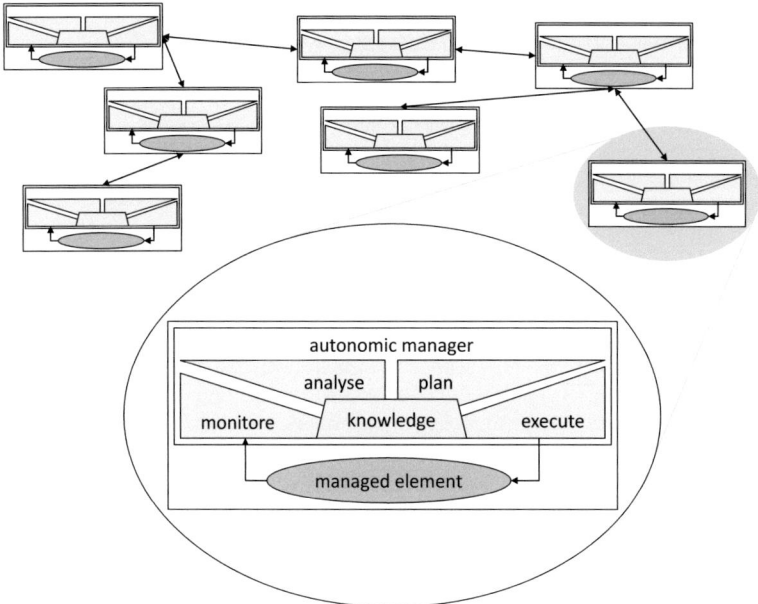

Figure 4.9: *Structure of an autonomic element, which interacts with other elements and with human programmers via its autonomic manager, see [KC03]*

the system and its policies, and is defined as an *autonomic manager*, see Figure 4.9. The autonomic manager has four functional areas. It *monitors* the managed element using embedded sensors, followed by *analysing* the resulting measured data. If this analysis results in necessary activities, the autonomic manager will *plan* and *execute* any specific action needed. These functionalities define a control loop, which is referred to as MAPE. The autonomic manager is guided by business goals manifested in the form of policies, which describe what needs to be accomplished. The manageability interfaces between the autonomic manager and the manageable unit basically consisting of sensors and effectors is called *touchpoint*. The autonomic manager will react – if necessary – to the circumstances observed in the system. It is possible to arrange the autonomic manager in a hierarchical manner, some autonomic managers manage other autonomic managers, which directly manage resources, and the upper manager – called *orchestrating* manager – is guided by high level business goals, which are translated into goals and objectives for the lower manager(s). Lower managers pursue the fulfilment of these goals by the managed resource.

While the underlying ideas of autonomic computing show great similarities to OC, the application field differs. In general, autonomic computing deals with the problem of IT-systems, which have become more interconnected and diverse. Architects are less able to anticipate and design interactions among participating components, leaving such issues to be dealt with at runtime. Systems are too massive and complex for the most skilled system integrators to install, configure, optimise, maintain, and merge, as argued in [KC03].

Thus, autonomic computing aims at solving these problems by computer systems that can manage themselves in a predefined framework, which allows self-optimising behaviour with some degree of freedom. Elements of an autonomic system contain resources and deliver services to humans and autonomic elements. They can manage their internal behaviour and their interactions to their environments in accordance with strategies established by humans. So it becomes apparent that autonomic computing focusses on the learning process of technical systems. IBM has implemented its autonomic architecture in its *DB2 universal database* [ZE04]. In comparison to OC, autonomic computing's focus lies on monitoring and analysing enterprise server architectures.

But, while autonomic computing is directed towards maintaining server architectures, which should be managed without active interaction between man and machine, OC's focus is more general in its approach and addresses large collections of intelligent devices providing services to users adapted to the requirements of their execution environment [Sch05b]. In other words, OC's focus is more on technical applications. Thus, besides showing the self-x-properties, interaction between man and machine is an essential part of OC systems. In particular, the two-level adaptation and learning architecture of the observer/controller is a powerful mechanism to autonomously adapt system behaviour to a continuously changing environment. Neither the need for autonomous learning capabilities on every level of the management architecture, nor a systematic investigation of patterns for collaborative behaviour is emphasised in autonomic computing. Another important OC aspect is controlled self-organisation, which is not addressed in autonomic computing.

4.5.2 Operator/Controller Module

The operator/controller module, as depicted in Figure 4.10, has been investigated in the collaborative research centre 614[2] to realise self-optimising systems of mechanical engineering [BGM+08, HBN01, HO03, OHKK02].

While the information processing unit of a mechatronic system has to perform a multitude of functions, the number of errors increases accordingly [HOG04]. E. g., control code works in a quasi-continuous mode, it controls motions in the plant, adaptation algorithms adapt the control to altered environmental conditions, error-

---

[2]http://www.sfb614.de/eng/index.htm

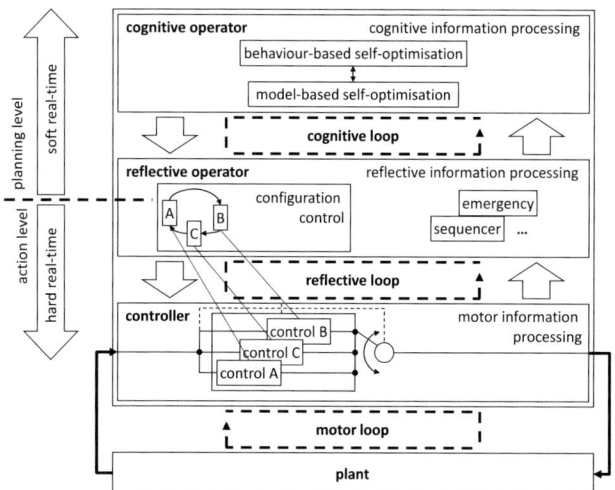

Figure 4.10: Structure of the operator/controller module, see [HOG04]

analysis software monitors the plant in view of occurring malfunctions, or different systems are interlinked. To cope with these increasing requirements and to allow safety and self-optimising systems, a new structure of the information processing of a mechatronic function module has been proposed.

The *controller* addresses the innermost loop (called *motor loop*), processes measurements, and produces control signals to directly affect the plant on the lowest level of the operator/controller module. Software that is processed on this level works in a quasi-continuous mode. Under hard real-time conditions the controller reads measured values, processes them, and outputs them continuously. This lowest level can be made up by one or by several controllers offering the possibility of switching and fading over in one time step between the different controllers.

The second layer, the *reflective operator*, complements the first layer. It executes monitoring and controlling routines, which do not affect the system directly, but modifies and switches between different configurations of the controller(s) on the lowest level. The reflective operator operates in an event-orientated manner under hard real-time constraints. Therefore, it uses quasi-continuous functions and adaptation algorithms.

The reflective operator is the connection layer between the upper layer, the *cognitive operator*, which asynchronously works to real-time requirements in software, and the controller operating under hard real-time constraints in hardware. It filters the incoming signals from the cognitive level and passes them through to the subordinate levels. Of course, the cognitive operator has to respond within a certain time limit. Otherwise and due to a dynamic changing environment, self-optimisation would hardly find useful results.

Using a cognitive loop, the cognitive operator gathers information on itself and its environment by applying various methods, e.g., learning, knowledge-based optimisation, and model-based optimisation. These methods are used to improve the cognitive operator's behaviour, but other cognitive functions are possible to achieve self-optimisation. In [HOG04], model-based and behaviour-based self-optimisation is divided. Model-based optimisation uses prediction for optimisation and is decoupled in time from the real system. Behaviour-based optimisation utilises functions for planning and evaluating the current objectives, see [HO03, OHKK02].

To conclude, the operator/controller module is divided into two loops. Both loops affect the system, the first directly operates in hard real-time (operator), the second does it with respect to soft real-time constraints indirectly (controller). In [GMM+06], the operator/controller module is compared to an early version of the organic observer/controller architecture.

> *A related practical approach, explained in [SMS05], is the observer/controller architecture for OC systems. Similar to the operator/controller module it is inspired in the brain system as low level structures, which reacts to sensory inputs and the limbic system as a high level structure, which observes and manipulates the first one. In contrast to this work, the operator/controller module also supports higher cognitive behaviour, which matches the planning layer of the touring machines [Fer92] (autonomous agents with attitudes) and tries to reach the goal of a general model for autonomous cognitive agents, as stated in [DF98],...*

This statement is misleading, since in [GMM+06], an early paper of the observer/controller architecture is used for the comparison of these two architectures. Comparing the operator/controller module with the generic observer/controller architecture, the following should be mentioned.

- In general, both architectures address similar goals investigating an adaptive regulatory feedback mechanism to control complex technical systems.

- Since the operator/controller module is focussed on mechatronic systems with a strong focus on real-time standards, the organic approach is more general where methods of quantifying emergent behaviour as part of the observer and learning as part of the controller have a strong relevance.

- As depicted in Table 4.1, the operator/controller module makes a difference between adaptation in hardware on level 0 and in software on level 1. The

Table 4.1: *Comparison of the different levels in the observer/controller architecture vs. the operator/controller module*

Level	Observer/controller architecture	Operator/controller module
0	SuOC, adaptation with fixed rules	Controller: Adaptation is done in hardware and follows fixed rules.
1	On-line (reinforcement) learning	Reflective operator: Adaptation is done in software and follows fixed rules.
2	Off-line planning using a model	Cognitive operator: Model- and behaviour-based learning

observer/controller architecture does not propose a separation of hard- and software. Thus, level 0 and level 1 from the operator/controller module could be mapped on level 0 of the observer/controller architecture.

• Furthermore, on-line learning, characterised as getting a reinforcement signal from the real SuOC, as proposed on level 1 of the observer/controller architecture, seems to be not included in the learning approach of level 2 of the operator/controller module. But, learning as part of the real system is important to slightly fine-tune the solutions produced by the planning module. When acting in changing environments the planning module on level 2 in both architectures cannot match the reality in all details or needs for customisation. Thus, the observer/controller approach allows more adaptation on level 1, thereby being advantageous in comparison with the operator/controller module.

4.5.3 Sense, Plan, and Act (SPA)

The SPA architecture is another approach, which was the predominate control methodology through 1985 in the area of (mobile) robotics. In SPA, a mobile robot has to perform complex information processing tasks in real-time and operates in an environment with rapidly changing boundary conditions. Typically, the problem has been decomposed into a series of functional units, as described in Figure 4.11. Firstly, gather all the information from the *sensors*. Secondly, create the world model using all the information and *plan* the next move. Thirdly, *act* as the plan dictates. After the acting phase, the sensing phase follows again [Nil86]. The SPA approach has two significant architectural features: First, the information flow from sensors to world model to plan to effectors is unidirectional and linear, never in the reverse direction. Thus, SPA proposes an open control loop, simple to understand. Second, the execution of an SPA plan is analogous to the execution of a computer programme. Both are built of primitives composed of partial orderings, conditionals, and loops. Altogether, SPA has tried an approach as simple as possible.

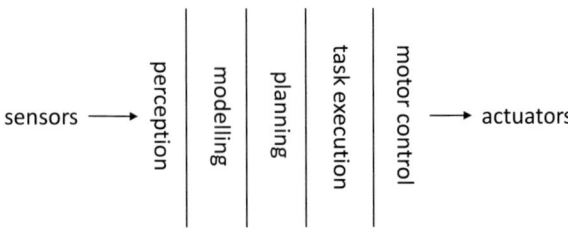

Figure 4.11: A mobile robot control system is decomposed traditionally into functional modules, see [Bro86]

However, in the mid of the 1980ies it became clear that the proposed simplicity, and at the same time SPA, has different drawbacks in planning and world modelling, which turned out to be very hard problems. In addition to that, executing open-loop plans turned out to be the wrong technique to cope with environments that are uncertain and unpredictable. Several approaches have been proposed to solve these shortcomings. One of these manifold approaches is the so-called *subsumption architecture*, as proposed by Rodney A. Brooks in [Bro86], which is based on the analysis of the (often limited) computational requirements for mobile robots. Thus in [Bro86], a decision is provided to use *task-achieving behaviours* as primary decomposition criterion of robot's tasks, as illustrated in Figure 4.12.

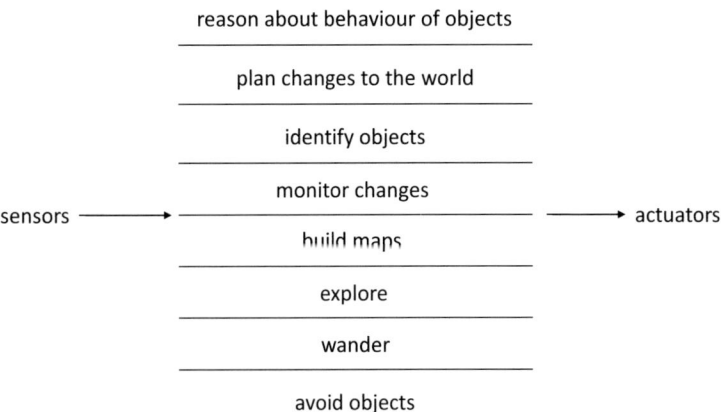

Figure 4.12: Task achieving behaviours as decomposition criterion for mobile robots, see [Bro86]

Each slice is explicitly implemented and forms a whole robot control system together with the other slices. This decomposition strategy is different to the work done before in terms of behaviours rather than in terms of functional modules and it is argued that it has plausible advantages concerning robustness, modularity, and testability. It follows nine dogmatic design decisions, made in [Bro86], e. g., things should be simple and complex behaviour is not necessarily a product of an extremely complex control system.

Since SPA decomposes the problem of building a robot into subsets of sensing, mapping sensor data into a model representation of the real world, planning, task execution, and motor control, decomposition forms a chain where information flows through the robot's logic/cycle. An instance of each subset has to be built in order to run the robot at all and later changes have to be done with respect to the whole functionality. Therefore, *task-achieving behaviours* split the problem on the basis of desired external manifestations and prefer *levels of competence*, which are an informal specification of the desired robotic behaviour. Each level of competence includes a subset of earlier subsets of level of competence. Furthermore, higher levels of competence provide additional constraints on the underlying levels. Thus, layers of a control system can be build that correspond to levels of competence. If a new layer is added to an existing set of layers, the system will move to the next higher level of competence. This hierarchically structured *subsumption architecture* is described in Figure 4.13. Building the first layer this framework provides a working control system for a mobile robot at a very early implementation step. Additional layer could incrementally be added and tested later – without changing the initial working system.

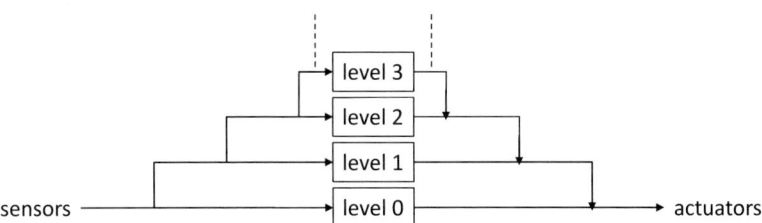

Figure 4.13: *Control is layered in a hierarchy of levels of competence, where higher layers subsume lower layers in the case of taking control, see [Bro86]: Partitioning the system is possible at every level, the lower layers form a complete operational control system*

Building each single layer includes decomposition in the traditional SPA manner, but the difference between SPA and the subsumption architecture might be that the designer does not need to account for all desired perceptions, processing, and generated behaviours in a single decomposition. For different sensor- and task-set

59

pairs the designer can choose different decompositions. Last but not least, the subsumption architecture has shown some drawbacks in practice, too, as mentioned in [HP91].

> *The most important problem we found with the subsumption architecture is that is it not sufficiently modular. The other problems described below are really side effects of this one. Because upper layers interfere with the internal functions of lower level behaviours they cannot be designed independently and become increasingly complex. This also means that even small changes to low level behaviours or to the vehicle itself cannot be made without redesigning the whole controller.*

Thus, more modern approaches of designing mobile robots combine hybrid reactive and deliberate behaviour and are inspired by a *three-layered architecture* [Fir89, Gat98] that consists of three main components: A reactive feedback control mechanism (controller), a reactive plan execution mechanism (sequencer), and a mechanism for performing time consuming deliberate computations (deliberator).

As described in [Gat98], the *controller* acts on the lowest layer of the three-layered architecture and consists of one or more threads of computation that implement one or more regulatory feedback control loops, respectively, where each loop matches sensors to actuators. At runtime the controller can change these sensor-actuator-mappings, the so-called *transfer function(s)*, which are stored in a library of hand-crafted transfer functions. Getting an external input the controller is determined, which transfer action is active at any given time and which not. Since the controller works on real hardware, several constraints have to be considered: First, computing one iteration of a transfer function should be executable in a constant amount of time and limited space complexity. This constant amount of time should be small enough to provide enough bandwidth to afford stable closed loop control for the desired behaviour. Second, an algorithm as part of the controller should fail recognisable. In other words: An algorithm should be designed to detect any failure to perform the transfer function, for which it has been designed. Since it is impossible to design algorithms on real robot hardware that never fail to detect a failure, the architecture allows other components of the system (the sequencer and deliberator) to take corrective actions to recover from a failure.

The *sequencer* performs its job on top of the controller in real-time. It selects the transfer function that is executed by the controller at a given time, and it supplies parameters for the transfer functions. By changing transfer functions at strategic moments the robot is induced to perform useful tasks. But, the resulting problem is that the outcome of selecting a particular transfer function in a particular situation might not be the intended one. In this way a simple linear sequence of transfer function is unreliable. Thus, the sequencer must be able to conditionally respond to the current situation, whatever it might be. Furthermore, the sequencer should not perform computations that take a long time in relation to the rate of environmental change at the level of abstraction presented by the controller. Usually, this constraint implies that the sequencer should not perform any computational intensive tasks, like search and optimisation tasks.

The *deliberator* acts on top of the sequencer performing time consuming computations, e.g., which includes planning and other exponential search-based algorithms. The key architectural feature of the deliberator is that several transitions of transfer function(s) can occur between the time a deliberate algorithm is invoked and the time it produces a result. The deliberator runs in parallel and as one or more separate threads of control. The architecture proposes no architectural constraints on algorithms in the deliberator, which are invariably written using standard programming languages. The deliberator can interface to the rest of the system in two different ways. It can produce plans for the sequencer to execute, or it can respond to specific queries from the sequencer.

[Gat98] mentions that the three-layered architecture is not derived from fundamental theoretical considerations. Instead, empirical observations of the properties of environments, in which robots are expected to perform, and of the algorithms that have proven useful in controlling them have led to this framework. Similarities with the before introduced operator/controller module could be mentioned. Both architectures provide regulatory feedback on technical systems and focus on real-time control, where hard- and software layers are distinguished and based on different constraints.

Table 4.2: *Comparison of the different levels in the observer/controller architecture vs. the three-layered architecture from the area of (mobile) robotics*

Level	Observer/controller architecture	Three-layered architecture
0	SuOC, adaptation with fixed rules	Controller: Fixed transfer functions acting in real-time in hardware
1	On-line (reinforcement) learning	Sequencer: Selection and modification of transfer functions in real-time
2	Off-line planning using a model	Deliberator: Time consuming computations

Furthermore and summarised in Table 4.2, the three-layered architecture is characterised by a hierarchy of control layers, each responsible for different tasks and equipped with different methods. This also seems equal to the proposed observer/controller architecture, even if the organic focus is more general and specially on the controller's side on different learning loops (no learning, on-line learning, and off-line planning). The term *learning* is still ignored in [Gat98].

4.5.4 Component Control, Change Management, and Goal Management

As in the area of robotics, similar three-levelled architectures exist in the area of software engineering to design *self-managed systems* consisting of *component control*, *change management*, and *goal management* [KM07, KM09], see Figure 4.14. Other termed approaches are described in [GS02, OGT+99]. Self-managed systems cope with a similar vision as OC systems do. For instance, goals, properties, and constraints, which a system is expected to achieve or preserve, and furthermore, a set of software components exist, which implement the required functionality. Then, the aim of self-managing means that the components should either configure themselves so that they satisfy the specification or are capable of reporting that they cannot.

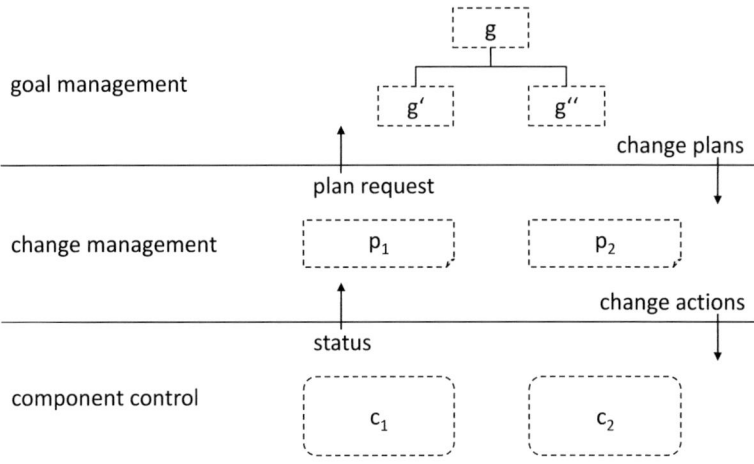

Figure 4.14: *Three-levelled architecture for self-managed systems, see [KM07]*

At the bottom of self-managed systems, *component control* is established by a set of interconnected components that provide the system functionality. Including facilities to report the current status of components to higher layers, this layer supports component creation, component deletion, or component interconnection. It contains behaviours to adjust operating parameters of components, e. g., the timeout values in a component implementing a communication protocol, e. g., the transmission control protocol. In summary, the bottom layer includes some kind of self-tuning algorithms, event and status reporting to higher levels, and operations to support modifications. If a situation is met that the current configuration of components is not designed to deal with, the component layer will detect this failure and will report it to higher layers.

The middle layer, the *change management*, reacts to changes in the underlying component layer in response to new reported states or in response to new required objectives given by the layer above. Given a new situation, this change management executes a single action or a sequence of actions to handle the new situation. Using a set of predefined plans, which are activated in response to modifications of the underlying layer, it introduces new components, reconfigures failed components, changes component interconnections, or modifies component operating parameters. Since plans are predefined, response and execution time of change management quickly adapt to new situations. If no plan exists to cope with a reported situation, the services of the higher *goal management* layer will be engaged. The same happens in the case of new goals involving new plans.

The highest layer is called *goal management*. In response to requests from the layer below and in response to the introduction of new high level goals this layer produces change management plans to achieve these goals using time consuming computations. Research issues on this level focus on how to represent high level system goals, how to synthesize change management plans from these goals, and how general or domain specific this layer should be?

Table 4.3: *Comparison of the different levels in the observer/controller architecture vs. the three-levelled architecture for self-managed software systems*

Level	Observer/controller architecture	Three-levelled architecture
0	SuOC, adaptation with fixed rules	Component control: Immediate feedback actions
1	On-line (reinforcement) learning	Change management: Activating of predefined plans according to reported and well known situations
2	Off-line planning using a model	Goal management: Synthesizing new plans from high-level goals in time consuming computations

Summarising this architecture as described in Table 4.3, immediate feedback actions are located at the lowest level, which has similarities to level 0 of the observer/controller architecture. Similarities on level 1 are also obvious, even if the controller's view on level 1, as described in detail in Section 4.3, needs not be limited to predefined plans. Since reinforcement learning may be an option that can be utilised on the controller's level 1, reinforcement learning methods specially include the risk of making mistakes in new and unknown situations. In comparison, change management will report new and unknown situations to level 2, if no plan exists to cope with this reported situation. Analogously, the longest actions requiring deliberation and time consuming computations take place on the highest level, which is the same in both approaches, see Section 4.3. In favour, the controller's view on level 2 utilises a simulation model. Moreover, the description, how the goal management produces change management planned by high level system goals, is not done precisely.

Thus, the predominant criterion of placing functions on different layers of the three-levelled architecture for self-managed software systems is specially guided by a view regarding the time scale. But, in comparison with the proposed organic architecture, the observer/controller architecture clearly covers a second criterion while the distinction of different time scales is also included. The observer/controller architecture explicitly sees differences in observing and controlling. Both tasks utilise different methods, which are not kept apart in this three-levelled architecture.

4.5.5 Control Theory

As stated in [Bro91], control theory is an interdisciplinary science of engineering and mathematics. It deals with the behaviour of dynamical systems, where the desired output of a system is controlled using *closed-loop controllers*. If one or more output variables of a system do not satisfy a certain predefined reference value, a controller will dynamically manipulate the input values of a system to obtain the desired effect on the output of the system. Every control system has to guarantee the stability of the closed-loop behaviour. By directly defining the lower and upper boundaries a closed-loop behaviour is easy to satisfy in the case of *linear systems*. However, more complicated in controlling are *nonlinear systems*, where control normally bases on specific theories, i. e., in most cases on Aleksandr Lyapunov's theory [Ele07]. The possibility to fulfil different specifications varies from the model considered and the control strategy chosen. E. g., the main control techniques include *adaptive control* or *model predictive control*.

Adaptive Control

In the 1950ies adaptive control [ÅW08] was applied for the first time in the aerospace industry, where it was successfully adopted. By obtaining strong robustness properties, adaptive control uses on-line identification of the process parameters. It involves modifying the *control law* used by the controller to cope with the fact that the parameters of the controlled system vary in time or are uncertain. For example, as an aircraft flies, its mass will slowly decrease as a result of fuel consumption. Thus, a control law is needed that adapts itself to such changing conditions. Adaptive control is different from robust control in the sense that it does not need *a priori* information about the bounds on these uncertain or time varying parameters. Since robust control guarantees that, if the changes are within given bounds, the control law will not need to be changed, while adaptive control is precisely concerned with control law that must change.

Model Predictive Control

Guaranteeing closed-loop stability two *optimal control* design methods have widely been used in industrial applications. These are model predictive control and linear-quadratic-Gaussian control.

Since the 1980ies model predictive control [CB04, DP04] has been an advanced method of process control that has been used in the process industries such as chemical plants and oil refineries. It explicitly takes into account constraints on the signals in the system, which is an important feature in many industrial processes. Model predictive controllers rely on dynamic models of the process, most often linear empirical models obtained by system identification. Model predictive control provides a multivariable control algorithm that uses an internal dynamic model of the process, a history of past control moves, and an optimisation cost function over the prediction horizon to calculate the optimum control moves. The generic observer/controller architecture has similarities with model predictive control, which only uses level 2 planning and an on-line adaptation of the level 2 simulation model.

Prediction also plays a role in the context of model predictive control. Models are used to predict the behaviour of dependent variables (i. e., outputs) of a dynamical system with respect to changes in the process independent variables (i. e., inputs). The model predictive controller uses the models and current plant measurements to calculate future moves in the independent variables that will result in operation that takes concern of all independent and dependent variable constraints. Then, the model predictive controller sends this set of independent variable moves to the corresponding regulatory controller setpoints to be implemented in the process.

Despite the fact that most real processes in chemical plants or oil refineries are approximately linear within only a limited operating window, linear model predictive control approaches are used in the majority of applications [GPM89, MRRS00]. When linear models are not sufficiently accurate because of process nonlinearities, the process can be controlled with nonlinear model predictive control [DBS+02] utilising a nonlinear model in the control application (e. g., artificial neural networks) directly. Together with *proportional integral derivative* controllers, model predictive control is the most widely used control technique in the area of process control.

4.5.6 Other Related Approaches

Architectures, which are mostly related to the generic observer/controller architecture, as proposed in this thesis, have been described before. Other related approaches are only mentioned shortly.

- The *organic robot control architecture* is developed in another OC project, which specially focusses the aspect of fault tolerance [ELM08]. Traditional fault tolerance relies on explicit fault models, which seem to reach their limits caused by increasing complexity. However, during their evolution living organisms have developed effective and efficient mechanisms, like the autonomic nervous system or the immune system, to adapt and self-organise in case of new unforeseen situations. These systems unconsciously operate in an emergent way to make them self-protecting, self-healing, self-optimising, and self-configuring. Using this nature-inspired principles the organic robot control architecture continuously monitors the *health status* of the system by so-called *organic control units*, which are closely attached to basic control units implementing the regular behaviours. Based on techniques like adaptive filters, the organic control units are able to learn on-line and thus adapt to new unforeseen (fault-) situations. The organic robot control architecture is evaluated on real, autonomous, mobile climbing robots.

- Other OC projects develop *system on chip architectures* [BZS$^+$06], which are inspired by and have similarities to the generic observer/controller architecture.

- As part of (simulated) robotic soccer [RGH$^+$06] or self-organising smart factories [Par98] *agent-based approaches* are investigated to realise controlled self-organisation.

- The *viable system model* [Bee72, LTS08] is a recursively defined model of the organisational structure of any autonomous system and is established in management cybernetics. This model is inspired by the architecture of the brain and the nervous system and describes organisations as adaptable systems to cope with changing environments.

4.6 Summary

The vision of OC systems is based on the urgent necessity to find methodologies for managing the complexity and controlling the behaviour of large scale distributed embedded systems. To build such systems, the generic observer/controller design paradigm has been introduced consisting of two architectural parts, an observer and a controller. This chapter shows how observer and controller should be designed, which functions should be implemented, and how the loop consisting of the SuOC, an observer, and a controller should work together. The observer, as presented in Section 4.1, measures and analyses the behaviour of the SuOC in terms of well defined system parameters. The controller has been explained in Section 4.2 and selects adequate actions to optimise the system behaviour with respect to certain global objectives. Furthermore in Section 4.3, the two-level learning approach as part of the controller has been especially explained. Although, this thesis focusses on the centralised variant of this design paradigm, the other variants have been summarised in Section 4.4. Finally in Section 4.5, related architectures and frameworks have been described that also propose regulatory feedback mechanisms to enable controlled self-organisation. As mentioned before, the components of the proposed OC architecture strongly relies on other established scientific areas e. g., data mining, time series analysis, machine learning, or control theory. Results and methods from these areas are used to extend the observer/controller toolbox. Based on the experience made in [MRB+07], this architectural framework will be evaluated for the control of multi-agent test scenarios from the predator/prey domain in the following chapters.

Chapter **5**

Learning to Control

Imagine that it is the year 2091 and your moon-Jeep is being repaired by a swarm of microscopic machines to fix some serious moondust damage. Do you trust them to do the job right? Now, imagine that it is the year 2061 and the city of New York launches a new surveillance system consisting of a swarm of autonomic microflyers. Do you feel secure? Imagine that it is the year 2031 and there is the first android team that challenges a human soccer team for the ceremonial opening game at the world soccer championships. Which team do you put your money on?

These future scenarios have one common denominator: They all involve complex systems consisting of (many) interacting parts that are self-organising and collectively intelligent. [Sch07]

It does not make any difference whether a swarm of microscopic machines is focussed on, a swarm of autonomic microflyers, the first android team, or any other futuristic idea, which is inspired by collective intelligence. Dynamically adaptive systems have to change their behaviour at runtime to operate in volatile environments. They alter their behaviour or composition in response to changes in their less predictable and less stable environment, they monitore, reconfigure, reconstruct, heal, and tune themselves at runtime. As summarised in Chapter 2, OC is specially interested in technical systems that fulfil the self-x-properties. Thus, this thesis is based on the question, how to design and build technical systems with greater autonomy establishing controlled self-organisation.

For all scenarios in the following sections, the requirement of dynamic adaptation is considered, which is imposed by the environment, in which the organic system has to operate. In terms of this thesis, dynamic adaptation is a strategy when the observer/controller recognises that the behaviour of the SuOC is incomplete, fails, or shows unwanted (emergent) observations. Situations serve as an indicator, where the environment is volatile, but understood sufficiently well to allow the observer/controller to anticipate, how it will change. Coping with fully unknown environments might be at the extreme end of the spectrum of dynamic adaptive systems.

Here, the environment is characterised as a set of discrete and stable states and the environment can change between theses states. Environments are typically not discrete or stable. For simplification, discrete and stable states are assumed. Thus, a dynamically adaptive/organic system can be understood to comprise a set of target systems and each target system is designed to operate within one of these states. It is the job of the observer/controller architecture to specify each target system and the adaptation behaviour, which defines, when the SuOC adapts from one target system to another target system.

Adaptation and learning capabilities seem to be key aspects of OC systems in general and of the generic observer/controller architecture in particular, as already mentioned in Section 4.2. In OC systems, the monitored agents of the SuOC and the controller itself could be endowed both with the capability of learning and adaptation. Agents of the SuOC learn to act in a dynamically changing environment. Moreover, the controller learns to control and to guide the behaviour of the SuOC. For this thesis, the learning capability of the controller is considered and discussed, as constituted in Section 4.3.

This chapter is structured as follows: After some general remarks about learning with a focus on challenges concerning learning in OC scenarios in Section 5.1, an introduction into the area of machine learning is given in Section 5.2. Then, LCSs are introduced as a machine learning technique that is specially investigated. But, LCSs have drawbacks in learning speed, as described in Section 5.4. The number of reinforcement learning cycles, an LCS requires for learning, largely depends on the complexity of the learning task. A straightforward way to reduce this complexity is to decompose the task into smaller sub-problems and learn the sub-problems in parallel. This idea of parallel and hierarchical structured classifier systems is explained in Section 5.5. Finally in Section 5.6, a second approach is introduced, how to apply the generic two-level learning architecture on an LCS. Therefore, a new *covering* mechanism is specified, which has not been used in traditional LCSs' implementations before.

5.1 General Thoughts on Learning

The research on (distributed) *artificial intelligence* is intensifying. A growing number of national and international conferences, workshops, and journals supports this trend[1]. Agents use machine learning techniques to adapt to changes in dynamic environments. They individually act in a coordinated or competitive way to achieve individual or common goals, as described later in Section 6.1.6.

---

[1] A comprehensive list is found on `http://www.aaai.org`.

In general, an agent or a system has the capability to learn, if it can autonomously improve its response to input values from some set X. That means, given time values t_1 and $t_2 > t_1$ such that for any $t > 0$ the response to an input from the set X at time $t_2 + t$ has a *higher quality* than the response to the same input at time t_1.

This learning capability requires some *learning mechanism* or *learning algorithm*, which may modify the behaviour of the system by

- changing the values of some attributes of the system or of its environment, or

- changing the behavioural repertoire of the agent's/system's control mechanism (which corresponds to the observer/controller architecture).

There is a broad range of possible learning mechanisms, reinforcement learning, neural networks, or meta-heuristics like genetic algorithms, ant colony optimisation [DS04], or simulated annealing, to name a few. These mechanisms could make use of learning by experience or trial-and-error.

In the case of the generic controller, see Section 4.3, the advantages of on-line learning on level 1 (the capability to tackle the real-time requirements of organic systems) are combined with the advantages of off-line planning on level 2 (that minimises the possible mistakes that may arise during on-line learning). By that, the main challenges of learning in OC scenarios may be summarised as follows, well knowing that the list is not complete and could be extended.

- OC systems act in highly dynamic (and nonlinear) environments and try to maintain a flexible and robust system behaviour. If components break down or produce fatal errors, OC systems should demonstrate their full technical power and intelligence. When components interact with each other, learning algorithms have to cope with these dynamics.

- Dynamic environments require learning algorithms that support quick decision making and provide fast response.

- The structure of the SuOC is often characterised by incomplete knowledge. Thus, learning has to cope with noisy environments and only partially observable system states.

- Furthermore, to control and to trust the output of a learning algorithm the learned solutions should be understandable by humans. This seems to be a more practical constraint, since OC focusses on the design of technical systems. However, human-readable learning processes (and results) are not in the focus of all machine learning techniques, e. g., artificial neuronal networks or evolutionary algorithms. The result of an artificial neuronal network can be human-readable, e. g., a value $f(x)$ for an input x, but the computed function f is hidden in the network.

Since it is a hard task to cope with all challenges simultaneously, the investigations, as presented here, are limited to level 1 of the proposed two-level learning architecture, as explained in Section 4.3. Especially, LCSs are in the focus of this thesis and are investigated as a special machine learning technique, since the idea of rule-based learning fits well into the observer/controller framework, see Section 5.3.

5.2 Machine Learning

> *Machine learning explores ways to get a machine agent to discover on its own, often through repeated trials, how to solve a given task. [HTP+05]*

In general, machine learning [Mit97] is concerned with methods and algorithms that allow machines/computers to learn (autonomously). From a limited number of observations or a description of the task and its goal, machine learning algorithms are able to classify data, learn about relations between entities, or achieve certain goals with a sequence of actions.

The use of machine learning algorithms is manifold, including handwriting and speech recognition, fraud detection, object recognition, game playing, natural language processing, path planning for robot locomotion, medical diagnosis, and many more. Machine learning provides no universal method to handle all these tasks and a large set of different approaches exist, which in the majority of cases are specialised for particular problem classes. Probably, the most distinct differences within the manifold machine learning methods are the type of task that they can handle, the approach that they are designed for, and the assumptions that they are based upon.

E. g., an interesting mechanism for learning by modifying parameters of the environment is the stigmergic use of pheromones by ant colonies, as shortly mentioned in Section 3.1.1. This aggregation of individual experiences combined with some degree of evaporation leads to the extraordinary capability of constructing shortest path ant roads even in a dynamically changing topography. As described in [DS04], this has inspired a whole range of new design patterns for optimisation algorithms.

Furthermore, the design of an organic traffic control system may serve as an example for a second type of learning method, see [RPB+06]: A modified LCS for selecting parameter settings for a traffic light controller (in the real traffic system) is combined with off-line planning. The LCS uses on-line learning by associating a fitness value to classifiers based on the performance of their parameter settings in real traffic situations. The off-line planning produces new classifiers for inadequately handled traffic situations by using a genetic algorithm, which generates new classifiers of some minimum quality level by evaluating their performance in a traffic simulator. In this way, the learning mechanism manages to improve the system performance on known traffic situations and it is also capable of generating adequate responses (i. e., control actions) to previously unknown traffic situations. This scenario adapts the proposed two-level learning approach, see Section 4.3, and is again focussed on in Section 6.2.5.

As a very general and powerful paradigm for acquiring knowledge through experience in an environment, reinforcement learning [SB98] is a widely studied area of machine learning, which is inspired by different techniques, e. g., temporal difference learning [Sut88], Q-learning [Wat89, WD92], or LCSs [Hol86]. In general, applications of reinforcement learning range from the design of situated agents (e. g., robotics or control of complex systems) to problem solving and pattern recognition, where an agent learns on-line. This means learning goes on forever and no preliminary training/learning phase exists that produces a generalised agent, which is capable to act when confronted with similar problems not explicitly learned.

By executing an action and receiving a feedback from the environment, an agent learns on-line about acting in the unknown environment. Using this feedback the agent modifies its behaviour and improves its performance over time. This is achieved by generalising past experiences using inductive methods. The feedback given by the environment does not specify the desired output, it has no instructive character, but it evaluates the agent's behaviour, how appropriate the agent has acted/performed, computing a scalar signal, called *reinforcement*. Thus, the agent tries to maximise the reinforcement improving its performance.

In several cases, the given feedback of the environment is sparse. The reinforcement is received at the end of long sequences of actions. In the context of LCSs the problem is addressed by modelling a learning task as a *single-step* or a *multi-step* problem, as explained in Section 5.3.2. Getting a reinforcement for a sequence of actions considerably increases the complexity of learning. An agent must correctly evaluate actions that are essential to behave in the right order, but do not receive an immediate reward.

This thesis focusses on LCSs and specially investigates their usability in the context of the presented observer/controller architecture. As described in the following, LCSs are a machine learning technique that combines genetic operators [Hol75] with reinforcement learning to evolve a set of rules, so called *classifiers*, which consists of condition and action parts that determine the behaviour of a learning agent. A classifier is activated when its condition part matches the sensory input of an agent.

5.3 Learning Classifier Systems (LCSs)

The field of LCSs, introduced in the 1970ies [Hol75, Hol76, HR78], is one of the most active and best-developed form of genetic based machine learning [KL00, Kov02, Lan08]. As mentioned above, much of learning classifier's theory is inherited from the reinforcement learning literature. The following section provides a brief overview, what an LCS is. In Section 5.3.4 a special LCS, the *extended classifier system (XCS)* [Wil95], is described, which is widely accepted as one of the most reliable LCSs.

As explained in Chapter 4, the controller uses some kind of *mapping* to choose an appropriate parameter set to configure the action that prevents (negative) emergence or enhances (positive) emergence, as measured by the observer. To keep the problem manageable, the input space is partitioned so that situations, which are sufficiently similar to allow usage of the same parameter set, will be covered by the same mapping entry. Since it is hard to anticipate, which situation can be handled by which action, and since a human developer would need tremendous effort to develop good (hard-wired) control strategies for all situations that can be imagined, the means for generating mapping entries have to be provided by the controller. To combine, these tasks are what LCSs are supposed to do: Classify input, find an appropriate action, and learn by gaining experience [HBC+00].

The architecture of an LCS has been modified over the past decades. Furthermore, an LCS is simple to study and the knowledge is encoded and stored in so-called *classifiers*. These classifiers consist of a condition part, which is matched against the input from the environment, an action part, and some kind of *fitness* or *strength* value. The rule syntax is very simple and a classifier can represent very fine-grained knowledge. This simple representation allows the LCS to use genetic operators for rule discovery.

The strength value is used to decide, which classifier should be chosen, if more than one classifier matches the current input. The encoding of conditions is done in such a way that different levels of *generality* are possible, hence the range of input values each classifier matches against may vary from a single point to the entire search space. In a step that is called *rule discovery* new classifiers are generated using genetic operators, like crossover and mutation, on existing classifiers, changing both, condition and action. Furthermore, every time no classifier matching the current input is available, one or more classifiers with a matching condition and randomly chosen action are created (this is called *covering*).

After a classifier has been generated, the system has to determine its strength value. Every time a classifier's action is chosen, the strength value of this classifier is updated using some *objective function*. Usually, the effect of an executed action cannot instantaneously be measured, therefore the current value of the objective function is used to update the value of the classifier that was active during the *previous* time step. The simplest way to increase performance would be to try and find classifiers, which maximise the objective function's value. This has also been the dominant approach, before the XCS has been introduced by Stewart W. Wilson, which uses another approach more suitable for complex problems. An XCS is also used within this thesis and described in detail in Section 5.3.4.

5.3.1 Pittsburgh vs. Michigan Style

Literature on LCSs falls into two broad categories: Pittsburgh and Michigan style classifier systems. The Pittsburgh style has been inspired by research done at the

University of Pittsburgh and introduced in [de 88, Smi80, Smi83]. This type of LCSs has a look on learning as an off-line optimisation process rather than an on-line learning process, as done in [Hol76, HR78]. The on-line learning approach has mainly been inspired by the University of Michigan.

The Pittsburgh style is characterised by a genetic algorithm, which is applied to a population of individuals, where each *individual* represents a *complete set of rules*. At each cycle, a reward is assigned to each rule set to obtain a performance measure that is then used by the genetic algorithm to guide the exploration of the solution space. Michigan style classifier systems have a different view. The whole population is a complete set of rules and an *individual* in evolution is only a *single rule*.

In [Lan08], it is discussed, which classifier style is the better design decision. But, no reasonable answer to such a question exists, since Michigan and Pittsburgh classifier systems are radically different in structure and no literature is known, which has bridged the two approaches. Furthermore, a fair comparison seems to be impossible and the competition between Michigan and Pittsburgh is still going on[2]. The Michigan style is usually considered as being more general, since it has tackled a larger variety of domains. Also, Michigan style has attracted most of research. Pittsburgh models on the other hand were awarded for their human-competitive results [BSH+07, LRMB07] and have recently gained more visibility.

5.3.2 Single-Step vs. Multi-Step Problems

Literature about Pittsburgh or Michigan style LCSs is also divided into *single-step* and *multi-step* approaches. This separation is based on, how to solve the reinforcement learning problem, and addresses a design decision, which has to be taken, when implementing an LCS. Some environments predefine this design decision, e. g., *Maze* environments, as explained in the following. This design decision refers to the question, *when* a reinforcement signal (reward) is achieved from the environment and *how* this reward is distributed to the past action(s).

In single-step environments, the external reward is received for every action and the environmental input for each time step has completely been independent of the prior time step. When a decision is made, the reinforcement is directly received and measures the quality of the decision. Single-step environments generally involve categorisation of data examples. A typical single-step benchmark problem is the *boolean multiplexer problem* [BKLW04, Wil95].

In multi-step environments, the external reward may not necessarily be received for every action, since the environmental input on a time step depends on at least the prior input and the system's last action. Typical multi-step environments are known as sequential environments or so-called *Maze* problems, e. g., *Wood1* [Wil94]

---

[2]A series of international workshops on LCSs (IWLCS 1999 to IWLCS 2009) or several books [But06, LSW00] support this trend.

or *Wood2* [Wil95]. These examples model the adaptive interaction of an agent with its environment and have been studied using a variety of methods. Most often, a Maze is defined as a given number of neighbouring cells in a grid-world. A cell is a bounded space and is the elementary unit of a Maze. When a cell is not empty, it can contain an obstacle, food, a so called *animat*, and eventually a predator of the animat.

An animat is randomly placed in the Maze environment (which could be some kind of a labyrinth) and it tries to set its position to a cell containing food, which is sparsely located in the environment. To perform this task, it possesses a limited perception of the environment. The animat's viewpoint is often limited to the eight cells surrounding the animat's position and it can also only move to an empty cell of this set of neighbouring cells. Moving step by step through the Maze in order to fulfil its goal the animat searches for a strategy (or adopts a policy), which minimises the effort undertaken to find the food in the selected Maze environment.

Maze environments offer plenty of parameters that allow to evaluate the complexity of a given environment and also to evaluate the efficiency of a learning method. A full description of these parameters is available in [BZ05].

More complex Maze environments are investigated in [BGL05] and the question is addressed, how to get a better learning performance in environments like *Maze6* and *Woods14* using XCS in combination with gradient descent methods. But, characterising the selected environments as *more complex* here means that the animat needs more steps to reach the food than it needs in other Mazes, e. g., in *Woods2*. The difficulty of searching and observing *moving* objects, e. g., well known by the predator/prey domain, as explained in Section 6.1.1, is not focussed.

Moreover, some Maze problems also offer perceptually similar situations that require different actions to reach the goal/food. This problem is often studied in the context of *non-Markov environments*, see [Bel57, How60, Mar54, Put05].

E. g., *Woods101* is a non-Markov environment, since it has two distinct positions, as indicated by the arrows in Figure 5.1, where the agent senses the environment as identical, but two different actions are required to solve the problem optimally. When the agent is in one of these two positions, it cannot decide, which is the correct action exclusively considering its current inputs. In the left aliased position, the optimal action is *go south-east*, and in the right aliased position, the agent should *go south-west* to achieve an optimal behaviour. The cell, marked with food Γ, denotes the animat's goal.

If the agent could remember, from which part of the grid it entered the aliased positions, the agent would be able to solve the problem, i. e., entering the aliased position from the left, the correct action will be *go south-east* and entering the aliased position from the right, the optimal action will be *go south-west*, respectively. Since it may not possible to enhance the agent's sensors to fulfil the Markov property in this environment, the agent needs some kind of memory to cope with the lack of information provided by its sensors.

76

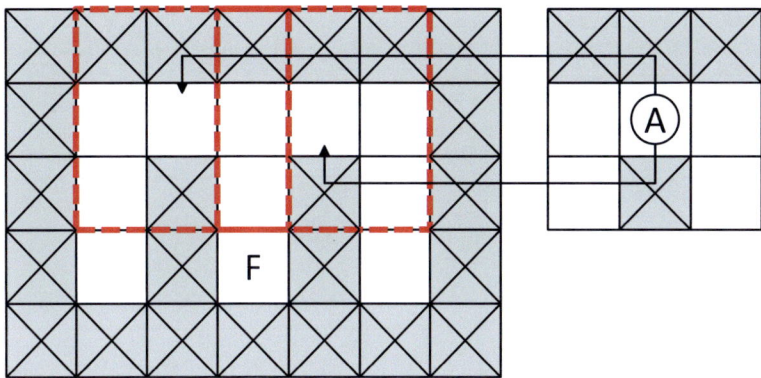

Figure 5.1: *The* Woods101 *example is a non-Markov environment*

Woods101 is a typical example of a *partially observable Markov decision process (POMDP)*, where a *single-agent* cannot distinguish different situations due to a lack of global environmental information. Using records of past situations/actions by adding temporary memory is a widespread approach to cope with such environments, as investigated in [Lan98, LW00].

A second non-Markov property is still embedded in *multi-agent* environments and this is related to a change of an agent's internal state. In scenarios with more than one learning agent, an agent has to evaluate actions that may be caused by its own internal state or that are the result of other agent's actions. It is difficult to recognise an environmental change, which is caused by the change of another agent's internal state, due to a lack of the other agents' information. Even if an agent stays in the same location, the agent cannot evaluate the environmental changes. In [TTS01], this second non-Markov property is defined as the *non observable Markov decision process (NOMDP)*. Thus, since multi-agent scenarios often include both non-Markov properties (POMDP and NOMDP), learning in multi-agent environments is more complex than learning in single-agent environments.

Furthermore, a concluding comparison of Michigan style XCS and an adapted Pittsburgh style classifier system in different Maze environments containing non-Markov situations is provided in [EP08].

5.3.3 Different Implementations

For LCSs a wide variety of different implementations, see [Kov02, MH06], has been proposed, most of them are based on [Wil95], which is an LCS implementation that maintains separate prediction and fitness values and where the fitness of a classifier is based on the accuracy of the prediction reward. While in [Wil94, Wil95] a binary coding of the *stimuli* for these rather simple LCSs is used, different approaches to represent real-valued input have been examined [DAL05a, SB03, Wil00a]. The rule representation depends on the problem being solved: Binary or ternary alphabets $\{0, 1, \#\}$ are most common, the $\#$ is known as the *don't care symbol*, integers, integer intervals [Wil00b], real intervals, or fuzzy rules [Bon98, Bon00, CFM96] are suitable, too. Since the investigations, as presented in Chapter 8, mainly bases on the XCS reference implementation [But00], more details about this special LCS are presented in the next section.

5.3.4 The eXtended Classifier System (XCS)

The *extended classifier system (XCS)* has been invented in [Wil95]. It is widely accepted as one of the most reliable Michigan style LCSs, which is able to handle both, single- as well as multiple-step tasks. The typical schematic overview of an XCS is depicted in Figure 5.2, which is described in the following. For a detailed algorithmic description the reader is referred to [But00, BW00, BW02].

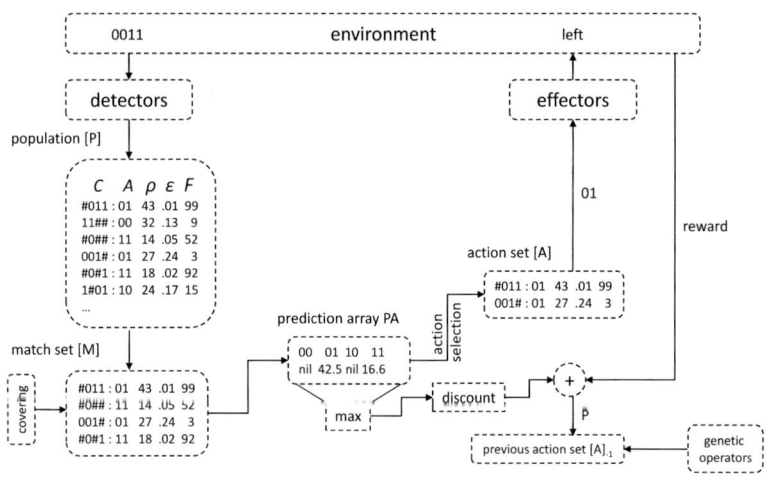

Figure 5.2: *Schematic overview of an XCS, see [Wil98]*

Generally, an LCS is an adaptive system that learns to perform the best action for a given situation (i. e., a vector of numerical values), where *best* is meant as an action that will receive the highest reward or reinforcement from the system's environment. The best action is chosen from a set of available actions, which depend on the investigated context. If the system is a mobile robot [WHRL03], the available actions may be physical and specifying actions like turn the robot *left* or turn it *right*. In a classification context, the available actions may be *yes, no,* etc. In a decision context, for instance a financial one, the actions may be *buy* or *sell* something. In a game theoretical context [SWd05], the actions may guide the players to play a *cooperative* or a *competitive* strategy.

The ability to choose the best action is improved with experience, which is realised as known from reinforcement learning. The environment provides a reinforcement, a so-called *payoff*, which may be 1.0 for a correct classification task and 0.0 for an incorrect decision. In a robotic context, e.g., the payoff could be a number representing the change in distance to a destination, which should be reached. Getting closer to this destination may be represented by larger positive numbers and the other way around. Receiving a reinforcement for a given action, the LCS is able to alter the likelihood of taking that action in similar situations again. Thus, the LCS consists and operates on sets of hundreds of rules, so-called *classifiers*, where every classifier represents a single *condition-action-mapping*.

A Classifier in XCS

Each classifier consists of a condition part and an action part. This mapping is expanded by some attributes that characterise the mapping and that are needed inside the XCS algorithm, as described in [But00, BW00, BW02].

- The condition C specifies the observed situation of the environment, in which the classifier can be applied.

- The action $A \in \{a_1, \ldots, a_m\}$ specifies the action the classifier proposes.

- The prediction p estimates the payoff expected, if the classifier matches and its action is executed in the system. The payoff refers not solely to the expected reward p, but is a combination of p and the payoff prediction of the best possible action in the next state.

- The errors made in the predictions are kept in the prediction error ϵ.

- The classifier's fitness is denoted by F. It is used to find classifiers suitable as input for the generation of new classifiers using genetic operators.

- The number of times since its creation a classifier has belonged to an action set $[A]$ is counted by the experience value exp.

- The time step of the last occurrence of genetic operators in an action set $[A]$, to which this classifier belonged is stored in ts.

- The average size of the action sets $[A]$ this classifier belongs to is stored in as.

- n reflects the number of micro classifiers this macro classifier represents. Classifiers in XCS are always macro classifiers, each classifier represents a number of micro classifiers having identical conditions and actions. This is done for practical reasons. Instead of having n identical classifiers (i.e., the condition-action-mapping is the same) XCS only contains one classifier with *numerosity* n.

The Different Sets in XCS

As depicted in Figure 5.2, an LCS operates on different sets of classifiers, which could be distinguished as follows.

- The population $[P]$ collects all classifiers that belong to a learning problem, which is solved using an XCS. When XCS is started from scratch, $[P]$ is initialised. This can be done in two ways and the two methods only slightly differ in their effect on the learning performance: $[P]$ can be empty or $[P]$ can be filled with randomly generated classifiers. In Figure 5.2 a population is shown that consists of six classifiers where each line is one classifier. The condition C is composed of four bits that are encoded using a ternary alphabet $\{0, 1, \#\}$. The action A consists of two bits.

- The match set $[M]$ is a subset of the population and includes all classifiers that match the measured situation.

- The action set $[A]$ is a subset of the match set and includes all classifiers that propose the executed action.

- $[A]_{-1}$ denotes the previous action set, which was active in the last execution cycle.

In the following section, a survey of the main functionality of an XCS is presented. For more details the reader is referred to the literature [BW02].

Functionality of an XCS

XCS perceives the environment by its sensors and encodes its observations into an environmental message. Then, the so-called *match set* $[M]$ of classifiers is formed, when a particular input occurs. This match set contains all classifiers of the population $[P]$, which satisfy the particular input value. A classifier's condition will match an input vector x, if a truth function $t(x)$ is satisfied $t(x) = 1$ (true). E.g., x_2 is a component of x and the truth function will return true, if $b_1 < x_2 < b_2$ is satisfied with b_1 and b_2 being lower and upper boundaries. In general, a classifier's condition consists of more than one constraint and the truth function will usually refer to all of them. All classifiers, which join the match set, influence the system's action decision. If the population is empty or no classifier(s) of the population match the observed situation, new classifiers will be generated using the *covering* mechanism. The condition is produced by encoding the observed situation and the action is generated randomly. Another covering operator has been introduced in [BW02], it inserts a new classifier for every possible action that is not covered by the classifiers in the match set, see Section 5.6.

For the example in Figure 5.2, the match set $[M]$ is composed of all classifiers from the population $[P]$ that match the input value 0011 coming from the detectors.

Typically, classifiers being in the match set will differ in their actions. Some will advocate an action a_1, others will advocate a_2, and so on. (This is also shown in Figure 5.2. Some classifiers advocate the action 01, others advise 11 as an action.) Furthermore, each classifier possesses an attribute that contains a prediction value p of the amount of payoff a classifier *thinks* it will receive, if the system takes the advocated action. But, how can the LCS decide, which action to take?

It is convincing that the system should execute the action, which in turn receives the highest payoff. Thus, XCS introduces a mechanism (the so-called *prediction array*) that decides, which prediction is the best, and computes for each action in the match set an average of the prediction values and chooses the action with the largest average. Furthermore, the computed prediction average is weighted by another classifier quantity, its fitness, which will be described later, but is intended to reflect the reliability of the classifier's prediction. Thus, $\frac{\sum F_j \cdot p_j}{\sum F_j}$ is computed for every action in the match set, where j are those classifiers having the same action. All classifiers, which advocate the action with the largest prediction average, form the so-called action set $[A]$. Referring to the example in Figure 5.2, an average of the prediction values is only computed for the actions 01 and 11, since no classifiers with an action 00 and 10 belong to the match set $[M]$. Thus, action 01 advocates the highest value in the prediction array and all classifiers of the match set facilitating this action are taken to the action set.

Then, the selected and best weighted action is executed in the environment and the LCS receives some amount of payoff P, which is used to alter the predictions of the classifiers being in the action set. To increase the classifier's accuracy κ, each classifier's prediction p is mathematically changed to bring it slightly closer to the received payoff using a Q-Learning-like algorithm [DB94, Wat89, WD92, She94], which is implemented as shown in Figure 5.2 by the combination of taking the maximum of the prediction array and *discounting* it by multiplying by a factor. Moreover, each learning cycle (receiving a payoff) is used to adjust each classifier's prediction error ϵ and fitness F. The prediction error describes the error of the classifier's prediction. The fitness value F is based on the accuracy of the classifier's payoff prediction and is arrived at in four steps. First, the classifier's accuracy

κ is computed. Then, the accuracies of all other classifiers in the action set are calculated. Third, the relative accuracy is calculated for each classifier in the action set by dividing its accuracy by the sum of the accuracies of the classifiers in the action set. Finally, the classifier's fitness value F is updated according to the relative accuracy value. Thus, the fitness value F of a classifier represents the accuracy of the classifier's payoff prediction relative to the prediction accuracies of other classifiers that typically occur in joint action sets. This provides the basis for the selective pressure in XCS towards more accurate classifiers.

However, an LCS is more than adjusting classifier attributes (p, ϵ, and F) in reinforcement learning cycles. I. e., classifiers evolve and the population of classifiers gradually changes over time. Classifiers with high accuracy values are reproduced more frequently than less accurate classifiers and the offspring are created using genetic operators. Evolution takes place each time an action set is formed and a predefined threshold Θ_{GA} is reached. Then, two classifiers are selected from the action set with probabilities proportional to their fitnesses. The two selected classifiers are copied and with certain probabilities the copies are mutated and recombined (crossed). Mutation and crossover are always customised with respect to the encoded information depending on the scenario. Mutation is interpreted as slight change of a classifier's condition and action. The crossover operator exchanges parts of the two selected classifiers and is often restricted on the condition. After mutation and recombination, the changed classifier copies are inserted into the population, where they have to compete with their parents. To keep the population size on a constant level, the maximal population size is always checked when new classifiers are inserted into the population. To add offspring can imply the deletion of other most inaccurate classifiers.

The effect of classifier evolution is to modify their conditions so as to increase the overall prediction accuracy of the population. This occurs because genetic operators are based on accuracy. In addition, however, the evolution leads to an increase in what can be called the *accurate generality* of the population [Wil98]. That is, classifier conditions evolve to be as general as possible without sacrificing accuracy. Here, general means maximizing the number of input vectors that the condition matches. The increase in generality results in the population needing fewer distinct classifiers to cover all inputs, which means (if identical classifiers are merged) that populations grow smaller, and also that the knowledge contained in the population is more visible to humans – which is important in many applications. The specific mechanism, by which generality increases, is a major, if subtle, side-effect of the overall evolution.

Concluding Remarks

Summarising, a LCS is an adaptive system that learns from external reinforcement and by an internal structural evolution derived from that reinforcement. In addition to adaptively increasing its performance, the LCS develops knowledge in the form of rules that respond to different aspects of the environment and capture environmental regularities through the generality of their conditions. Research has shown that XCS evolves accurate, complete, and minimal representations on different problem domains. The learning of *boolean functions* is well explored [Kov97]. Furthermore, XCS has been investigated on several other problems, as mentioned in Section 5.3.2, but more research has to be done in complex environments. As mentioned at the beginning, LCSs are in the focus of many OC projects (e. g., [BFR08, PRT+08, ZBSH08]) and they fit well into the observer/controller architecture. One of their great advantages is that classifier systems aim at the autonomous production of potentially human-readable results (if this condition is met, then this action is applied). This helps in understanding, how the system is adapting to a specific problem or to a varying environment.

However, as the experimental results in Chapter 8 will show, LCSs have drawbacks in learning speed, especially in high-dimensional complex problems. The number of reinforcement cycles for learning a given task depends on the complexity of the classifiers (i. e., on the number of encoded condition and action parameters), which in turn depends on the complexity of the learning task. This problem is explained in the following section and solutions are also proposed. Furthermore, LCSs have drawbacks in dynamically changing non-Markov environments as multi-agent scenarios, where the answer to the problem does not uniquely depend on the actions by the agent itself, but by all the agents.

5.4 Drawbacks of LCSs

In LCS, learning a set of classifiers with high prediction values and low prediction errors requires a substantial amount of computation time, this includes even simple learning tasks. As the complexity of the task – the dimension of the condition-action-mapping – increases, the demand of computational time to solve a problem becomes more and more a bottleneck, because theoretically, every possible condition has to be mapped to each possible action. The mapping has to be applied to the environment. Moreover, the utility of the mapping has to be tested, rewarded, and evaluated over time. In other words, the number of learning cycles increases dramatically, when the complexity of the learning task increases. As a matter of fact, the strength of a classifier can only be updated by a small amount at each cycle, in order to preserve the stability of the whole system. Furthermore, the genetic operators (crossover and mutation) are also used as background operators to avoid drastic changes in the population, which in turn could affect the stability. Consequently, the high computational costs required to get to a population of classifiers with high performance turns out to be a major drawback.

5.5 Parallelism in LCSs

I am working to improve my methods, and every hour I save is an hour added to my life. (Ayn Rand)

To speed up the learning process (in terms of the number of learning cycles to solve a problem) different strategies could be useful. In the following, it is specially focussed on *parallelism*, so that LCSs can be applied to more complex learning tasks. Parallelism is distinguished as follows.

1. Parallelism as part of a centralised *single-agent* learning approach.

   a) Parallelism is based on the implementation onto *parallel architectures*. An LCS is decomposed into a set of parallel activities that run on distinct processing elements of a parallel architecture. Thus, speed up is achieved by running the problem on parallel hardware. The number of learning cycles will be equal to the sequential algorithm.

   b) Moreover, the learning task of an LCS can be *decomposed* into a set of parallel learning subtasks that are solved in parallel. Then, speed up is achieved by modifying the learning problem, which may decrease the number of learning cycles.

2. Parallelism as part of a *multi-agent* learning scenario, where agents periodically interact and exchange classifiers: The exchange of knowledge that is represented in classifiers constitutes a kind of cooperation, which can help running the search towards the fittest elements of the search space – the best condition-action-mappings. (An agent of this multi-agent learning approach could also be extended by the aspects of the single-agent approaches, as mentioned above.)

5.5.1 Single-Agent Learning Approach

An LCS is normally implemented as a sequential algorithm. Designing parallel LCSs is often analysed by thinking of how to parallelise the sequential implementation by executing it in a parallel architecture to speed up the computation. In general, the overall behaviour of the algorithm is not modified. Parallel hardware only reduces the amount of time to learn a problem, but does not affect the process. The amount of time, which may be saved by a parallel implementation, depends on the number of independent parallel tasks, the amount of time that is used to synchronise the independent tasks, and the number of parallel processing units.

As described in [Gia97], LCSs exhibit some sources of *data parallelism*. Most operations, e. g., building match and action sets, or computing a strength update, can be independently performed on each classifier or can be done in parallel by using standard parallel algorithms. The genetic operators can be independently applied on distinct classifiers, or on sets of classifiers. Since data parallelism is a natural programming paradigm for *single instruction and multiple data (SIMD)* architectures [Fly72], it can also be applied to *multiple instruction and multiple data (MIMD)* machines, which allow many simultaneously active flows of control operating on different classifier sets. Moreover, *control parallelism* can be exploited in an LCS by overlapping distinct activities that can be recognised as independent. This could be achieved by decomposing an LCS into concurrent processes, which focus on different data. One process may operate on the classifiers, the other on the detectors, and the third on the effectors. Since some techniques usually adopted in sequential LCSs are not totally suitable for parallel implementations, it is sometimes not practical to parallelise a given sequential algorithm. Thus, a parallel LCS is designed by adopting new algorithms that are more suitable for a parallel implementation, which may result in algorithms that are not equivalent to the original sequential algorithm.

Decomposing a Learning Problem

The second single-agent learning approach to design parallel LCSs is based on the higher level idea of *decomposing* a problem into several modules/sub-problems, which can be solved independently. Difficult learning tasks are tackled in a modular/hierarchical way and the performance is improved by decreasing the number of learning iterations. Figure 5.3 summarises the different ideas of designing parallel implemented LCSs. The choice between a monolithic and a modular approach is orthogonal to the parallel implementations mentioned before. A modular LCS can also be implemented in parallel.

Related Work Concerning the Single-Agent Learning Approach

Parallelly implemented and hierarchically arranged LCSs have been investigated to reduce the number of reinforcement cycles, necessary for learning a given task. However, the problem of increased convergence times, i. e., the increased number of learning cycles, in the case of big search problems still does not seem to be fully solved. A survey of work that has been done before 1996 is available in [Bar96], more recent work is briefly reviewed here.

Hardware

First parallel hardware implementations on early versions of LCSs have been investigated in [Rob87], where each process of the parallel implementation on a connection machine (CM–2) [Hil85] manages a data structure that references a single classifier. As a result independent operations on distinct classifiers are independently computed. A similar approach is investigated in [Rio88]. Investigations on LCSs on parallel hardware are also presented in [Gia97]. A general framework is defined in order to exploit the computational power of parallel hardware architectures to speed up

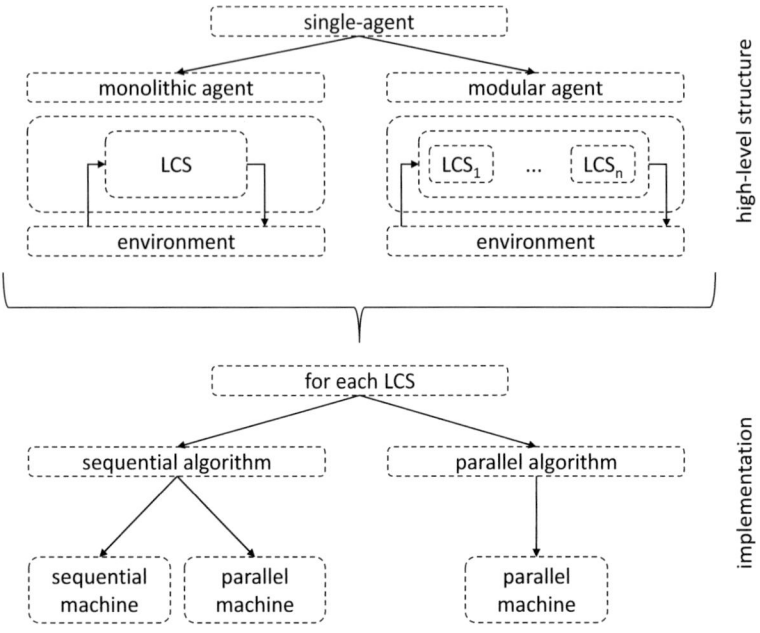

Figure 5.3: *Variants of parallel LCSs as part of the single-agent learning approach: Parallelism is distinguished on different levels, see [Gia97]*

the learning process. The experiments were run on a parallel system, where each processing node is a complete computer and an interconnection network supports the exchange of information among the nodes.

Robotics

In [Dor95, DS93], LCSs are investigated as a tool for building adaptive control systems for real robots. It has been investigated that it is possible to let the AutonoMouse, a small real robot, learn to approach a light source under a number of different noise and lesion conditions. A modular/hierarchical approach is merged by a parallel implementation of each module. In [Dor95], this is called high level and low level parallelism, respectively. On the lower level, each module/LCS is implemented on a transputer-based MIMD architecture providing both, data and control parallelism. On the higher level, different LCSs are organised in a hierarchical architecture, where each LCS is responsible for solving a simpler sub-problem or for coordinating decisions learned by other LCSs. An idea to enhance the learning speed of complex simulated robot behaviours is also presented in [BST07]. The work seems similar to that, presented before in [Dor95]. Five hierarchically arranged LCSs are used, where three LCSs learn basic robot behaviours (chasing, avoidance, and escaping) and two other LCSs combine these basic behaviours to more complex behaviours.

An interesting example of the modular approach is also proposed in [BFS95], where a quadrupedal robot is controlled. Distinct LCSs learn the behaviour of one leg of the robot. The modular approach promotes the formation of behavioural niches in order to obtain modular and scalable structures to deal with more real world applications.

Data Mining

In [DAL05b], an XCS is used in combination with a client/server architecture for distributed data mining. Each client has its own XCS that learns classifications based on a local database and reports the learned classification model to the server. The server aggregates the models to its own XCS and additionally learns all unsolved problems that could not be locally solved by the clients. This distributed XCS architecture is compared to a traditional XCS implementation and the performance evaluation shows that the distributed XCS is competitive to the traditional XCS, when the disturbance level is small. When the level of noise in the data is increased, the distributed XCS needs more time to converge.

In [GS07], a similar idea is proposed. The authors try to improve global XCS performance by solving smaller sub-problems and combining the solutions. Results are demonstrated on the binary coded multiplexer problem.

The idea of data parallelism is investigated in [SQN06]. An LCSs is implemented as an agent-based system on parallel hardware. The performance of the agent-based system is compared on grid data mining tasks (like character recognition and classification) with a monolithic implementation to perform these tasks. Thereby, the whole population of classifiers is distributed among a number of so-called *knowledge agents*. The study compares the execution time of several operations on populations from 120 up to 20 400 classifiers, which are distributed among two up to ten different knowledge agents, and determines the attained speed ups. A measurement of the system efficiency is used, which implicitly incorporates the latency times in relation to the global execution time. The results show that the amplitude of the gains increases in the direction of a bigger number of classifiers, and a bigger number of knowledge agents. On the other hand it is visible that for a number of classifiers less than 2 000 the use of parallelism is not computationally advisable in this scenario. Furthermore, the variation of the global speed up in comparison to the number of classifiers and the number of knowledge agents points to a linear growth.

Concluding Remarks on the Single-Agent Learning Approach

To solve a global learning problem and to improve the learning speed, all cited papers mainly follow the idea of parallelism related to the single-agent learning approach. Two aspects can be distinguished. Firstly, a learning problem is decomposed into sub-problems, which are separately learned and afterwards combined into a global result. However, no work on distributed Michigan style LCSs using the XCS algorithm [But00] is known that uses decomposition and focusses on real- or integer-valued inputs instead of binary coded classifiers. This thesis will specially make contributions to this lack of research. Investigations of task decomposition are done on integer-coded classifiers.

Secondly, the single-agent learning approach has been examined from a viewpoint of parallel hardware in literature. While previous work has focussed on learning in robotic environments or data mining problems with parallelism on hardware level, the provision of a fast on-line learning mechanism is here investigated that can be integrated in the general observer/controller architecture. This general view is independent of hard- and software constraints, since the evaluation of the observer/controller architecture is done as a start in simple multi-agent scenarios using simulated environments.

The single- and multi-agent LCSs' approaches differ in one specific aspect. Agents, equipped with an LCS, can communicate. Thus, they can cooperatively solve a learning problem in parallel, e. g., in [FB95], a multi-agent Pittsburgh style classifier system as part of a two-tracked vehicle is investigated to find trails (as ants) as part of the tracker task, where each motor of the robot is controlled using a single LCS. Each LCS learns actions for one motor moving the robot forward, backward, or doing anything to stay, where it is. Then, coordinated behaviour of the two motors depends on the sum of both separated motors and is achieved using communication between the two LCSs. Rule sets of the left LCS are exchanged with the LCS on the right side and *vice versa*. A comparison of the performances between the two-agent approach and a monolithic LCS that learns the whole problem in a single system significantly shows that the robot will learn the tracking problem faster, if the problem is learned in parallel using cooperation between the two rule sets. The reason for these significant differences is that the fitness landscapes of the communicating classifier systems are smaller and probably less complex than the global landscape of the equivalent single system. Thus, progress for the parallel LCSs is less difficult within the defined niches of left and right. More parallel multi-agent learning approaches are presented in the following.

5.5.2 Multi-Agent Learning Approach

To improve the sequential models regarding learning speed as well as execution time, the multi-agent learning approach is based on the idea of several independent LCSs that work in parallel on the same learning problem. Moreover, they *cooperate* by *sharing* their learned knowledge. Then, the system is characterised by a collection of (homogeneous) agents, where each agent interacts with an instance of the environment that represents the global task to be learned. No agent will outperform all the other agents. The principle of this multi-agent learning approach is to cooperatively combine the output of several agents to find an overall solution that makes use of the strength of the constituents and compensates the individual weaknesses. Similar (cooperative) approaches, as introduced here in the case of LCSs, are known from the research on *genetic algorithms*, when non-trivial problems have to be solved, which forces computationally expensive solutions. Parallel implementations of genetic algorithms come in two flavours.

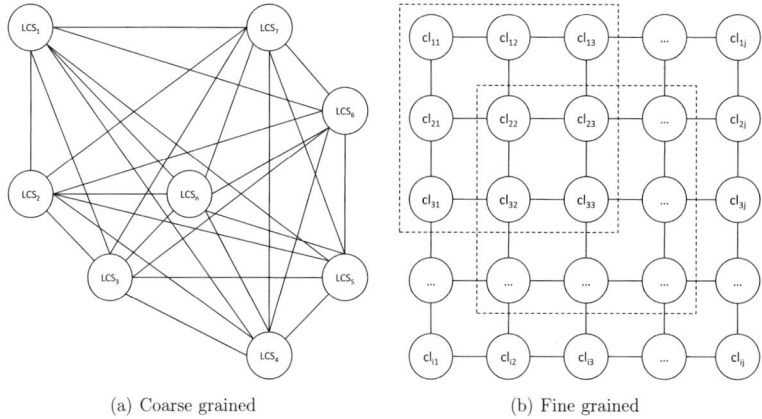

(a) Coarse grained   (b) Fine grained

Figure 5.4: *Population structures for parallel multi-agent LCSs*

Coarse grained parallel genetic algorithms assume a population on each processor node and periodical migration/sharing of individuals among these nodes. This approach is depicted in Figure 5.4(a) and is also well known under the term *island model*, e. g., [CHMR87, NG95]. Each node independently evolves a population of individuals and periodically interacts with other nodes. Then, some selected individuals are exchanged and introduced into the other population. I. e., focussing a Michigan style LCS, each node independently evolves its own population of classifiers. When nodes interact with each other, classifiers are exchanged and introduced into the population of a neighbouring node. In some coarse grained models a neighbourhood relationship is imposed among the nodes. Each node may only interact with a fixed subset of neighbouring nodes. The figure depicts a complete neighbourhood. This is

89

similar to a global communication pattern, where each agent can communicate with each other agent.

Fine grained parallel genetic algorithms assume an individual on each processor node, which acts with neighbouring individuals for selection and reproduction. Good solutions *diffuse* by localised breeding, e. g., [FPS00, MS89]. This is depicted on a two-dimensional grid with a typical neighbourhood in Figure 5.4(b). I. e., one classifier is evolved on each node assuming a Michigan style LCS. After some time the classifiers with high fitness diffuse across the grid. Thus, the population tends to become homogeneous.

In [CP00], it has been shown that performance improvements can also be obtained by such parallel approaches, along with reductions in execution time, due to an increased level of diversity within the global population from the restricted mating schemes.

As stated in [BSBW07], the multi-agent learning approach as a whole will receive many more reinforcement learning cycles as the traditional single-agent LCS, caused by multiple learning processes on each agent. But, under a parallel implementation this increased number of reinforcement learning cycles is not the main concern. With very large data sets and complex problems, the actual data processing time – the time that is needed until an LCS converges to a steady result – to build effective models is the critical factor.

Furthermore, a coarse grained model of parallel (Michigan style) classifier systems consists of independent LCSs, which run in parallel, which operate on the same problem, which periodically interact with each other, and which exchange learned knowledge. Each LCS interacts with an instance of the task environment and the instances of the environment are identical. I. e., the same chosen action in the same situation has the same effect. Additionally, an action in an instance of the environment does not manipulate the other instances. In other words, the multi-agent learning approach replicates the whole learning agent and is based on cooperation, as depicted in Figure 5.5. By comparison, the single-agent learning approach decomposes the learning problem or exploits the parallelism among the internal structure of one agent.

Each LCS searches for a complete solution of the problem. The multi-agent learning approach does not include any explicit decomposition of the learning task. If the problem can be decomposed into sub-problems, an agent will likely find a partial solution. The cooperation between the agents allows to exchange partial solutions. Agents can communicate parts of the whole solution and they can focus on subtasks in parallel. Thus, task decomposition seems to be possible, but is not statically imposed. The main advantage of this multi-agent learning approach is that parallelism is potentially unlimited. A problem can be solved with the cooperation of one up to n agents, where each agent can be implemented in parallel as stated in Section 5.5.1. A further advantage of this multi-agent learning approach is *agent polymorphism*. I. e., each agent can be internally structured in different ways. Thus,

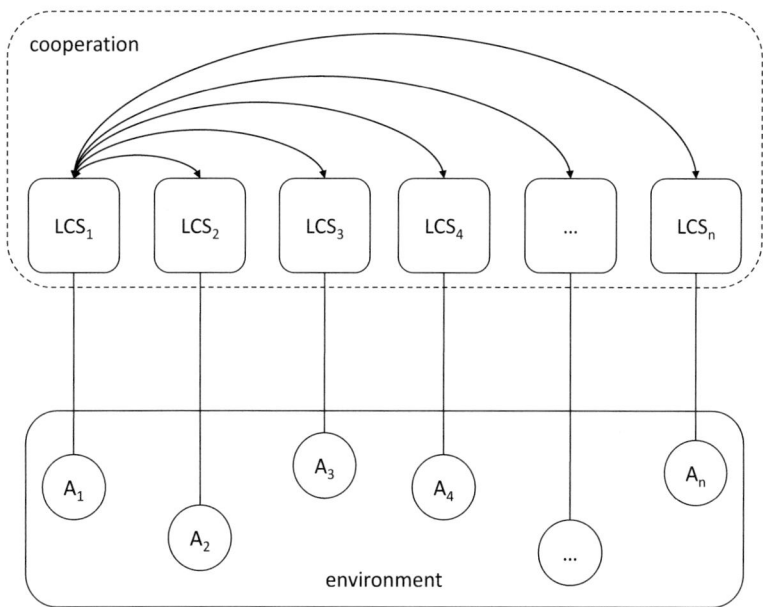

Figure 5.5: *Multi-agent learning approach*

several agents can explore a problem in different ways. This will be of advantage, if little knowledge about the whole learning problem is available and agents start learning from scratch.

Cooperation Strategies between LCSs

Any learning process is an iterative process that calls for progressive refinements. Then, the desired global solution may be a piece of a classifier, a whole classifier, or a set of classifiers. Using the multi-agent learning approach, distinct agents may search in parallel for partial solutions of the problem. As outlined before, one agent may discover a classifier or a set of classifiers, which respond to one situation presented in the environment. Another agent may discover a classifier or a set of classifiers that covers another situation. Thus, agents focus on partial solutions. Parallel cooperative agent behaviour is achieved, when already found partial solutions are exchanged between the agents. In this way, the effort of an agent's search to find a complete solution to a problem is lower than that of an isolated single-agent.

The time that is needed to solve a problem should be significantly decreased. But, the cooperation mechanism has to be aware of the problem of *preserving* and *integrating* the knowledge coming from other agents. If proper *cooperation strategies* are defined, useful knowledge will be shared each time, when agents cooperate, which increases learning speed. However, knowledge exchange can be hindering, if exchanged classifiers are not suitable in the context of the new classifier set. Thus, cooperation between LCSs is characterised by a cooperation strategy among the incorporated agents. This depends on several constraints. A theoretical survey is given in the following.

Firstly, the *genetic granularity* concerns the kind of material that is changed, when agents cooperate. Pittsburgh and Michigan style LCSs learn on different granularities and therefore require special cooperation strategies. The Pittsburgh approach evolves individuals, where each individual is a whole population of classifiers. The Michigan approach evolves individuals, where each individual is equal to a single classifier. A fruitful integration depends on the utility of the exchanged material.

Secondly, the *cooperation mechanism* describes, how the genetic material is exchanged between the agents.

- *Simple* cooperation is achieved, when genetic material is periodically *migrated* from one agent to another agent. This approach corresponds to the island model. This cooperation strategy is also related to other parameters. When LCSs cooperate by migration, both, the *migration rate* (number of migrated individuals) and the *migration interval* (interaction frequency), determine the quality of the final solution and the learning speed.

- *Complex* cooperation describes population *merging*. Two or more agents
  1. merge their populations into a single larger population,
  2. e. g., apply a genetic algorithm to the resulting population, and
  3. redistribute the offspring among the agents according to some criteria.

  The interaction frequency is also important in this case of merging.

Thirdly, the cooperation strategy is based on a communication pattern between the agents. The *interconnection topology* might be either *complete*, i. e., each LCS can cooperate and communicate with any other LCS. Moreover, the interconnection structure can be *partial*, i. e., an LCS can only cooperate with a fixed set of neighbouring agents, since a spatial distribution may define the structure of the neighbourhood.

Not depending on genetic granularity, migration or merging, and complete or partial topologies, the question has to be addressed, *which* classifiers are selected to participate in cooperation. In other words, which individuals are good enough to be exchanged?

The choice of the Michigan approach poses different problems. The fitness value F of a classifier depends on the overall population, a classifier belongs to. Thus, this value is not an absolute measure of the classifier's utility. I.e., a good classifier may not be useful in every population, when it is exchanged. A consequence could be that a set of classifiers is exchanged and not only a single classifier. If a classifier belongs to a cooperating subset (a multi-step chain of classifiers) and is migrated as a single classifier from one population to another one, then it may not find any cooperating classifiers in the new population. Hence, the migrated classifier will not be chosen and will be replaced after some time. Moreover, cooperation happens without effect on convergence and learning speed. In other words, to be effective the cooperation among LCSs should preserve the cooperation among classifiers (which are part of one set).

The relationship between cooperation and premature convergence is also worth mentioning. High interaction frequency or large numbers of migrated classifiers forces premature convergence. Both effect diversity among the affected populations. Moreover, the import of a large number of classifiers may result in instability, since the internal structure of a population is drastically changed.

The discussion highlights the diverse problems, when classifiers are exchanged among populations. It seems to be the designer's choice to speed up the learning process and to preserve the stability of an LCS using a cooperation strategy. Thus, promising related work on the multi-agent learning approach is summarised in the following.

Related Work Concerning the Multi-Agent Learning Approach

In [BSBW05, BSBW07], different classifier *migration* mechanisms are investigated to improve learning speed in comparison to equivalent single-agent learning approaches. Improvements in learning speed are demonstrated on the 20-bit, the 37-bit, and the 70-bit multiplexer problem using an island model as the basic rule migrating mechanism. Studies have been conducted on one hand with a simple accuracy-based derivative of XCS, which is named YCS [Bul05], and on the other hand with a simple payoff-based LCS, which seems to be equal to the *zeroth-level classifier system (ZCS)* [Wil94].

With some predefined probability, some fraction of the population is chosen, based on fitness, to be migrated. A recipient LCS is chosen at random from the other ensemble members. The recipient inserts the new rules into its population. Thus, as in island model systems, the learning process is augmented by the influx of diverse classifiers selected based on their good (local) fitness to be used in further search by a given LCS. This is opposed to purely relying upon the standard stochastic search operators.

The effects from varying the rate, at which rule migrating occurs, and the amount of rules then shared have been examined in a scenario of ten agents on the multiplexer problem and have shown that rule sharing is beneficial. Furthermore, a *niche-based rule migrating mechanism* is investigated, where migration is only applied within the current action set when the average number of system cycles since the last rule migrating in the set is larger than a predefined threshold. If this condition is true, a single rule will be chosen according to the fitness using the standard roulette-wheel selection, before being inserted into the population of another member of the ensemble as described above. Again, this only occurs on explore trials. Investigations on the different multiplexer problems have also shown that time necessary to reach optimal behaviour is reduced. When task difficulty increases (37-bit and 70-bit multiplexer problem), it could be shown that an increase in the relative difference in performance is obtained by the rule migration scheme; the speed up is better than linear here.

In multi-agent scenarios, where the environment is highly dynamic, where information is limited, where response is immediately required, where agents cooperate to reach a common goal, and where agent's specialisation is necessary, other rule migration and rule reuse mechanisms may be needed to increase the learning speed and to keep the agent's diversity, respectively. Thus, a more complex mechanism is provided in [LTSK06, TNS02, TTS01].

Agents administrate local/individual learned populations on one hand, and contribute to global/shared rule sets on the other hand. In multi-agent scenarios, this may be useful, when agents have to cooperate with and contribute to their local behaviour to a global goal fulfilling *different roles*. In dynamic environments, agents have to cope with changes, which require different behaviour. This corresponds to different roles an agent can take. Global rule sets, which contain the whole knowledge of all agents, are stored on a centralised node (or with redundancy on every agent). In [TTS01], the idea of so-called *organisational-learning oriented classifiers* is presented. All classifiers of all agents are stored on every agent and are used to administrate different roles of agent's behaviours. Thus, classifier sets can be shared and reused between the different agents. This rule reuse mechanism depends on the local situation of an agent and specially on the task, which is fulfilled by this agent. In [TNS02], the organisational-learning oriented LCS is investigated on a space shuttle crew task scheduling problem (similar to a job-shop scheduling problem under hard resource constraints) as a real world application. It demonstrates robustness in finding good solutions at small computational costs, even after disturbances occur.

In [BN06], another cooperative multi-agent learning approach using LCSs is investigated, where agents aim at learning the same rules as the others and where agents attract other agents to an unexplored region in the search space. The idea is that agents learn until a consensus between the agents is reached, which means, e. g., that all agents have the same opinion on a classification problem. Since agents attract each other an action-reaction-effect may appear, which leads to an equilibrium status. This effect is implemented using direct communication between the agents, on one hand a *result-based cooperation* is established and on the other hand a *rule exchange mechanism* is used. At each learning cycle a sample from the learning set is given to all agents. Every agent tries to classify this sample and decides, which action to chose. Each agent sends its chosen action to all other agents. Thus, an agent can compare the decisions of the other agents with its own decision. If the degree of agreement between the other agents and itself is greater than a predefined threshold, agents will have the same knowledge and can stop learning on this sample since an equilibrium status is reached. The second cooperation mechanism is based on knowledge sharing. When an agent receives a sample and covering should occur, since no knowledge exists (no classifier of the population matches the given sample), an agent asks other agents for help. When another agent receives such a request and can provide the needed help, it responds with the needed classifier.

A similar rule exchange mechanism is also investigated in [EE99] and focusses on distributed elitism. Pittsburgh style LCSs are used to learn the control of nine junctions in a Manhattan network. Each junction is realised as one (homogeneous) agent and agents exchange best classifiers using a centralised pool. The pool is filled with the best individuals of each agent, where best means the global strength of each agent. Then, the redistribution occurs according to rules. The worst agents take the best individuals from the pool and the best agents take the worst of the best of the pool. Experimental results show that distributed elitism provides robust learning in the case of changing traffic flows.

Since cooperation in multi-agent scenarios is not only limited to rule migration and rule merging, other approaches using LCSs are introduced in short.

Other Multi-Agent Learning Approaches

Another multi-agent learning approach adopting a Michigan style LCS for each agent is presented in [SCK95]. The simulation uses a simple *ring-game* environment with eight agents, where each agent has two neighbours, one on the left hand side, another on the right hand side. At each time step all agents are active and all agents are allowed to observe the actions of their direct neighbours. Depending on a predefined observation horizon an agent is able to observe the number of played games (as state representation of a classifier). Furthermore, all agents simultaneously have to generate an action according to their current decision policy and receive a reward from the game environment at each time step. Then, two experimental studies are compared, one with *reward shaping* among neighbours as local cooperation strategy, the other one without reward shaping. Reward shaping defines a mechanism that a reward, which is achieved in response to an action, is passed to the two agents in the local neighbourhood. The results suggest in the case of this investigated game with limited interactions (i.e., where states of a game are defined in terms of actions executed by neighbouring agents) that reward shaping results in better convergence properties to the global maximum payoff point.

In [HF02b, HF02a], XCS is investigated for modelling social problems. E.g., the *El Farol bar problem* [Art94] is introduced, where agents learn in parallel a cooperative behaviour in studies of ten up to hundred individuals. The El Farol bar problem is based on a bar that weekly offers entertainment. But, the place inside the bar is small and uncomfortable, if overcrowded, and boring, if not full. Thus, a comfort threshold is defined, at the number of people, which makes the place an enjoyable one. Now, the agents have to decide, based on their local strategies, whether or not to go to the bar each week. If an agent decides to go to the bar and the comfort threshold is not exceeded, then the agent will be rewarded. Additionally, if an agent decides to stay at home and the threshold is exceeded, then it will be rewarded, too. Otherwise an agent is not rewarded. Different *global reward functions* are compared that differ in their influence on a cooperative vs. selfish agent behaviour. Thus, this work proves the feasibility of using XCS in a multi-agent scenario, where agents learn to adapt to a complex environment. The focus is not on rule exchange or profit sharing to enhance convergence, but instead global reward functions are investigated.

In [ITS05], a simplified multi-agent soccer game is investigated, where one or two XCS agents have to learn to kick a ball against zero or one randomly moving opponents. The goal is reached, when the ball is kicked over the vertical line of the right or the left side of the 5×9 grid-world. The agents have limited sensors to observe teammates in the upper, lower, left, and right direction, and also sensors to observe the ball, respectively. Learning in this cooperative multi-agent scenario is not improved by rule sharing, but instead by a kind of *reward/profit sharing*. If a team consisting of two agents gets a goal, a reward of 1.0 will be given to the agent, which kicks the ball last, and 0.9 will be given to the other.

Concluding Remarks on the Multi-Agent Learning Approach

LCSs have been investigated on manifold problems. However, their drawback of learning speed has not often been solved. Specially, research on LCSs in the context of cooperative multi-agent scenarios seems to be open for more research. Cooperation has been presented as *rule migration* and *rule merging* mechanisms. Moreover, cooperation has been achieved through *local reward shaping* or *global reward functions*. Accordingly, the capabilities of multi-agent based LCSs have not consistently and comprehensively been investigated yet. Due to this lack of cumulative processes of proposed ideas, it has been difficult to determine the applicable ranges of these manifold approaches. This dilemma prevents industry from employing such ideas for given problems, which is a serious problem, when research results should be transferred to real engineering techniques. To overcome this problem step by step, more research is certainly needed on problems, which do not fulfil the Markov property. Then, it could hopefully be shown that LCSs have the following potential: *Generality* to show a good performance on more real world problems, *scalability* to maintain the same level of performance in large-scale problems, and *high performance*, which corresponds to better results than could be achieved with traditional LCSs.

5.6 Level 2 and Another Covering Method

Since speeding up the learning behaviour of LCSs is in the focus of this thesis, another approach is introduced in the following. The proposed idea adopts the generic observer/controller architecture from the viewpoint of LCSs.

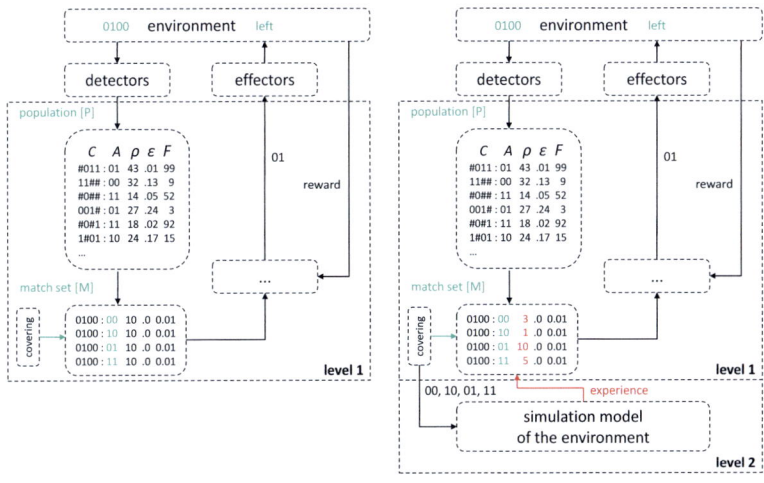

(a) XCS with covering on level 1   (b) Covering uses an simulation model on level 2

Figure 5.6: *Two-level learning architecture is applied to an XCS*

As depicted in Figure 5.2, two discovery mechanisms coexist in an LCS. The genetic operators are inspired by evolution and have been mentioned in Section 5.3.4. The other mechanism, so-called *covering*, is not inspired by evolution. Covering will generally occur, when the minimal number of different actions that must be present in a match set $[M]$ is not achieved. This mechanism provides classifiers for every possible action, whose condition matches the detected situation. In general, the action is randomly chosen. When the parameter, which controls covering, is set to the available number of different actions, *full covering* takes place. A classifier generated by covering can be directly added to the population, since it must differ from all current classifiers. The default value of the covering operator of the XCS reference implementation [But00] is equal to the number of available actions, in other words, *full covering* takes place. In the example depicted in Figure 5.6(a), the input value 0100 coming from the detectors is not known to the population. Thus, full covering generates new classifiers in the case of all possible actions (00,

10, 01, and 11) and introduces these classifiers to the match set $[M]$. New covered classifiers are initialised with default prediction, prediction error, and fitness values. These default values are often badly initialised and many reinforcement learning cycles are necessary to adapt these predefined default values. The inherent problem is that little is known about new classifiers. The LCS randomly covers missing condition-action-mappings and evaluates this relationship by trial and error on the real problem.

In Section 4.3 the organic two-level learning architecture has been introduced to overcome this trial and error behaviour using a simulation model on level 2. Thereby, it has been argued that an agent can test and compare different actions off-line, and thus can plan its next actions without actually acting in the environment. This approach has the advantage that testing potentially bad strategies does not occur in the real world, which can initiate tremendous costs and cause the system to fail permanently.

Thus, it seems possible to extend the default covering operator and to add some kind of off-line planning, as depicted in Figure 5.6(b). When covering occurs, new classifiers are evaluated through simulation on level 2 and initialised through this simulated experience instead of worse default initialisations. Since model-based planning is always limited by the necessary simplifications made in the model, the best action with respect to the model is not necessarily the best action with respect to the real world. However, investigations, as presented here, are limited to simulated scenarios and therefore, the model on level 2 is equal to the real (simulated) world. This new mechanism is investigated in Section 6.2.4, experimental results are presented in Section 8.4.

5.7 Summary

This chapter has introduced the idea of learning as part of an organic controller. Many machine learning techniques coexist that are applicable on the controller's side to implement its proposed functionalities. Thus, a limited view on LCSs has been presented, because they fit well into the observer/controller framework.

Since LCSs have drawbacks in learning speed, the idea of parallel LCSs is explained. Different approaches of parallelism are discussed that depend on the instance that is suitable for learning. A single-agent learns on its own and parallelism on a single-agent is limited to a parallel implementation or task decomposition. A learning problem is decomposed into sub-problems that are solved in parallel. The multi-agent learning approach is based on the idea of several *independent* LCSs that work in parallel on the same learning problem. Moreover, these independent LCSs cooperate by *sharing* their learned knowledge. Experimental results will specially focus on the single-agent learning approach. Furthermore, the two-level learning architecture proposes another learning approach to speed up learning, which combines on-line learning and off-line planning capabilities. In the following chapter, test scenarios are introduced that have been used to evaluate and to compare the different learning approaches.

Chapter 6

Test Scenarios

In order to evaluate the proposed observer/controller architecture as a framework to build organic systems and specially the learning task as part of the controller, some simple test scenarios are required for demonstration of the achievements. To allow for a generalisation of the results, the test scenarios should exhibit a variety of emergent phenomena. On the other hand, they should be rather simple to implement and easy to understand.

This chapter starts with a general introduction to the area of multi-agent systems in Section 6.1 and summarises concepts that have been achieved by other scientists (concerning the aspect of learning). The (quick) reader's thought can concentrate on the nature-inspired chicken scenario in Section 6.2, which is in the focus of most experiments, as presented in Chapter 8. Other test scenarios, as described in Section 6.3, only serve as a pool of inspiration. Experimental results of these scenarios are directly summarised in Section 6.3.

6.1 Multi-Agent Systems

> *In order to live, man must act; in order to act, he must make choices;*
> *in order to make choices, he must define a code of values; in order to*
> *define a code of values, he must know what he is and where he is – i.e.,*
> *he must know his own nature (including his means of knowledge) and the*
> *nature of the universe, in which he acts... (Ayn Rand)*

In general, for less than two decades distributed artificial intelligence has existed as a sub-field of artificial intelligence and is mainly characterised by systems that consists of multiple independent entities that interact with each other in a domain. Multi-agent systems [Woo02] are an emerging research field, which provides principles for construction of complex systems consisting of multiple agents. In the same way, multi-agent systems offer mechanisms for cooperation and/or coordination of independent agents' behaviour. Thus, it is assumed that an agent acts in an environment and is considered to be an entity, e.g., a robot, with objectives, personal/individual actions, and private knowledge – since there is no generally accepted definition of *agent* [RN02]. The way an agent (inter-) acts in the observed environment or with other agents in the environment respectively is called the agent's *behaviour*.

It has several advantages to concentrate on multi-agent systems as a possible domain of test scenarios for research on OC systems. Reasons for that are shortly listed in the following.

- OC *requires* multi-agent technologies. In particular, OC systems consists of a number of (homogeneous or heterogeneous) components with different (or possible conflicting) objectives. These components interact and communicate with each other in a self-organised way and form together the SuOC, which is controlled regarding to some higher objectives. Technical components act in an environment and this dynamics can be observed by other components. In addition to the uncertainty of sensing the other components, a technical component can affect the environment and other components in unpredictable ways. Multi-agent systems seem to be an adequate approach for the design and engineering of such dynamically changing OC systems. This relieves studying the resulting emergent behaviour. Each component could be modelled as a single-agent, which reflects its own capabilities and priorities. Then, a multi-agent system is needed to handle the interactions between the different sub-systems. Furthermore, the collective, collaborative, or emergent behaviour is studied using multi-agent simulations.

- A common objective of OC systems is the capability to maintain a reasonable system performance by adapting to different situations in case of disturbances occurring in the environment. The standard notion for this issue is *robustness*. The requirement to modify the behaviour because of certain changes in system objectives would correspond to the notion of *flexibility*.

Robustness has different meanings depending on the context. Typical definitions include *the ability of a system to maintain its functionality even in the presence of changes in their internal structure or external environment* [CNSW00], or *the degree, to which a system is insensitive to effects that have not been explicitly considered in the design* [SL90]. In engineering, robust design generally means that the design is capable of functioning correctly, (or, at the very minimum, not failing completely) under a large range of conditions. It is also often related to manufacturing tolerances, and the corresponding literature is immense, see [Tag92]. In scheduling, robustness of a plan generally means that it can be executed and will lead to satisfying results despite changes in the environment [Sch01], while in computing, robustness is often associated with fault tolerance [Jal94].

Robustness in multi-agent systems can be achieved by having redundant agents. If control and responsibilities are sufficiently shared among different agents, the system will tolerate failures by one or more agents. A single point of failure may not occur.

- OC systems are no monolithic systems. Since they are compositions of many components, they can flexibly adapt to new situations and changing environments. Multi-agent systems are inherently modular. Therefore, it should be easier to add new agents with different capabilities to an environment than adding new capabilities to a monolithic system. Thus, being *scalable* is an advantage that can be used in OC systems.

- From the viewpoint of a programmer's perspective the modularity of multi-agent systems can lead to simpler programming. A programmer can identify subtasks and can assign these subtasks to different/distributed agents, which decreases the complexity of the whole task on the one hand and speed up possibly a system's operation by providing a method for parallel computation on the other hand. Several independent tasks could be handled by separate agents that run in parallel on different machines. Multi-agent systems support *modularity*, *parallelism*, and *distribution*.

- Finally, multi-agent systems are often used as test scenarios to validate concepts before engineering real world applications and systems. Therefore, they have benefits in terms of the work/cost ratio. This *cost effectiveness* is not a specific characteristic in the domain of OC systems, but rather a general advantage.

The remainder of this general overview about multi-agent systems follows in its argumentation the work done in [HTP+05, SV00], and highlights, how multi-agent systems are often used to build complex systems.

However, many possible ways exist to divide and characterise research that has been done in the field of multi-agent systems, see [Dec87, Les95, Par96]. The overview, as presented in the following, is limited and organised along to main dimensions – agent heterogeneity and amount of communication among the agents. Thus, it starts with the simplest multi-agent scenario, homogeneous and non-communicating agents, followed by a summary of the full range of possible multi-agent systems, through highly heterogeneous and communicating agents. Thereby, communication is not described as the aspect of communication protocols that are available to the agents. It characterises the degree of communication between the agents. E. g., do the agents directly communicate with each other? Or do they not? Furthermore, communication may be limited to a local neighbourhood, where agents only communicate with agents that act in a limited visibility range. Global communication is also possible.

6.1.1 The Predator/Prey Example

As an example of a multi-agent approach, the predator/prey domain is an appropriate example that has successfully been studied in a variety of instantiations. It does not serve as a complex real world domain, but as a test scenario for demonstrating and evaluating manifold research ideas. Introduced by [BJD86], researchers have investigated different instantiations of its original formulation in the context of different application areas. Usually, the predator/prey domain is studied with four predators and one prey acting in a two-dimensional grid-world. However, different numbers of predators and preys are possible. Both, predator and prey, can move typically into four different directions – north, east, south, and west. Additionally, diagonal instead of horizontal moves are a possible variation. Mostly, predators follow a capturing strategy as a goal, while the prey randomly moves or stays still with a certain probability in order to simulate slower movements than the predators. An active escaping strategy, where the prey adapts and learns its behaviour, may also be possible. A cell of the two-dimensional grid-world can only be occupied by one agent. Worlds with other shapes as spaces (e. g., hexagons) or continuous/toroidal worlds without edges (predators and prey can move off one end of the world and come back on another end) are possible. The predators try to capture the prey in such a way that the prey cannot move to an unoccupied position. If the grid world has edges, it might be possible that fewer than four predators can catch the prey by surrounding the prey against an edge of obstacles or in a corner of the world. Other parameters of the predator/prey domain are: Do the agents move simultaneously or successively – one after the other? Is the local view of an agent limited or does an agent see the whole environment? And last, but not least, is direct communication between the agents allowed? While predators and prey(s) have limited actions and follow well defined objectives, the predator/prey domain is simple to understand, easy to implement, and flexible enough to demonstrate a range of different scenarios, which have been emerged over the past decades. The general approach of the predator/prey example, the possibility to customise and adopt the scenario to manifold applications, or the widespread experience that is documented, not only in multi-agent literature, result in the assumption that the predator/prey example can be used as a valid testbed for OC scenarios.

6.1.2 Homogeneous and Non-Communicating Agents

In homogeneous and non-communicating environments all agents have the same *structure*, which consists of same goals, sensors, actions, and domain knowledge. Agents follow the same objectives. They have the same procedure for selecting the next action/movement, but they decide on their own. Agents do not communicate with each other directly. They only differ in their sensory inputs and the actions they take in their individual situations, respectively. Thus, agents have limited information about each other's internal state and sensory input. Moreover, they may not be able to predict each other's actions. As illustrated in Figure 6.1(a), the homogeneous and non-communicating version of the predator/prey example is characterised by one identical agent per predator.

The dominant characteristic of homogeneous and non-communicating environments is that agents have different sensor input and effector output, since they are identical in their structure. Based on the position in the environment and the local observation the agents decide on their own, which actions to take. If all agents act as a unit, they will essentially show the behaviour of a single-agent. In other words, different effector output serves as a necessary condition for multi-agent systems. In order to realise this difference in output, homogeneous agents must have different sensor input as well. Otherwise they will show an identical behaviour.

6.1.3 Heterogeneous and Non-Communicating Agents

Heterogeneous agents combine the advantage of having a great deal of potential power being heterogeneous with the drawback of having more complexity (in developing and controlling heterogeneity in such systems). Agents might be heterogeneous in a number of different ways. Similar to the homogeneous case, the agents are differently situated in the environment, which causes them to have different sensory inputs and necessitates taking different actions. Moreover, they could differ in goals, in actions, or in domain knowledge. As explained in Section 6.1.6, agents can show a cooperative or a competitive behaviour. Even if agents follow different goals, they will cooperatively act to each other's goals, or they will compete and will actively try to inhibit each other.

Figure 6.1(b) depicts a heterogeneous and non-communicating predator/prey scenario, where every predator is controlled by a separate agent. It is shown that agents differ in goals, actions, and domain knowledge (every agent has a different colour, which denotes this context) and cannot be subsumed by one identical agent. Additionally, the prey can be modelled as a single-agent with a different goal compared to the predators' goal.

As described in [SV00], numerous issues arise in this scenario and deal with topics like cooperation vs. competition, static vs. learning agents (problem of credit-assignment), or modelling of other agent's goals, actions, and knowledge.

6.1.4 Homogeneous and Communicating Agents

In this third category, multi-agent systems with directly communicating agents are described. Communication is not interpreted as simply part of an agent's interaction repertoire with the environment. Equipped with communication skills, agents have the ability to coordinate much more effectively than they would act without communicating with each other, even if communication introduces several challenges. As in the homogeneous and non-communicating case, the predators are identical agents except that they are differently situated in the environment and that they can directly communicate with other agents. From a practical point of view, communication might be realised as broadcast, as posting on a blackboard for all to interpret, or as point-to-point communication from one agent to another one.

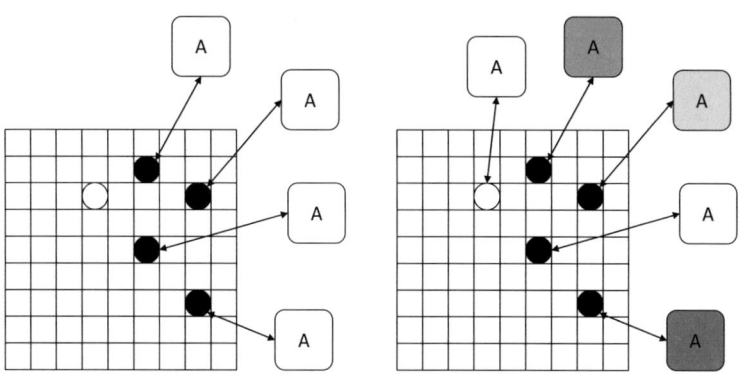

(a) Homogeneous predators using one identical agent per predator

(b) Heterogeneous predators may differ in actions and goals

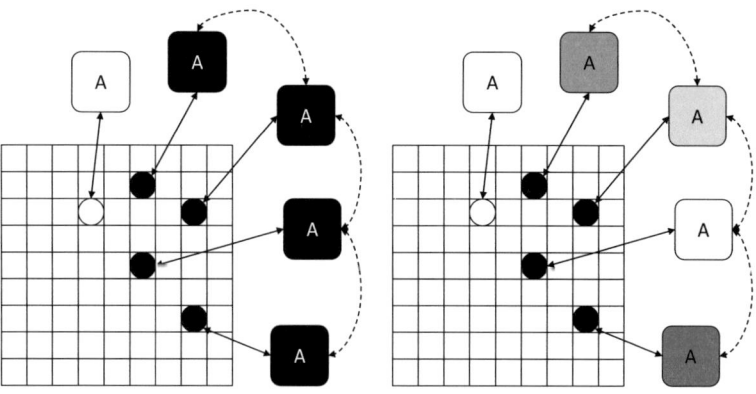

(c) Homogeneous predators that can also communicate directly

(d) Predators are heterogeneous and communicate with each other

Figure 6.1: *Variants of the predator/prey example, see [SV00]*

As illustrated in Figure 6.1(c), communication creates new possibilities in the predator/prey scenario. In a scenario having only one prey, the prey cannot profit from communication. But, the predators can exchange information and more effective capturing strategies can emerge.

In Section 6.2, a nature-inspired multi-agent scenario is described that belongs to this category of homogeneous and communicating multi-agent scenarios. Certainly, OC focusses on the problem of increasing complexity in *technical* scenarios, and it is admitted that this nature-inspired *chicken scenario* has no obvious technical relevance on its own. But, this scenario can also be seen as an instance of the predator/prey example with a more technical background, where e.g., robots explore unknown environments, robots observe and control other robots, or autonomous swimming robots operate in inner harbours and clean the water from oilslick using swarming techniques. The resulting problem of clustering, see Section 6.2, where all agents move and meet at one place of the two-dimensional grid world, is a general problem from the investigated point of view and does not only depend on the selected application domain.

6.1.5 Heterogeneous and Communicating Agents

Heterogeneous and communicating agents in the predator/prey example are shown in Figure 6.1(d). The agents can differ in any number of ways, including the sensors, the goals, the actions, and the domain knowledge. These heterogeneous and communicating multi-agent systems can be very complex and powerful. They reflect the full power of multi-agent systems.

6.1.6 Cooperative and Competitive Multi-Agent Learning

The presented categories above do not cope in detail with the issue of cooperation and competition in multi-agent *learning* scenarios. Thus and following the reasoning of [HTP+05], two major types of *cooperative* and *competitive* multi-agent learning approaches should be added – which may result in a third dimension of categorisation of multi-agent systems in addition to degrees of heterogeneity and communication. Main concepts are only summarised, and the link between multi-agent systems and (evolutionary) game theory [Smi82] is skipped, which is a common standard of modelling cooperative and competitive multi-agent behaviour.

In cooperative learning systems agents pursue a common goal and the group utility is maximised. Designers of multi-agent systems are free to design (cooperative) agents. The algorithm that learns the cooperative agent's behaviour is fully controlled. Thus, extensive knowledge of the system can *explicitly* be built into the agents, which can always anticipate and expect cooperative behaviour and good intentions from other agents.

In comparison, agents in competitive multi-agent scenarios are solely focused on maximising their own utility having selfish goals. Competitive settings are often created by separate designers, where all affected parties try to achieve their own goals. As a result, cooperation between selfish agents seems to be a more difficult and risky task. A designer of competitive agents must also expend effort in considering the types of exploitive behaviour that will be encountered. This increases the range of strategies the agents can choose and the complexity of programming and controlling competitive settings.

Cooperative Team Learning

Cooperative team learning summarises approaches, where a single-agent searches for new behaviours for the entire team of agents. Such approaches are equal to traditional machine learning techniques and straightforward, but they have unsolved scalability problems within increasing team sizes. Team learning can be divided into homogeneous and purely-heterogeneous team learning (the aspect of communication is skipped). Homogeneous agents develop a single-agent behaviour that is used by every individual. A single behaviour of every agent drastically reduces the search space of new rules and is well studied for cellular automata [MCD96]. Purely-heterogeneous agents (e. g., typical in the case of robotic soccer) learn a unique behaviour for each agent. This has the advantage of agent specialisation, and the disadvantage of a larger search space.

Cooperative Concurrent Learning

Reducing the joint search space into n separate spaces, multiple concurrent agents search for new behaviours, and every agent has its own learning process to modify its behaviour. This field requires new learning methods, because multiple learning agents make the environment dynamic, and this is contrary to the assumptions of most traditional machine learning algorithms (which is also known as the *Markov property*, see Section 5.3.2). Concurrent learners adapt their behaviour depending on other adapting agents, and they have no control on this process of coadaptation. Even the agents' own adaptation to the dynamically changing environment can change the environment itself. This makes learning complex and divides research of concurrent learning into three research areas: Firstly, the credit assignment problem (How to divide team reward among the individuals?), secondly, the dynamics of learning (How to cope with the problem of coadaptation?), and thirdly, modelling of other agents (How to model other agents to improve collaboration?).

Competitive Learning

Competitive multi-agent learning systems are characterised by agents, which do not share the goal to work together. The overall utility of all agents is not in the focus of these systems. The agents compete, they have their own, possibly conflicting goals, and they search for local optimisation. Competitive agents are often used in business scenarios, where negotiation and auctioning play a role between competing companies or autonomous departments within bigger organisations.

Competitive multi-agent scenarios are based on the principles known from the field of economics, where *game theory* is broadly used to mathematically analyse the strategies of competing players. Typically, research has covered scenarios coping with e-commerce, market-based games, markets and market mechanisms, auctions, or matrix games.

6.1.7 Concluding Remarks

Multi-agent scenarios have been used widespread and successful in research. Therefore, the use of multi-agent scenarios is anticipated in order to evaluate the proposed observer/controller architecture. Especially, this thesis is interested in and focus on the learning task of the controller.

Evaluating the observer/controller architecture completely, all variants of this architecture, as proposed in Section 4.4, have to be tested in all mentioned multi-agent categories starting with a scenario of homogeneous and non-communicating agents, and tackling then the full range of possible multi-agent systems, through highly heterogeneous and communicating agents. Since this may be overwhelming, the investigations are started with the case of applying the centralised observer/controller architecture to homogeneous and communicating agents.

6.2 Chicken Simulation

The multi-agent system described below and used for the experimental validation of the observer/controller architecture in Chapter 8 is inspired by nature and shows clustering from a macroscopic point of view as an emergent behaviour of local interactions. The simulation reproduces the collective cannibalistic behaviour of densely housed chickens in cages and tries to explain the unwanted behaviour of clustering, also known as *feather pecking* [BA84, JPF06, RKE+08, RvB+04]. This behaviour is frequently observed, when a chicken is wounded. Moreover, it leads to a major loss of animals (up to 50% of the animals).

If chickens perceive a wounded chicken, they will chase this chicken and pick on it, until it dies [MRB+07]. Chasing and picking wounded chickens leads to the emergent building of chicken swarms (or clusters), see Figure 6.2. A swarm disperses, when the wounded chicken is killed. The emergent behaviour is spatial, but swarms move over time. This is a case of *negative*, i.e., undesired, emergence.

While simulating this behaviour, order patterns emerge as expected in form of chicken swarms. Currently, in agriculture these patterns are interpreted by human

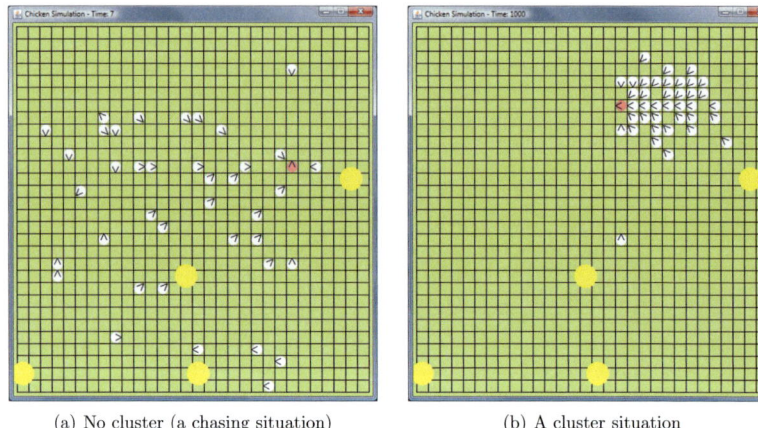

(a) No cluster (a chasing situation)	(b) A cluster situation

Figure 6.2: *Snapshots of the chicken simulation: Unwounded chickens are white, wounded chickens are dark (red), and feeding troughs are represented by four bigger (yellow) circles.*

experts. But, from the viewpoint of OC it is the goal to observe, classify, and control (global and macroscopic) system behaviour automatically. To achieve this goal and to reduce the chicken death rate, the observer/controller paradigm is used, as introduced in detail in Chapter 4. A quantified context of the underlying system is reported to the controller, which evaluates the situation and reacts with adequate control actions to disperse chicken swarms or to prevent their formation.

Referring to Section 6.1.4, the organic approach is evaluated in a homogeneous and communicating predator/prey example, where healthful chickens (predators) search and chase wounded chickens (preys). To be a predator or prey depends on the individual energy level of each chicken, as outlined in Section 6.2.1. It is a scenario with communicating agents, since chickens know about the internal state of all chickens in their local neighbourhood. As explained in the following, a chicken can be a *following* chicken, which means that it perceives a wounded chicken and other chickens follow this following chicken.

The scenario has been taken from an interdisciplinary research cooperation between the Leibniz Universität Hannover and the University of Veterinary Medicine Hannover. In its first implementation without an organic observer/controller architecture the multi-agent scenario shows that very simple local rules suffice to explain the global complex behaviour and reproduces the swarming behaviour well known from nature, see [Ost04, von05]. The simulation followed the goal to assign the nature behaviour to a technical multi-agent scenario, which is explainable by human beings. A snapshot

110

of this *Eurovent*[1] simulation is presented in Figure 6.3. But, the outlined original simulation programme does *simply* simulate a chicken population showing clustering behaviour without providing any means for the user to intervene in the course of the simulation. Within the limits of this thesis, the existing simulation programme has been rebuilt and extended to incorporate additional functionality. The scenario has been uncoupled from the nature context and OC research questions have been focussed. The major requested modifications are listed in the following.

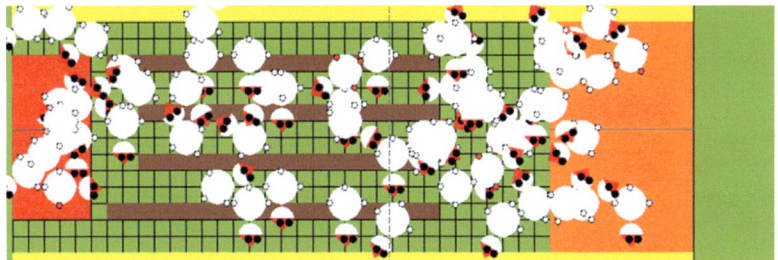

Figure 6.3: *An Eurovent cage with 60 chickens*

- Controlling and learning to control the unwanted behaviour of the chickens a control mechanism has been implemented, which bases on the generic *observer/controller architecture*. Even if both, an observer and a controller, were implemented, the focus will be on the controller's side, specially on the (on-line) learning task using LCSs.

- The *observer* should be able to recognise and to quantify clustering. The quantification is necessary, because it is the prerequisite for the interventions of the controller. Additionally, the observer is provided with the capability to predict the near future. This ability presumes either the existence of a system model within the observer or competence to approximate the future course of the system. Work on the observer's side is shortly described and for more details the interested reader might have a closer look at [Mni09].

- The *controller* should be able to intervene somehow in the course of the system, if clustering is detected by the observer. Interventions of the controller or its control strategies should reduce clustering and as a direct consequence the number of killed chickens should decrease.

Implementing an observer/controller architecture on top of the chickens creates an instrument to observe the development of clustering in the system in a quantitative

---

[1]http://www.bigdutchman.de

111

way (i.e., to measure clustering). On the other hand, controlling the clustering behaviour improves the whole system performance. System performance is expressed in terms of life times and number of killed chickens. The observer and the controller have to satisfy the general guidelines of OC. Thus, these components are realised with respect to certain constraints, which are mainly the properties of the generic observer/controller architecture.

- The controller should never be a centralised authority, as known from classical and centrally organised control systems. Therefore, the interventions of the controller have only a guiding nature (the autonomy of the agents is not compromised). In Section 6.2.4 these interventions are described in detail.

- Ordinary operation of the chickens should be guaranteed, if observer and controller are turned off. This constraint results from the principle that the chickens (i.e., the SuOC) do not rely on the actions of the controller. Most certainly, the number of killed chickens will increase in absence of the controller, however, the agents are able to fulfil their strategy further on, where they are explicitly programmed for.

6.2.1 Agent Behaviour

It should be mentioned that the notions of agent or chicken have the same meaning in the here presented context. The item *chicken* is used in analogy to the nature-inspired paradigm and abstract from the animal to presume that the single chicken is an autonomous technical agent, which shows no life of its own and instead reacts as specified by its developer.

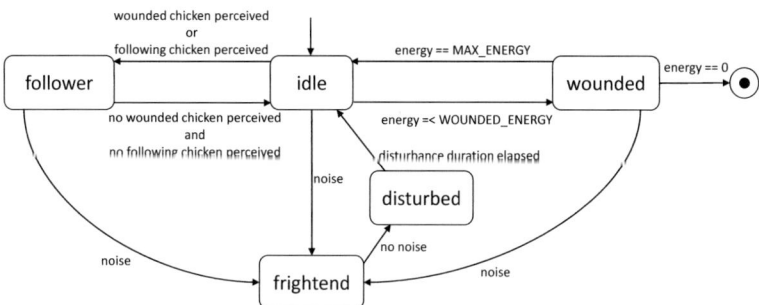

Figure 6.4: *Finite state machine of a chicken representing the local behaviour rules of a single chicken*

In the simulation, every chicken can move to eight different directions (north, north-east, east, south-east, south, south-west, west, and north-west) at the speed of one movement per simulation tick. A chicken is characterised by the attributes heading, position (x-, y-coordinates), and energy/vital force. As depicted in Figure 6.4, a chicken is directed by a predefined fixed *finite state machine* and it will be influenced by the behaviour of other chickens in its local neighbourhood or by changes in the environment, e. g., noise that frightens the chickens, see Section 6.2.4. Chickens are considered as autonomous agents with simple fixed rules and local goals, they aim to survive as long as possible, and they are attracted by wounded conspecifics.

Whether a chicken is wounded or not depends on its personal energy level. Five different internal states of a chicken have been defined – the scenario has been simplified and the effects of food have been blinded out. Because of this the finite state machine, as pointed out in Figure 6.4, is quite simple.

Idle — In this state a chicken is not wounded. The chicken moves according to a simple mobility model, is initially placed at a random position in the cage, a two-dimensional grid, and randomly chooses a new position to move to in its direct neighbourhood. Arrived at its destination the chicken chooses another random destination for the next simulation step. One simulation step is characterised by a movement from one field to another one in the direct neighbourhood. Typically, a chicken can choose its new position from a set of eight possible positions. Alternatively, it stays, where it is.

Follower — A chicken will move to this state, if a wounded chicken or a following chicken is perceived (the distance to this chicken is lower than a fixed perception horizon given as simulation parameter, see Table 6.1). Then the chicken tries to get as near as possible to the wounded (or the following) chicken using the *Euclidean distance*. If it is immediately close to the wounded chicken, it will begin to pick on it (and the wounded chicken will loose energy).

Wounded — A chicken will get to the wounded state, if its energy level passes a threshold that is lower than a given energy level, which is set by a simulation parameter, see Table 6.1. In this case, the wounded chicken tries to escape attacks, it maximises the distance between itself and the chickens in its direct neighbourhood, and the energy level will increase with each tick of the simulation, only if it is not picked.

Frightened — A chicken will be frightened, if it is confronted with noise. It moves as fast as possible (one field per simulation step) outside the fields that are affected by noise. If the chicken has been in the state of a *follower*,

113

Table 6.1: *Parameters of the chicken simulation*

Number of agents	40
Size of the two-dimensional grid	30×30 fields
Simulation time	Varied (maximal 1 000 000 ticks)
Generation of wounded chickens	Every 60 ticks, after a wounded chicken is killed or healed
Maximal energy level in the case of a wounded chicken	100 energy units
Energy level of a randomly generated wounded chicken	70–80 energy units, which are uniformly distributed
Energy lost per received pick	One energy unit
Healing rate	One energy unit/tick
Radius of the perception horizon of a chicken	15 fields
Number of moving directions	Eight plus one (stay at position)
Disturbance duration of a chicken after a controller intervention	Five ticks
Number of feeding troughs	Four

it will try to maximise the distance between the wounded chicken and itself.

Disturbed – After leaving the noise affected fields a chicken changes to the disturbed state for a fixed duration, see Table 6.1. A chicken does not react to wounded chickens and randomly moves as it does when being idle.

The simulation environment is set up with the parameters, as listed in Table 6.1. A scenario of 40 chickens is observed that randomly move on a two-dimensional grid, which has a dimension of 30×30 fields, see Figure 6.2. The two-dimensional grid is limited through the borders on the left, on the top, on the right, and on the bottom side. Thus, the agents cannot move outside the grid or they cannot move out of the grid on the right side and enter the grid on the left side (like a torus). If a chicken is set to a border or it reaches an edge of the playground, it will be obvious that five or three possible movements are not possible for these special situations.

Each cell of the grid can only be occupied by one agent or by one feeding trough. The feeding troughs have the function of obstacles. To achieve endless simulation runs, a new chicken is generated and randomly placed in the cage, when another chicken is killed. Thus, the simulation always runs with a complete chicken population (of 40 agents).

6.2.2 General Simulation Structure

As mentioned before, the simulation programme is an implementation of an observer/controller architecture following the generic model. The SuOC is formed by the chickens moving on the grid. The programme itself runs in form of a loop; during operation, the loop is cycled once every tick. After programme initialisation the simulation begins iterating trough the loop. At first, (a) the chickens act, i. e., move to another position on the grid or pick a wounded chicken, then (b) the task of observing starts, and (c) the task of controlling is executed. The focus of the following explanations is on steps (b) and (c).

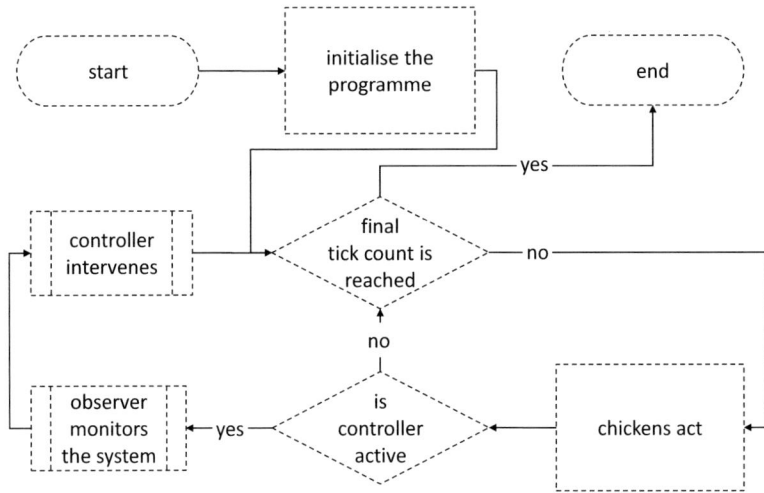

Figure 6.5: *Operational sequence of the chicken simulation, the contained observing and controlling steps are shown in Figures 6.7 and 6.12*

Before starting the simulation the user is able to turn on or off the observer/controller functionality (via a parameter file). Deactivating the controller does also deactivate the observer as the monitoring process of the observer is a necessary prerequisite for the controller. (There exists no functionality for deactivating the controller only.) As postulated before, the simulation will technically run flawless without an observer/controller. Of course, there will be more clustering without an observer/controller. Nevertheless, the simulation is runnable without an observer/controller. The just outlined course of operations is shown in Figure 6.5. In the following section the actual implementation of the observer/controller architecture is introduced.

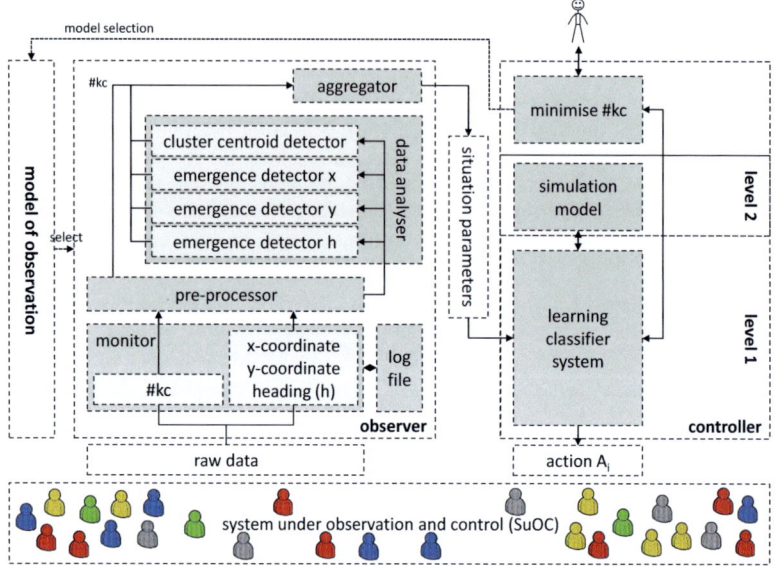

Figure 6.6: *The generic architecture is applied to the chicken scenario*

6.2.3 Observing the Chickens

The primary task of the observer is to monitor the system behaviour, to aggregate, and to generate the system parameters based on the current system state. In the chicken scenario the relevant system state for the controller is mainly determined by the present degree of clustering, as the controller has to alleviate it. Therefore, the observer has to measure clustering and quantify it. In the following, the procedures taking place within the observer as well as the actual parameters being monitored by the observer are outlined.

The generic observer/controller architecture is applied to the scenario, as depicted in Figure 6.6. The observer fulfils its task on-line, i. e., the status of all relevant system components (the chickens) is checked at every simulation tick within the observing process. For this purpose, the observing process is made up of five steps: Monitoring, pre-processing, data analysing, predicting, and aggregating. The whole process is illustrated in Figure 6.7 and explained step by step in the following. E. g., monitoring is limited to the number of killed chickens, the x-coordinates, the y-coordinates, and the heading of all chickens. Data analysing computes three emergence indicators.

116

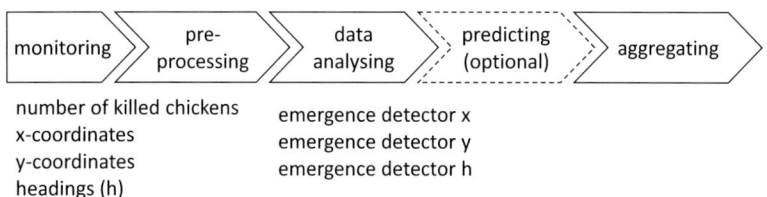

number of killed chickens
x-coordinates
y-coordinates
headings (h)

emergence detector x
emergence detector y
emergence detector h

Figure 6.7: *Steps of the observing process*

Observation Range

In order to develop metrics to quantify the clustering behaviour of the chickens, all parameters have to be specified, which can actually be observed and that are relevant for attaining the objective. However, before the observer is able to monitor or pre-process raw data, the intended data have firstly retrieved. Data retrieval raises the question, which parameters of the SuOC can actually be *seen* by the observer, i.e., how far does the observer's *visibility range* reach? The visibility of parameters is certainly not a serious constraint in the present straightforward test scenario, but it could be a rather important factor at more comprehensive real world applications.

The visibility of model parameters to the observer seems to be ambiguous. Within this test scenario all parameters could be made visible to the observer easily. However, in real world systems of larger scale such a request would be infeasible in many cases. E.g., in large collections it may be impossible to observe all components of the SuOC in detail. There may not be enough sensors, the communication bandwidth may not be sufficient, the used hardware may not be able to process so much data, the collection of data would consume too much energy, etc. As described in Section 4.1.1, it may be necessary to adjust the *model of observation* in the presence of such constraints in terms of granularity. In the chicken scenario the parameters, as listed in Table 6.2, may be observable.

Since Table 6.2 potentially shows all observable parameters, the observer's view has been limited in the chicken scenario to some special parameters. These could be measured by observing the cage with a simple camera from a global point of view, where the camera is installed above the cage. Such a simple camera would be able to identify the moving agents, but not to view inside a chicken. The camera has no information about the individual energy level or the local destination of a chicken. I.e., the energy value is an intrinsic property of the agents, which is not available to an external observer. Thus, a camera can only decide, if a chicken is wounded, if a chicken is killed, or if a chicken is completely healed.

Model parameters like the dimension of the grid or the total number of chickens will definitely remain *constant* during operation. Other parameters as the number of wounded chickens or the position of the agents will *vary* over time, e.g., when a

117

Table 6.2: *Observable parameters*

Agent parameters	Model parameters
Position (x- and y-coordinates)	Horizontal and vertical dimension of the grid (number of fields)
Heading	Position of feeding troughs
Energy level	Number of feeding troughs
Destination	Total number of chickens
...	Number of wounded chickens
	Number of killed chickens
	Position of clusters
	Number of involved chickens in a cluster
	...

noise signal is applied. It is suggested that these constant parameters will not be observed, but rather known by the observer, if their observation is desired.

Therefore, in the *monitoring* task data are collected from the system at a fixed sampling rate (one data set each simulation tick). As depicted in Figures 6.6 and 6.7, this data set consists of a *system-wide* attribute (the number of killed chickens in the last sampling period, denoted with $\#kc$) and of *individual* attributes of each chicken (x-coordinate, y-coordinate, and heading).

Observation Functionality

During operation, the observer is ought to measure the current level of clustering among the chickens. In the chicken scenario the focus on the observer's side has strongly been set on a validation of the methods of the *data analyser*, see Figures 6.6 and 6.7,

The functionality of the *pre-processor* is reduced to passing the individual parameters to the data analyser and the number of killed chickens to the aggregator. The *data analyser* determines the *emergence fingerprint* of the system by computing the (relative) emergence indicators (e_x, e_y, e_h) of the collected three chicken attributes at every simulation tick, as described in more detail in [MMS06] and summarised in Section 4.1.5. Additionally, the data analyser determines the coordinates of the population centroid (x_c, y_c). The results of the data analyser (three emergence indicators and the population centroid) are passed to the aggregator.

Predicting is an optional step, which has not been investigated in detail. Therefore, prediction is left out of this thesis. Instead, the reader is referred to [MMS06], where a trajectory-based prediction method of chicken positions is presented, which can be used to predict and prevent future unwanted clustering. By extrapolating the trajectories of the chickens, this prediction method measures the positions of every chicken at two consecutive points in time. Based on these two points and the heading of each chicken the trajectory of a chicken is computed by extending the line between them, as illustrated in Figure 6.8. This method results in an early indicator of clustering and allows to react in time.

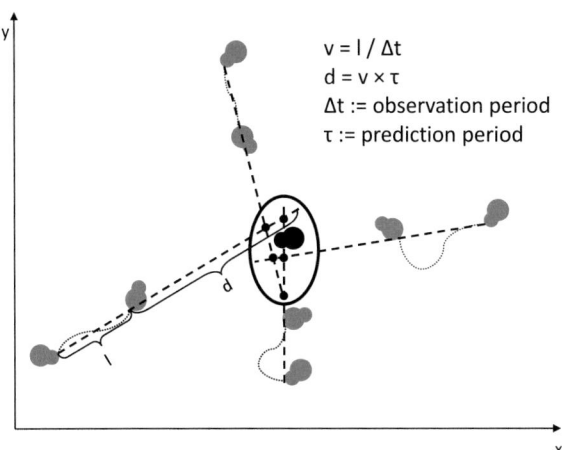

$$v = l\,/\,\Delta t$$
$$d = v \times \tau$$
$$\Delta t := \text{observation period}$$
$$\tau := \text{prediction period}$$

Figure 6.8: *Method to predict clustering, see [MMS06]*

The *aggregator* forwards the situation parameters $S_t = (e_x, e_y, e_h, (x_c, y_c), \#kc)$, composed of the computed data analyser values and the number of killed chickens, as a combined vector to the controller. E. g., typical values of the relative emergence indicator of the *x-coordinates* can be seen in Figure 6.9.[2] The figure shows the trend for one run of simulation and the recurrence of a cycle is observed that constitutes of three phases: The formation phase of clustering (the curve increases from values around 0.25 to 0.6 or higher), a clustering phase (the values oscillate on a high level), and a dispersion phase (the curve decreases from high level to low level). The interpolated values show a more exact disjunction of the three phases, as depicted in Figure 6.10.

During the absence of a wounded chicken, the chickens are uniformly distributed over the area. When a chicken becomes wounded, a cluster is formed after a short delay and the emergence indicator increases. After each clustering phase a chicken is killed, as depicted in Figure 6.11. Then, a short distribution phase follows and a new

---

[2]Typical values of the relative emergence indicator of the *y-coordinates* and the *heading* are not presented. However, they show a similar behaviour.

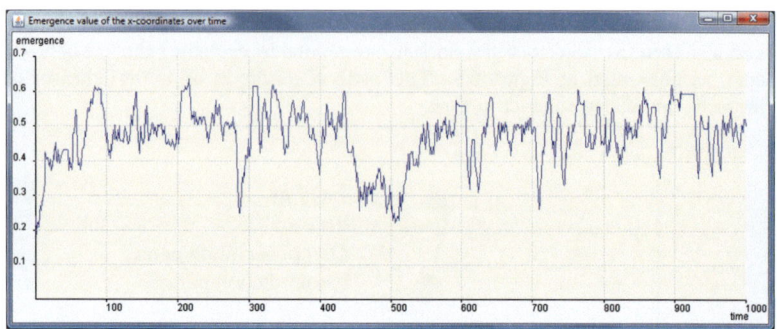

Figure 6.9: *Emergence value of the x-coordinates over time without any control action*

cycle begins. E. g., a chicken is killed at time 280. Similarly, a cluster decreasing phase starts as well as at time 280, see Figures 6.9 and 6.10.

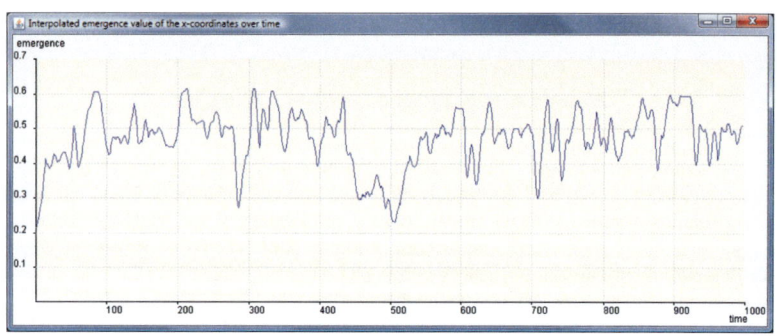

Figure 6.10: *Interpolated emergence value of the x-coordinates over time without any control action*

The figures indicate that there is a correlation between the different emergence indicators, the clustering behaviour of the chickens, and the total number of killed chickens. Furthermore, the observations suggest that an optimal control intervention should be triggered, when a certain emergence value is exceeded, as explained in the following.

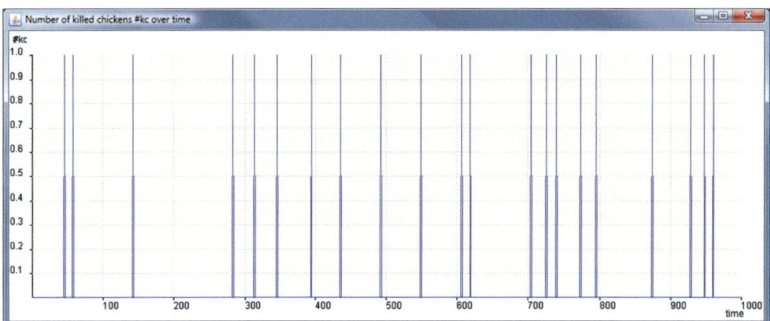

Figure 6.11: *Number of killed chickens #kc over time (every peak denotes a killed chicken) without control action*

6.2.4 Controlling the Chickens

After the observer has finished evaluating the current system state including the unwanted clustering behaviour, the controller becomes active. As stated before, the task of the controller is to maintain a proper system behaviour. The controller assesses the system's situation, based on the information given by the observer. Afterwards the controller intervenes in the course of the SuOC, whether a control action is considered as necessary or not.

Like the observer, the controller acts at every tick and the process of controlling directly starts after the observer has submitted its situation parameters to the controller. The process consists of a receiving and an action selecting step. Between these two steps on-line learning and off-line planning may take place. The whole investigated process is depicted in Figure 6.12.

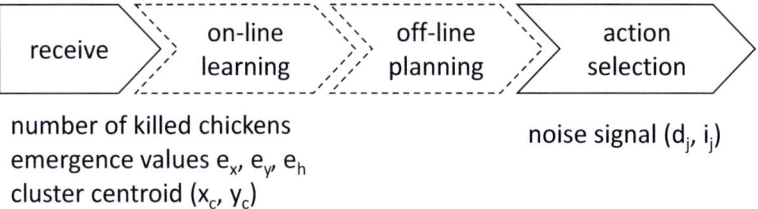

Figure 6.12: *Steps of the controlling process*

Within the receiving step the controller assesses the situation. Based on the situation parameters, it will decide, if the situation is in accord with the desired course of the system or if it is not. In the present case, the decision is based on three emergence indicators (e_x, e_y, e_h), reported by the observer, as the task of the controller is to prevent the clustering behaviour of the chickens (or to minimise the number of killed chickens). The situation will be considered as undesirable, if the number of killed chickens drastically increases or if the clustering behaviour surpasses a certain predefined threshold. Thus, if the observations reach a critical situation, the controller will intervene using the cluster centroid (x_c, y_c). If otherwise, the process of control will come to an end without further intervention. The controller checks the clustering behaviour every tick, so it will decided at every tick anew, if interventions have to be started, ended, continued, or to be omitted further on. Finally, when no learning steps are implemented the action selector step will follow, if the controller decides to intervene. Within this step the controller performs its interventions. The actual form of the interventions depends on the implemented control actions. Different control actions are possible in this chicken scenario.

1. The controller can change the local decision rules of the agents, which modifies the local behaviour of the individual. Doing so the controller has to know the encoded dependencies about the finite state machine that allows the chickens to move and behave on the grid. In this nature-inspired scenario such an intervention seems not realistic, the genes of a chicken cannot be modified. Thus, this way of control has not been addressed in this scenario.

2. The controller can influence the system structure. As assumed in Chapter 4, the elements of a SuOC base their actions on local information, where *local* is defined by a neighbourhood and an interconnection network. Modifying this network, in particular with respect to global characteristics, will change the global behaviour of the system. Also, changing the absolute number of elements influences neighbourhoods and at last the behaviour of the SuOC. In the chicken scenario this would mean, e. g., that the controller could introduce new wounded chickens to the population or that chickens, which pick too much on a wounded chicken, are directly wounded by the controller. Since the controller should rescue and not kill the chickens, such actions seem not reasonable. Placing more feeding troughs or some other kind of blinds on the grid to distract the chickens from a wounded chicken may assumed to be a better and more realistic strategy of control.

3. At least, the controller can influence the environment, which allows *indirect* control of the chickens and will only work, if the agents have sensors to measure and react to a modified environment.

Thus, it has been decided to control the chickens with some kind of *noise signal*. A noise signal with variable intensity i and duration d can be applied at an arbitrary position in the cage to frighten the chickens and scare them off, which leads to the dispersion of a possible existent cluster. Moreover, the noise signal also has a negative effect: If the noise is too loud or occurs too long, then chickens will (eventually) be killed through noise intervention. Therefore, it is not beneficial to continuously apply a noise signal to prevent clusters.

A powerful light source or putting food in the cage may have similar consequences on the group behaviour. The powerful light source may blind the chickens and scare them off. Food may also attract them and lure them away from a wounded chicken. More strategies of control may be possible, but this thesis will concentrate on frightening the chickens with applying a noise signal.

As shown in Figure 6.13, in the course of noise control with duration d some fields of the playground around the population centroid (x_c, y_c) and within a radius that depends on the intensity i are highlighted with a noise flag. A chicken reacts to this flag and uses this information within its decisions of movement and behaviour during the duration of noise control. A chicken will change its status to frightened, if it perceives noise. The personal energy value of the chicken decreases with the noise level depending on the field of the grid, where the chicken is positioned. A frightened chicken moves one field per simulation step outside the fields highlighted with noise. All chickens try to maximise the distance between the wounded chicken and themselves, move as fast as possible to fields, which are not highlighted with noise, and change their personal status to disturbed.

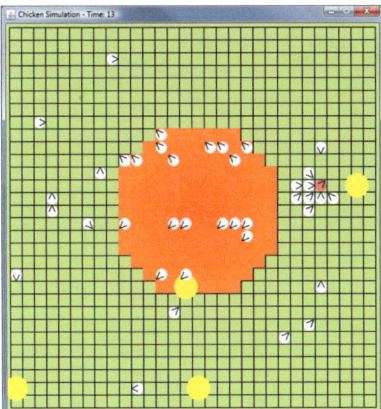

Figure 6.13: Snapshot of the chicken simulation with noise control

The actions taken by the controller have the form $A = (d, i, (x_c, y_c))$, which can be simplified to $A = (d, i)$, because the duration d and the intensity i of a noise intervention only need to be defined, since the centroid (x_c, y_c) of the chicken population has already been determined by the observer. The controller will only interfere, if the observer measures a critical clustering situation. However, what is a critical situation? Which clustering behaviour seems to be critical? When can the controller rescue a chicken and when is the controller's intervention applied too late? Which level of computed emergence indicators seems to be critical? To validate the observer/controller architecture, different controller types have been developed varying from completely static ones using fixed rules to control the clustering behaviour, see Figure 6.14, to adaptive ones using both, on-line learning and off-line planning, as depicted in Figures 6.18, 6.19, and 6.20.

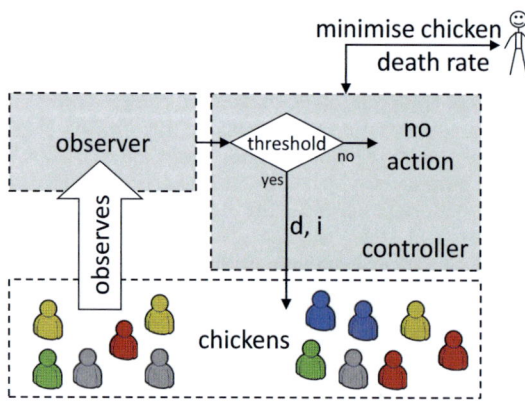

Figure 6.14: *Controlling with fixed single rules*

Single Fixed Rules Controller

As shown in Figure 6.14, using a freely applicable noise emitter with interim fixed duration and intensity, the chickens are frightened and the cluster will disperse, if a predefined threshold is exceeded that indicates critical clustering behaviour.

In comparison with Figure 0.9, the emergence values with noise intervention show no possible separation into three phases any more, see Figure 6.15. The interpolated curve in Figure 6.16 shows this effect in detail. The values are characterised by continuous increasing and decreasing phases. The cluster phase is skipped.

Comparing Figure 6.11 with Figure. 6.17, a significantly lower number of killed chickens is observed. Thus, the total number of killed chickens has decreased due to the control interventions. However, not all interventions have been successful, and for some cases many control interventions have been necessary to deal with the emergent situation. Whether a controller decision is successful or not depends on the

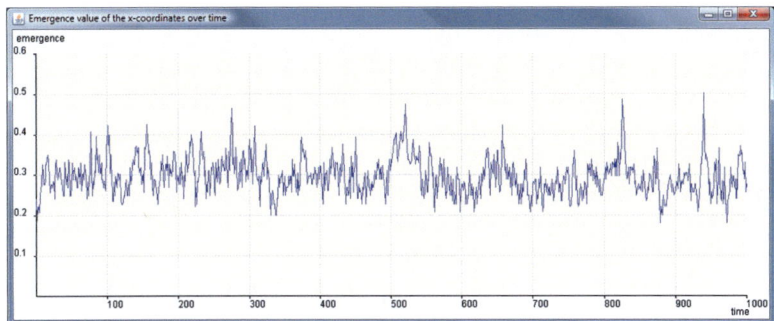

Figure 6.15: *Emergence value of the x-coordinates over time with control action*

energy status of the wounded chicken. The odds that a chicken will heal during the duration of a controller intervention depend on how many other chickens randomly run away in the same direction as the wounded chicken does, so that they can attack it again after getting out of the intervention area and after the disturbance time has elapsed. Furthermore, the relationship between critical values of emergent clustering indicators and applied noise interventions has been investigated in parameter studies, as described in Section 8.1.2.

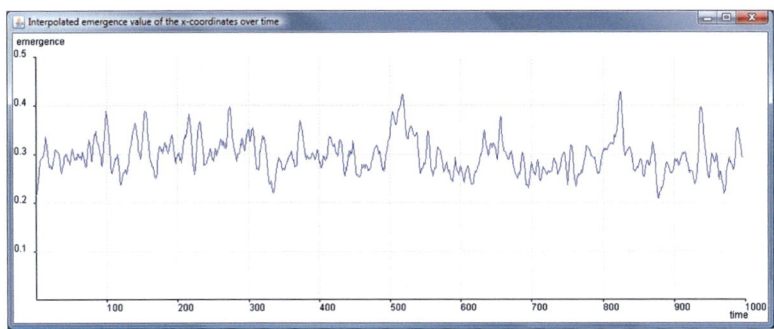

Figure 6.16: *Interpolated emergence value of the x-coordinates over time with control action*

Adaptive Controllers

With respect to the proposed generic observer/controller architecture and especially having a focus on the two-levelled learning aspect of the controller, different adaptive

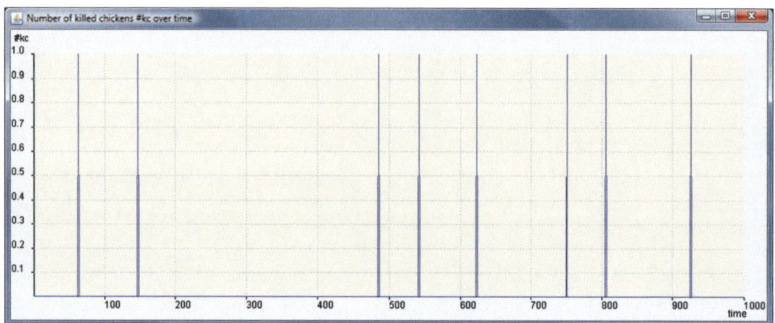

Figure 6.17: *Number of killed chickens #kc over time (every peak denotes a killed chicken) with control action*

variants are investigated, corresponding to different implementations. As depicted in Figure 6.18, the investigations have been started with a limited on-line learning controller and left out the second level, which focusses on off-line planning capabilities and is based on a simulation model. This controller uses an XCS, which will only be triggered, if predefined critical emergence values are exceeded. In other words, learning only takes place in situations, which are recognised as critical and where the information of being critical has been hard-wired into the control loop by the designer.

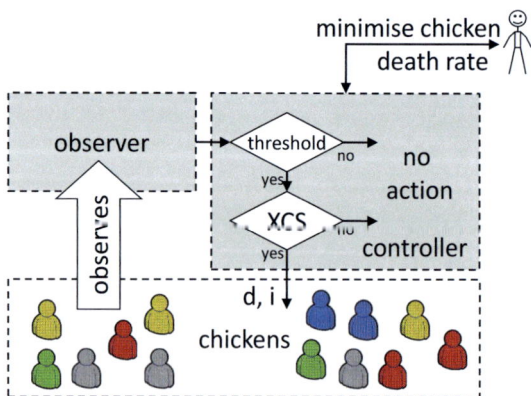

Figure 6.18: *If a predefined threshold exceeds, learning will start using an XCS*

126

Secondly and as described in Figure 6.19, the adaptive controller has been modified, and the barrier of surpassing a predefined threshold has been removed. Thus, the XCS will learn on its own, if a noise intervention is needed or not. If an action is triggered on the chickens, then the XCS will learn, which parameters of this noise signal (duration and intensity) should be selected referring the measured emergence indicators. The idea behind this approach has been that the same noise signal would not lead to the same effect on the clustering behaviour in different situations. The XCS should be able to support different kinds of clustering with different parametrised noise signals. Investigations on this second adaptive controller type are described in Section 8.2.6.

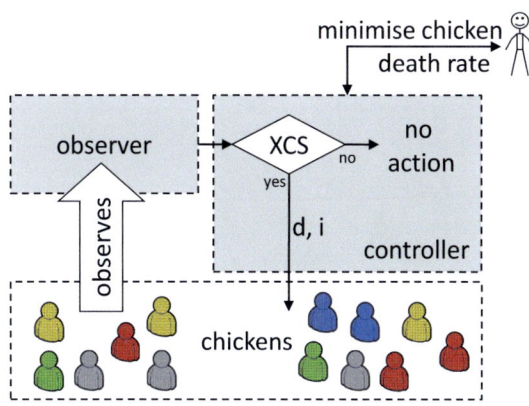

Figure 6.19: *Learning all possible situations using an XCS*

A special implementation detail refers to the encoding of applying a noise signal and applying no noise signal as part of the XCS. As already described, the noise signal is set up of two parameters duration and intensity. These two parameters are limited to values taken from sets with upper and lower boundaries, which could be defined, before a simulation run is started. The duration is limited to values of $d \in \{1, 2, \ldots, 15\}$. Intensity is taken from a set with $i \in \{0, 10, 20, \ldots, 50\}$. Every combination of these two parameters characterises a single noise signal. All noise signals having an *intensity of zero* $(i = 0)$ are defined as an action, which is translated into an intervention, where *no noise* is applied. Using this workaround, the XCS is able to distinguish and respectively learn situations, where controlling using noise is needed or is not needed.

Thirdly, Figure 6.20 shows an adaptive controller type, which learns on-line and off-line the best noise signal with respect to the proposed two-level learning architecture,

127

see Section 4.3. If situations occur, which are not known to the XCS on level 1, the XCS will trigger level 2, where the impact of different noise signals is evaluated using an off-line simulation model. The results are introduced on level 1 and support the decisions taken by the XCS. This third learning approach is simplified as much as possible: Level 2 is realised through cloning the real simulation. Thus, the effect of unknown noise signals in special situations can be verified on-line. On level 1 all working processes are paused until level 2 is acting.

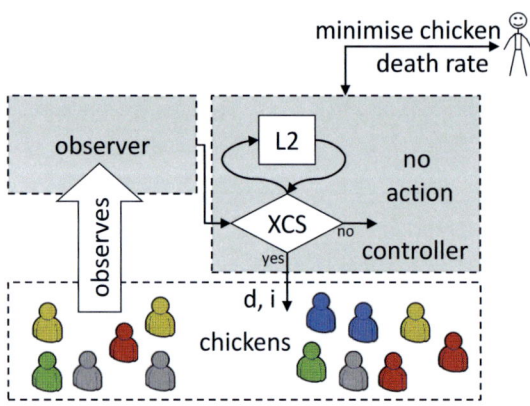

Figure 6.20: *An XCS is equipped with a simulation model on level 2*

Furthermore, a more complicated instance of this two-level learning approach is in the focus of organic traffic control [BMMS⁺06], which has also been mentioned in Section 4.4 and where the observer/controller architecture is used to control an urban traffic network. There, level 2 uses evolutionary algorithms and runs in parallel to level 1. This approach is again discussed in Section 6.2.5. All implementations have been investigated with respect to different parameter combinations, as presented and discussed in Chapter 8.

6.2.5 Discussion of Special Aspects

Depending on special characteristics of the implemented chicken scenario, some important aspects are shortly discussed in the following.

Grid Structure

Using a two-dimensional grid structure is a very simple and widespread way to design and implement multi-agent scenarios. In the case of special clustering situations, all agents are positioned very near by each other on a small part of the whole grid, particularly, when simulating a population of 40 agents on a grid of 30×30 fields. When a noise signal is applied to such a situation, the chickens that are only located at the border of the cluster have the chance to quickly run away. The chickens, which are located in the centre of a cluster, have to wait until the positions around them are not occupied any longer by other agents. This behaviour could be mitigated a little bit using other grid structures, like hexagons, where the local neighbourhood allows more positions for escaping possibilities.

Short- and Long-Term Benchmark Criteria

To rate the mapping of situations and actions, it is often useful to differ between short- and long-term criteria. In the case of this simple chicken scenario, one single criterion has only been identified to evaluate the controller actions – the number of killed chickens $\#kc$ (or counting the number of interventions that are needed to achieve and to maintain a special level of killed chickens, respectively). Referring to Chapter 8, this criterion seems to be limited in its statement about the improvement of learning to control local behaviour tackling a global goal. In most cases, the number of killed chickens is zero or it often counts one or two killed chickens, after a noise intervention has taken place. The range of this fitness criterion is normally characterised by zero, one, or two killed chickens. No gradual values between these values exist. Thus, in other scenarios it may be easier to define a reward function with more gradual differences coping the problem of quantifying the fitness of control actions in different situations.

Simple Feedback Mechanism

The chicken scenario seems to be a scenario, where a very simple feedback mechanism might be sufficient to control the clustering. If critical emergence values occur, a lot of noise will be made to frighten all chickens. Then, no chicken will pick on other chickens any more, and chickens will only be killed through a noise signal, which is applied too loud. Then, if the number of killed chickens increases, the controller will stop or will reduce interfering with noise, until the chickens start again their picking activities.

This argumentation is true, but every control action could also correlate with costs (e. g., chickens cannot eat food and cannot quickly grow until they are frightened) and the application of any control actions should be minimised. The controller should learn to achieve its goals with a minimum number of control actions. In situations, which are not quantified as critical, no control actions should be applied. In critical situations, the controller should interfere with an action that is best parametrised in this special situation.

Uniqueness of Quantitative Emergence

Always interfering with the best noise signal specially depends on the utilised metric that characterise the emergent clustering behaviour. Even if *quantitative emergence* has been used with respect to the fruitful research cooperation between the involved project partners from Hannover and Karlsruhe, some critical remarks concerning this design decision should be discussed.

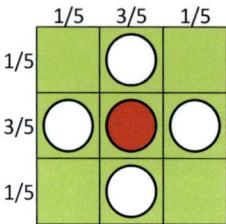

Figure 6.21: *Simplified chicken scenario*

Quantitative emergence seems to be a very general approach to quantify emergent behaviour, but this metric may not be the best answer to quantify clustering behaviour in the case of the chicken scenario. As depicted in Figure 6.21, this critic is clarified using an example, where the emergence indicators e_x and e_y are measured in a simplified scenario of 5 chickens on a grid with 3×3 fields. The emergence values are computed, as proposed in Section 4.1.5,

$$
\begin{aligned}
e_y &= e_x \\
&= \frac{H_{x_{max}} - H_x}{H_{x_{max}}} \\
&= \frac{\left(-\frac{\ln\left(\frac{1}{3}\right)}{\ln(2)}\right) - \left(-\left(\frac{1}{5} \cdot \frac{\ln\left(\frac{1}{5}\right)}{\ln(2)} + \frac{3}{5} \cdot \frac{\ln\left(\frac{3}{5}\right)}{\ln(2)} + \frac{1}{5} \cdot \frac{\ln\left(\frac{1}{5}\right)}{\ln(2)}\right)\right)}{\left(-\frac{\ln\left(\frac{1}{3}\right)}{\ln(2)}\right)} \\
&= \frac{1.585 - 1.37}{1.585} \\
&= 0.136.
\end{aligned}
$$

By comparing the situations that are presented in Figure 6.21 and in Figure 6.22, the conclusion is drawn that many different situations have a similar emergence value of 0.136. An observed emergence value is not explicitly correlated with a single situation. Quantitative emergence is not unique in its characterisation of self-organising behaviour. Moreover, it will be impossible to theoretically distinguish critical and non critical situations, if the only use of quantitative emergence is aimed as a metric on the observer's side to observe clustering in the chicken scenario.

But in practice, quantitative emergence shows acceptable results, as it is shown in Chapter 8. Many theoretical and possible situations do not occur during simulation, since the chickens behave as they have been programmed for. Chickens are always attracted by wounded chickens. This gravity/attraction leads to the effect that chickens would never occupy widespread positions, as it is admitted in the theoretical discussion before and shown in Figure 6.22. To conclude, the controller can trust the emergence indicators. If an emergent behaviour is observed, the emergence values have really identified a critical clustering situation.

Nevertheless to compare the fitness of quantitative emergence, another very simple metric has been implemented, which strictly depends on the investigated scenario and instead shows unique results of quantifying clustering. If a grid of 30×30 fields is observed, this whole grid will be separated into nine equal smaller grids with 10×10 fields. The metric computes the density of chickens in each smaller grid and passes the information about the grid with the highest density to the controller. Then, the noise intervention takes place in the centroid of the chicken cluster that relies on the most densely packed (smaller) grid. Experimental results are also presented in Section 8.5.

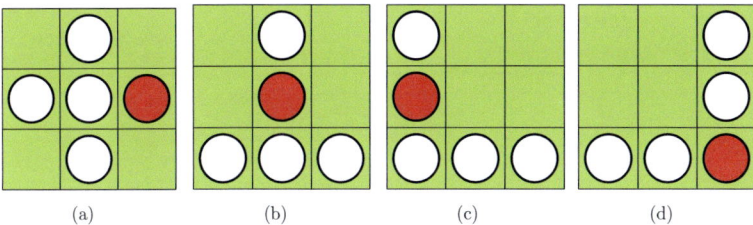

(a)   (b)   (c)   (d)

Figure 6.22: Example with identical entropy and emergence values, respectively

Parallels and Differences to Organic Traffic Control

As mentioned above, organic traffic control is a more complicated instantiation of the observer/controller architecture, as described in detail in [BMMS$^+$06]. It focusses on an approach based on principles of self-organisation, where every junction of a traffic network is controlled using the two-level learning architecture. Fast reaction to changing traffic conditions is a vital prerequisite to reach good performance in such a scenario. However, since the junction controllers should be kept as generic as possible, they have to adapt to the environment they are placed in, i.e., they have to learn.

The capability of learning always includes making mistakes, which is detrimental to performance. To cope with this challenge, the necessary functionality of a junction controller has been realised as an organic system, as depicted in Figure 6.23.

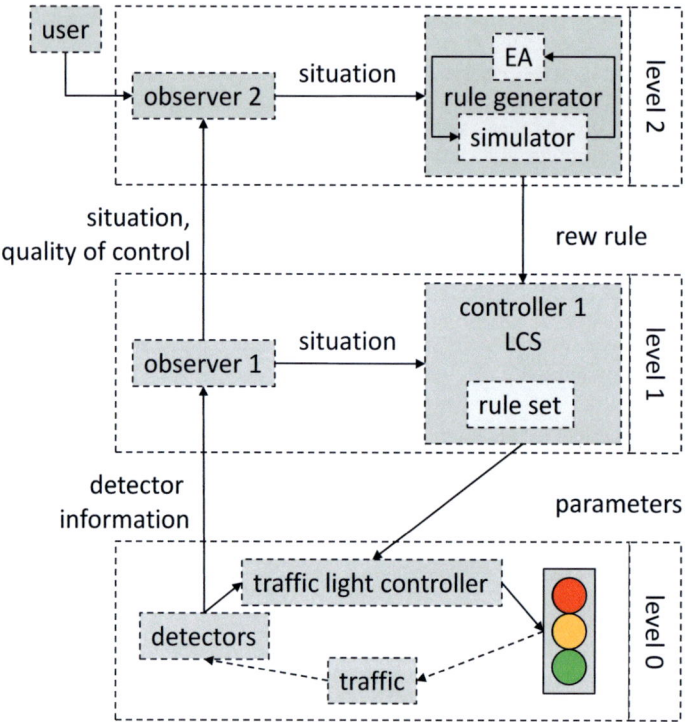

Figure 6.23: *An architectural overview of organic traffic control: Level 0 represents the traffic node, levels 1 and 2 are organic control levels responsible for the selection and generation of signal programmes, see [RPD+06]*

The SuOC in this traffic scenario consists of a signalled junction equipped with detectors, traffic lights, and a parametrisable traffic light controller. This traffic light controller can instantly act on small changes in the traffic situation by slightly varying its phase timings within predefined boundaries and in a predefined way. Its behaviour is defined by a set of parameters that have to be adapted, whenever the traffic situation significantly changes. While the observer is responsible for analysing the traffic situation, the controller decides, when and how to change the parameter set for the traffic light controller. Therefore, the controller maps traffic situations to parameter sets and keeps track of how well each parameter set performs. Alternative parameter sets are generated on level 2 of the controller using an evolutionary algorithm and a simulation of the traffic network, adjusted to the traffic situation in question. This way, trial-and-error search in the real traffic network can be avoided.

The task of the observer in this traffic scenario is to analyse the traffic situation and generate macro level situation parameters. Generally, the collected data are used to calculate the traffic flows (measured in vehicles per time unit) for all signal groups installed at the junction.

As said before, the controller uses some kind of mapping to choose an appropriate parameter set to configure the traffic light controller for each traffic situation presented as input by the observer. To keep the problem manageable, the input space in terms of different traffic situations has to be partitioned. Situations, which are sufficiently similar to allow usage of the same parameter set, will be covered by the same mapping entry. Since it is hard to anticipate all traffic situations that might occur at the controlled junction and since it would need a tremendous effort of a traffic engineer to develop good control strategies for all situations that can be imagined, the means for generating mapping entries have to be provided by the controller. These tasks combined are realised using a modified LCS on level 1.

Obviously, the mechanism used for the generation of knowledge is of crucial importance. As it is not a viable approach to let a system learn using a real traffic network as testbed, a modified classifier system similar to XCS is used, but with its functionality divided between two components: A basic classifier system and a separate component for rule discovery. This separate component utilises a model of the real traffic network running on a simulator to search for optimal traffic light controller parameter sets. Such a parameter set together with the encoded situation forms a classifier that is then fed into the population of the LCS. Classifiers from this population are applied by the LCS in the real network and their valuation is further improved based on feedback from reality. Both components (basic LCS and rule discovery) use the same objective function to update the value of a classifier or to find the optimal parameter set, respectively. Evaluation criteria incorporated into the objective function might be the average waiting time or the average number of stops.

Since the explorative behaviour of the system is moved to an external component, the task of the basic system is to find the best action among those available. This will be simple, if classifiers exist that match the current input: The classifier is chosen, whose prediction is best. If no classifier matches, a new matching one will be generated. The proposed approach is to choose the classifier, whose condition is closest to the current input, copy it, widen its condition just enough to match and discount its value slightly. This way a quick response is possible (waiting for a new solution to be generated using the simulator would take too long) and the probability that the chosen action will show an acceptable behaviour is greater than randomly choosing an action. If this widening exceeds a certain threshold, the current situation will simultaneously be passed to the rule discovery component so that, when a similar situation is encountered again, a specifically optimised classifier is available.

Within the rule discovery component, an evolutionary algorithm is responsible for producing new classifiers. It generates populations of traffic light controller parameter sets and evaluates their applicability for the current situation using a simulation model. The parameter sets are used to configure a simulated traffic light controller that controls the simulated junction for a defined period of time. After a warm-up period allowing the traffic to build up, a number of quality measures (like the average waiting time or the average number of stops) are recorded. These results are used by the evolutionary algorithm by means of the objective function to evaluate the different parameter sets in the same way as action values are updated after execution in real traffic. At the end of this process, a new classifier is created that maps the simulated situation to the best parameter set found by the evolutionary algorithm. The classifier's value is initialised based on the simulation results.

By using a simulation model to generate new classifiers, not useful traffic light controller parameter sets can be identified without negative consequences for the SuOC. Furthermore, the employment of a simulation software allows the fast evaluation of many parameter sets, which should result in an improved learning speed of the architecture.

Comparing organic traffic control to the chicken scenario and having a focus on the realisation of the two-levelled learning, organic traffic control is driven by the motivation of defining a solution towards a real world application. Learning suitable traffic light controllers cannot only be done on-line and with getting feedback from the experience of testing new traffic light controllers in the real world. Thus, level 2 with its simulation model and its evolutionary algorithm has a very important function in this scenario. The simulation model serves as testbed to validate new traffic light controllers and the evolutionary algorithm actively searches for new solutions testing them by simulation. The XCS on level 1 is reduced in its functionality, since covering and genetic operators have been moved to level 2.

Thus, it seems obvious that the chicken scenario only has a testbed character, which allows for more degrees of freedom in the design and the technical realisation of learning, respectively. The covering mechanism of the XCS (searching for new actions) is here *supported* by level 2, but not fully removed from level 1 to level 2, as done in organic traffic control. Furthermore, the impact of new noise signals is completely learned on-line and just *supported* by level 2. In other words, simulating new actions in a cloned simulation model on level 2 (which shows the same situation, as observed in the main simulation) and counting the killed chickens after the action has been applied, helps to initialise new classifiers that occur by covering on level 1.

However, as already discussed in Section 4.3, model-based planning as part of organic traffic control's level 2 is always limited by the necessary simplifications made in the model or by incomplete model calibration due to the fact that the modelled environment changes continuously. Thus, the best action with respect to the model is not necessarily also the best action with respect to the real world. In the chicken scenario, level 1 and level 2 are designed and implemented as two completely identical simulations (because the designer can freely decide and has full control about everything), which seems to be an unrealistic constraint in real world scenarios like organic traffic control.

6.3 Other Multi-Agent Scenarios

The main research, which has been done in this thesis, is based on results from the presented chicken scenario. However, during this work, several instances of the predator/prey scenario have been developed and investigated to validate special research topics and to generalise the preliminary results achieved with the chicken scenario. E. g., this has predominantly been done in the context of a diploma or bachelor's thesis. To give an overview of these even more technical scenarios, the following section shortly summarises the achievements.

6.3.1 Lift Simulation

A more technical scenario is the emergent (clustering) behaviour of a group of lifts, as depicted in Figure 6.24. Thus, lift group control has served as another testbed to develop and evaluate the specified generic architecture for OC systems.

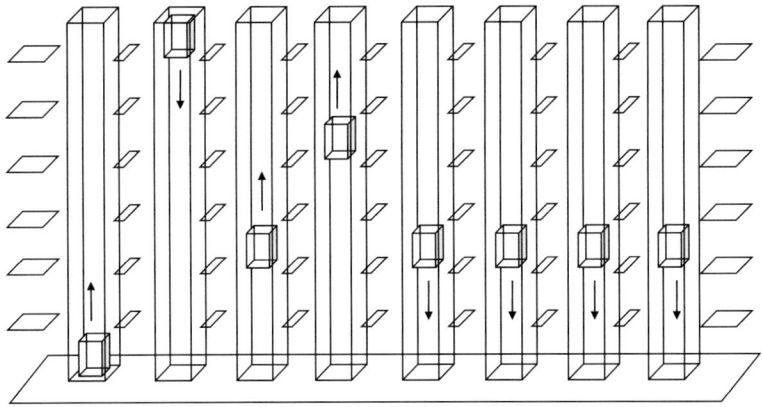

Figure 6.24: *Lifts synchronise, move up and down together, and show the emergent effect of bunching*

135

Lift group control is a familiar problem to everyone, who has used a lift system in high office buildings or skyscrapers. After pressing a button, the passengers wait for a lift to arrive travelling in the right direction. Passengers may have to wait a long time, if there are too many passengers or not enough lifts, which could handle the needed capacity. How long passengers wait, depends on the *dispatching strategy*, the lifts use to decide, where to go. For example, if passengers on several floors have requested to be picked up, which should be served first? If there are no requests to be picked up, how should the lifts distribute themselves to await the next request? Lift dispatching is a good example of a stochastic optimal control problem of economic importance that is too large to solve by classical techniques. Its conceptual simplicity hides significant difficulties. Operating in continuous state spaces, non-stationary behaviours of lifts and passengers, or changing passenger arrival rates are just some indicators that should be mentioned. In the last decades, lift group control has been studied as a well known example within different research domains [BB05, CB98, HU97, MKKBB06, Sii93, Sii97a, Sii97b, SSE03], but an optimal and globally valid policy for group control is not known and depends on many determining factors.

For a *single lift* in a building, a good heuristic is to follow the oldest known principle of *collective control* [Bar03, HR05, Str67, Str98]: A cabin always stops at the nearest *hall call* in its current running direction. A lift only changes its direction, when there are no more requests to be satisfied in the current direction, and stops at every floor with an issued request. However, if there are *several lifts* in a building, all working with that simple rule, they will tend to synchronise in the sense that they move up and down as a parallel wave, which is an undesired emergent behaviour and known from literature as the so-called *bunching effect*. This bunching effect leads to an increase in the average waiting time of the passengers and is quite inefficient [Pic06]. Lifts, the participants of the bunching effect, could be substituted with one huge single lift with a capacity equal to the sum of the individual synchronised cabins. This *super cabin* looses the advantage of flexibility and the possibility to serve hall calls on different floors at the same time. In summary, this technically motivated example depicts emergent behaviour that can only be observed as a pattern over time.

In the testbed implementation using the *recursive porous agent simulation toolkit (Repast 3)* [NCV06, SM06], a decentralised scenario has been assumed, where every lift is responsible for its own behaviour. A lift does not know, what the other lifts are doing. It just reacts to the hall calls, which are driven by passenger arrivals. A lift moves up and down, while the remaining capacity is positive and passengers have entered the cabin and follows a simple moving strategy like collective control. The performance is evaluated with respect to the global average waiting time of passengers. Different arrival patterns during the day need different strategies, but initially investigations have been concentrated on *inter-floor traffic*. (*Up-peak traffic* in the morning rush hour of a typical office building, where every lift is filled up in the lobby with passengers and stops at many different upper floors, or *down-peak traffic*, which shows a reversed situation, many arrival floors and one destination, are ignored.)

From the viewpoint of OC the bunching effect represents an interesting emergent behaviour in a technical scenario. The SuOC operates with a larger degree of order, but inefficiently, the average waiting time increases, and the system performance decreases. A lift group, which uses collective control and does not have any interaction between the cabins (e. g., the lifts could have information about the direction or the position of the neighbouring lifts), produces bunching. In [Pic06], several dispatching strategies for lifts have been compared by intensive simulations. The results of this study indicate that different dispatching strategies have different effects on the behaviour and the capability of the lift group. However, with an increasing intensity of passengers, the chosen strategy is irrelevant and has no further impact on the continuously increasing average waiting time. The studies demonstrate a correlation between the capability of the lift group and bunching effects on the one hand. Moreover, bunching and the average waiting time are directly related on the other hand.

In [Rib07, RRS08], the potential of applying concepts of OC are investigated to control this group of self-organising lifts, showing a macroscopic behaviour that only depends on local rules. Providing feedback and decision capabilities to this group of lifts, it is shown that bunching can be observed and autonomously prevented with respect to a global objective function. A metric is used, which is based on ideas of [AS93, AS96, ASB92a, ASB92b, Pow95] to detect bunching effects. For controlling the lifts, two simple methods have been implemented that modify the perception of the environment and thus affect the local behaviour of the lifts. The basic idea behind both implemented strategies is to accelerate delayed lifts. By passing a hall call, a lift is accelerated. Thus, this lift saves time compared to the other lifts, since the blinded lift will stop less frequently and finally speeds up. The experimental results validate the idea of using the observer/controller architecture to modify the environmental parameters of the SuOC without modifying the local rules of the lift cabins directly. This led to significant improvements in the performance of the lift group system.

Open issues in this scenario, which have not investigated yet, are learning and prediction capabilities. First, endowing the controller with adaptation capabilities, as designated in the generic architecture, the controller should be able to recognise and react to different traffic patterns. The investigations have only focused on inter-floor traffic, but it seems to be interesting whether bunching is the correct measurement to characterise the effectiveness of the group behaviour during up-peak or down-peak phases (this may require an extended observation model). Second, [Rib07] has done investigations of integrating a prediction module into the observer that computes the bunching value with respect to history data. Better performance of observer and controller functionalities are expected, but this could not be verified so far.

137

Referring to Section 6.1.2, the lift simulation can also be viewed as a cooperative, homogeneous, and (non-) communicating[3] agent scenario. Comparing it with the predator/prey example, the lifts can be seen as predators, which *chase* the travelling passengers from their arrival floor to their destination. This analogy may be ambiguous, but the generality of the predator/prey domain is demonstrated one more time.

6.3.2 Cleaning Robots

Based on the experiences with LCSs in the chicken scenario [RM08, RPS08] and presented in detail in Chapter 8, the power of other machine learning techniques has been investigated in another homogeneous and (indirectly) communicating multi-agent scenario in [Pat08]. A group of learning and self-organising cleaning robots follow a local strategy to search in their local neighbourhood for dirty places, clean these places, and evolve a better cooperative group behaviour over time. As machine learning technique evolutionary modified artificial neural networks are investigated, which are similar to the research project NERO[4] by the University of Texas at Austin.

As explained in Section 6.1.6, the cleaning robots perform a cooperative concurrent learning task. A group of cleaning robots searches in parallel for new cleaning strategies. Every agent has its own learning process to modify its behaviour and the environment, respectively. Following the common global goal of maximising the cleaning performance the robots indirectly communicate with each other by placing pheromones[5] on fields of the two-dimensional grid, where they have performed their cleaning task before. Since the group of learning agents make the scenario dynamic, the already mentioned *Markov property* is violated. Concurrent robots adapt their behaviour depending on other adapting robots, but they have no control on this process of coadaptation. Even the robots' own adaptation to the dynamically changing environment can change the environment itself. This makes learning complex in this scenario and results have shown that the investigated machine learning technique is not able to satisfactorily cope with the dynamics of the cleaning scenario. In ongoing work [Fri09], the results of the evolutionary modified artificial neural networks algorithm are compared with an approach based on LCSs.

---

[3]Collective control is a non-communicating strategy. However in [Pic06], other dispatching strategies have been investigated, which are based on simple communication patterns between the lifts. Lifts change status reports between neighbouring lifts, which contain information about travelling directions, next lift calls, etc.

[4]http://www.nerogame.org

[5]Communication through stigmergy has shortly been summarised in Section 3.1.1.

6.3.3 Multi-Rover Scenario

A similar approach of concurrent learners has been investigated in [Lod09], where the *credit assignment problem* (How to divide team reward among the individuals?) is specially addressed. Moreover, the investigated approach is focussed on the dynamics of learning (How to cope with the problem of coadaptation?) in a *multi-rover scenario* as an instance of the homogeneous and (non-) communicating predator/prey example.

Following the global task to observe one or up to n (randomly) moving targets (preys), a number of rovers (predators) has to achieve a common goal with local and distributed behaviour, e. g., maximising the global observation time or catching moving target(s). The scenario shows technical relevance to OC scenarios and it seems to be very flexible in its parameterisation, as explained in Section 6.1.1.

Thus, the challenge of concurrent learning agents is addressed in [Lod09], where all agents are equipped with a single XCS. It has been ascertained that neither the single-step nor the multi-step approach of XCS, see Section 5.3.2, could be used to learn this dynamic observation task. Thus, a promising modified XCS approach has been investigated to overcome the drawbacks of the classical XCS algorithm. The proposed idea is mainly based on a local cooperative reward function and some kind of temporary memory, which stores past actions sets. Thus, local payoffs can be delayed and the reward function reflects in a better way the local agent behaviour. Cooperation (incorporated in the reward function) is more or less achieved through rejection and attraction. Predators reject each other, the prey attracts the predators. Thus, agents try to uniformly distribute on the grid and observation time of the prey seems to be maximised.

6.4 Summary

This chapter has presented an overview of multi-agent test scenarios, which have been investigated from a learning perspective. In Section 6.1 the field of multi-agent systems has been introduced as a series of four increasingly complex and powerful categories. The simplest systems are those with homogeneous and non-communicating agents. The second category involves heterogeneous and non-communicating agents. The third deals with homogeneous and communicating agents. Finally, the general multi-agent systems involve communicating agents with any degree of heterogeneity. The aspect of cooperation vs. competition has been added as a third axis of organisation of multi-agent research in Section 6.1.6. To summarise, multi-agent scenarios are an active field with many open issues that have shown their usefulness as OC test scenarios validating the generic observer/controller architecture.

A nature-inspired chicken scenario has been presented in Section 6.2. This scenario serves as dominant testbed to investigate the learning approaches in the following chapters. To generalise the achievements made within the chicken scenario and to focus on special topics, other investigated multi-agent scenarios (i. e., lift simulation, cleaning robots, or multi-rover scenario) have been summarised in Section 6.3. The parallels between the different scenarios and the generic predator/prey example have always been mentioned.

Chapter 7

Experimental Design

As stated in Section 6.2, an observer/controller architecture has been developed on top of a chicken simulation to evaluate the concepts and methods, as described in Chapter 4. In order to demonstrate that these components fulfil their intended task and to examine the impact of the observer/controller architecture experimental tests have been performed. A special focus has been set on different learning approaches using LCSs. Within this chapter, general design decisions concerning the experiments are outlined. The actual analysis of the results is given in Chapter 8. Overall design guidelines are presented in Section 7.1. General thoughts in designing the experiments like defining the exact aim of the experiments are presented in Section 7.2. Finally, the used experimental design is introduced in Section 7.3.

7.1 Design Guidelines

In order to avoid that a whole experiment becomes meaningless before performing experimental studies, special attention has to be drawn to planning and developing an experimental design. The presented work follows the guidelines given by [Mon05].

1. Recognition and statement of the problems

2. Selection of the response variables

3. Choice of factors, levels, and ranges

4. Choice of experimental designs

5. Performing the experiments

6. Statistical analysis of the data

7. Conclusions and recommendations

However, this thesis will not go into the details of experimental design, but will shortly outline the approach and some essential underlying concepts. The tasks (1), (2), and (3) are performed in Section 7.2. Task (4) is described in Section 7.3. And tasks (5), (6), and (7) are covered in Chapter 8.

7.2 Pre-Experimental Planning

The first step is to define the *objectives* for the experiments. As mentioned before, the concepts and methods of the proposed observer/controller architecture should be evaluated in the context of the nature-inspired chicken scenario: Can the total number of killed chickens be decreased leading to an increase of the global system performance?

The component exerting influence on the system behaviour, and hence producing measurable effects, is the controller. Therefore, tests will be performed, if the controller does actually alleviate clustering within the chicken population, and will thus reduce the total number of killed chickens. While doing this, the influence of the controller will be examined as well as selected system parameters, as for example the choice of different duration and intensity parameters of the noise signal. In addition, the correlation of the number of killed chickens and the number of triggered actions/interventions is checked, which might be an indicator of the quality of the reward function and the learning performance of the XCS. Thus, the goals of the implemented experiments can be summarised, as explained in the following.

1. Gain insights of the influence of the controller on system performance

2. Gain insights of the influence of system parameters on system performance

3. Gain insights of different learning approaches on system performance

4. Gain insights of different metrics on system performance

5. Check the correlation between clustering and total number of killed chickens

7.2.1 Selection of the Response Variables

The second step is to define *response variables*, i. e., variables that provide information about the process under study. The goals (1) to (4) deal with the influence on system performance, which is measured in terms of the number of killed chickens $\#kc$ or the number of control interventions needed to control the clustering behaviour. An optimal system performance is equal to a minimum number of killed chickens, or a minimum of control interventions decreasing the number of killed chickens, respectively. Therefore, varying parameters, which influence the whole system performance, will also change the number of killed chickens. In other words, the number of killed chickens is a measure of the effects of parameter variations on the system performance. Additionally, changing parameters in a way that the number of killed chickens is affected, the clustering behaviour will also change, if the correlation assumption does hold. As stated before, it is considered that clustering is the main effect degrading the system performance in the present simulation and thus assumes the existence of this correlation. To verify goal (5), a regression model may be performed, which shows that the number of killed chickens corresponds to clustering. Such a calculation is explicitly not presented in this thesis, but Figures 6.9, 6.10, 6.11, 6.15, 6.16, and 6.17 admit that these two values are correlated – the death rate depends on the emergence values, which serves as indicator of clustering. However, it should be mentioned that the noise signal also has a negative effect on the chicken death rate.

7.2.2 Choice of Factors, Levels, and Ranges

The third step is to consider the factors, which may influence the performance of the system. These are *nuisance factors* and potential *design factors*, which split up into *design factors*, *held constant factors*, and *allowed to vary factors*, see [Mon05].

Factors

In the chicken scenario, the *nuisance factor* only present in the system is the *random seed* for the random numbers generator. This value is responsible for the starting positions of the chickens and is used within the XCS, as outlined in [But00, BW02]. *Design factors* are factors, which are actually selected for study in the experiment. I. e., the influence of these design factors on the system should be examined. *Held constant factors* are factors, which are not varied within the experiment. Additionally, they may exert some influence on the system performance. However, for the purpose of the experiment they are not of interest.

Moreover, held constant factors could be *allowed to vary factors*. These factors are mostly very difficult to vary and have only negligible effects on the system. If those factors exist, they will often be balanced out by repeatedly performed experiments. However, these factors may particularly exist in the case of an adaptive controller using an XCS, see the work done in [BW00, BW02], where all parameters are listed, which are used to control the learning process. A (simplified) list of factors affecting the system is investigated in the following and depicted in Figure 7.1.

As stated before, not all of those factors are varied, since not all of them will affect the system in such a manner that justifies the necessary effort. Held constant factors are the chicken number, the number and the starting place of feeding troughs, width and height of the grid, most parameters of the XCS (without the maximal number of classifiers), and some other factors, which are also mentioned in Table 6.1.

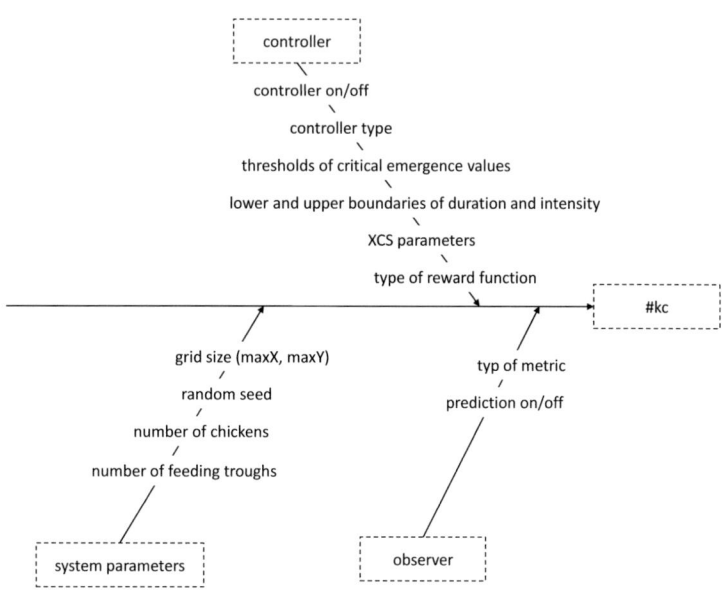

Figure 7.1: *Simplified cause and effect diagram of the chicken simulation*

All remaining factors will be varied. However, there are some peculiarities. The initial seed of the random numbers generator is considered as a nuisance factor that has to be averaged out by replication, i. e., by repeated runs of the experiment under the same conditions. If it is explicit unless otherwise noted, all runs will be preformed with 20 different seed values to sufficiently gain low variances and standard errors.

The selected covering mechanism, the maximal number of classifiers in a population, the reward function, and the observer type are normally held constant at all. However, some experiments are performed to investigate the effect of varying theses parameters, see Section 8.2. Therefore, these parameters are considered as design factors.

Among other parameters there are some dependencies that one has to be aware of. On the one hand, the type of the chosen reward function, the predefined XCS parameters, lower and upper boundaries of duration and intensity, and the thresholds of critical emergence values depend on the chosen controller type. Moreover, the controller type depends on the parameter, which activates and deactivates the controller. On the other hand, the variable, which turns the predictor on or off, is not explicitly considered for analysis. The effects of prediction are not investigated.

Levels and Ranges

At last, the *levels and ranges* of the design parameters have to be chosen. The parameter, to turn the controller on and off, takes two discrete values. The same is applied to the type of the chosen metric on the observer's side. Quantitative emergence is normally used, but a second metric has been developed, as outlined in Section 6.2.5. The parameter, which corresponds to the controller types, can take four different values. It distinguishes the so-called *single fixed rules controller* and the three different adaptive controllers, as explained in Section 6.2.4.

Depending on the controller type the thresholds of critical emergence values, lower and upper boundaries of duration and intensity, an the XCS parameters have to be set. The three critical emergence thresholds t_x, t_y, t_h are limited to values from 0.0 to 1.0, since the relative emergence values have been defined as $e_x, e_y, e_h \in [0.0, 1.0]$, see Section 4.1.5. The values of duration and intensity are normally taken from predefined sets, as explained in Section 6.2.4. Furthermore, XCS parameters are generally not varied. Experiments have been implemented using initialisation values, as proposed by the XCS reference implementation [But00]. The parameter, which controls the covering mechanism, allows different modes. If the XCS uses full covering, this parameter will be set to the possible number of control actions in the scenario. Moreover, a minimal covering mechanism or covering using level 2 learning is possible.

The maximal number of classifiers in a population has been varied to investigate its effect on the learning process having small and huge populations. The maximal number of classifiers should be chosen in relation to the dimension of the searched condition-action-mapping. It also depends on the predefined values of lower and upper boundaries of possible duration and intensity values. These dependencies are investigated in detail in Section 8.2.

As shown in Section 8.2.4, some investigations of learning have been done with different reward functions to evaluate the influence of varying this function. However, similar to the parameter, which controls the chosen type of metric, the reward function is defined as a design factor, but most experiments have been taken with the same reward function.

7.3 Choice of Experimental Designs

The choice of the experimental design depends on the initial situation and on the desired goals of the experiment. No previous knowledge existed to anticipate the influence of the parameters on the system. Furthermore, this observer/controller architecture has been built from scratch.

In fact, the effects of parameters on the outcome and the dependencies among the parameters should be discovered: How much does the response variable (the number of killed chickens) change, when each factor is varied, and does it make any difference to vary factors simultaneously instead of one at a time. In literature, this request is called *parameter screening* and forms the basis for further investigations, see [Mon05]. Under the given constraints, the usage of a *factorial experimental design* is suggested, which is a very efficient approach to investigate the parameter influence with respect to parameter interactions. This is not considered in detail here and interested readers are referred to the viable introduction given in [Mon05], where some other experimental designs are presented. Based on results taken from factorial design steps, further studies have been performed depending on the outcome of parameter screenings.

At factorial design, all possible subsets of the design parameters are varied with the other parameters held constant. Since parameters are varied together, interactions of the parameters can be revealed. Within experiments aiming at parameter screening, it is general practice to perform so-called 2^k *factorial experiments* to keep the experimental effort within certain bounds. Within such an experiment, each of k parameters are tested at two levels. These levels are most apparent at a relatively high and a relatively low value of a parameter and can be quantitative as well as qualitative (for example a functionality is turned on or off). Therefore, such a design *only* requires $2 \times 2 \times \cdots \times 2 = 2^k$ observations. It is the most efficient way to analyse both, the influence of single parameters as well as their interactions on a given parameter set. Analysis of only two levels for each factor requires an approximately linear response over the range of the chosen factor levels.

The assumption for every factor needs to be verified in preliminary examinations utilising several factor levels. The chosen levels for the factors are obtained by prior investigations. The levels are chosen in a manner that they produce a significantly different response in *one factor at a time experiments*. Performing such experiments one factor is varied apart from the others in every run of the experiment and no insights of parameter interactions can be attained.

Since the analysis of such a highly parametrisable scenario can never be complete and it has been a tremendous effort to perform all preliminary factorial experiments, the (theoretical) discussion about the choice of experimental design stops here. Some selected results are presented in the following chapter.

Chapter 8

Results

An inventor is a man, who asks why *of the universe and lets nothing stand between the answer and his mind. (Ayn Rand)*

Based on the general thoughts given at the end of Chapter 7, several experiments have been performed. At the beginning extensive preliminary investigations have been carried out to find reasonable levels for the parameters. These investigations are not presented in detail and the results are only mentioned. Some preliminary experiments can be found in Section 8.1. Subsequently, several experiments have been carried out to gain further insights based on those preliminary observations. These are described in Section 8.2. Finally, the investigations are examined that have been taken to speed up the learning process. Section 8.3 describes the experiments, which are based on parallelism and decomposing a learning problem into sub-problems. Section 8.4 summarises the results, which have been achieved by combining on-line learning and off-line planning capabilities. Furthermore, all experiments are based on using quantitative emergence. To show the influence on the number of killed chickens reflecting another metric, a comparison between quantitative emergence and a metric, which simply measures the density of the chickens based on assumptions made in this scenario, is presented in Section 8.5.

8.1 Preliminary Experiments

Several preliminary experiments have been performed. To get a feeling of the implemented multi-agent scenario, results without control interventions are presented in Section 8.1.1. Section 8.1.2 describes preliminary experiments, which investigate the clustering behaviour, when the chickens are controlled with static noise signals.

8.1.1 Chicken Simulation without Control

As shown in Table 8.1, without controlling the global chicken behaviour approximately 336 chickens are killed during a simulation with 10 000 ticks. Simulations are done up to 1 000 000 ticks. The number of killed chickens $\#kc$ linearly increases. Thus, approximately 32.65 chickens are killed per 1 000 ticks. This average is used as benchmark to evaluate the different approaches in controlling the chickens in the following.

Table 8.1: *Chicken simulation without control*

Ticks	1 000	...	10 000	...	100 000	...	750 000	1 000 000
Average #kc	31	...	336	...	3 323	...	24 506	32 692
Per 1 000 ticks	31.00	...	33.60	...	33.23	...	32.67	32.69

8.1.2 Parameter Studies Using Single Fixed Rules Controller

Applying a static noise signal with fixed intensity and fixed duration around the computed cluster centroid to frighten the chickens and disperse the cluster works well and decreases the number of killed chickens $\#kc$, see [MRB+07] or Section 6.2.4.

Essentially, the number of killed chickens is a function that depends on the mapping of a situation to an action, where a situation is described by three (critical) emergence values. Moreover, an action is characterised by the noise signal, which is divided into duration and intensity. The fitness landscape is depicted in Figure 8.1.

However, a static control loop, as introduced in Figure 6.14, does not satisfy the idea of adaptation in changing environments, but investigations with the fixed single rules controller will help to search the search space step by step to find an existing global minimum – if any global minimum does exist. Since the fitness landscape is completely unknown, these investigations are helpful as preliminary results to understand the multi-agent behaviour and the dependencies of the programmed logics. Furthermore, the results can be used to benchmark the adaptive controllers.

Different simulation runs have been performed by varying the characterisation of a critical situation (the if-part of a rule) and the corresponding action. The if-part of a rule is characterised by a boolean combination (i. e., AND, OR, XOR, etc.) of three conditions, where each condition is related to one of the three emergence values $e_x, e_y, e_h \in [0.0, 1.0]$. To reduce the computing time resulting from this immense search space, it is assumed that the best possible if-part would have the form $((e_x \geq t_x)$ AND $(e_y \geq t_y))$ OR $(e_h \geq t_h)$ with $t = (t_x, t_y, t_h)$ being the critical emergence thresholds. The two conditions, which are related to the x- and y-coordinates, are connected using an AND-operator, since the x- and y-emergence values are correlated due to the topology of the simulation. If a cluster emerges, the

148

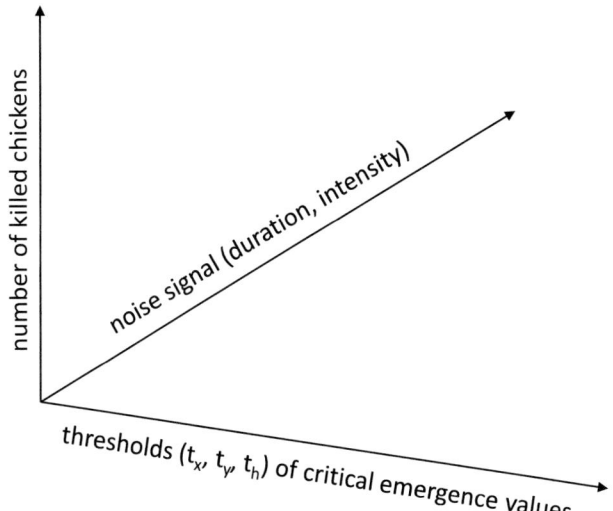

Figure 8.1: *Fitness landscape of the chicken simulation depends on three thresholds of critical emergence values and two parameters of a noise signal*

x- and y-emergence values will jointly increase. The condition, which reflects the aggregated heading, is assumed as a separate condition.

Furthermore, it is supposed that $t_h = 0.3$ is a reasonable threshold for the critical heading emergence, see [MMS06]. To simplify the investigations for presentation, the real-valued search space is searched step by step in discrete distances. The other two threshold values t_x and t_y are restricted to values as shown in Table 8.2. Moreover, it should be mentioned that other different boolean combinations of these three critical emergence values are possible, but they have not been investigated here.

Each line of Table 8.2 corresponds to a parameter set of a group of 36 tests, which should be read as follows: Taking the first line in the table, it corresponds to tests with fixed single rules controllers with a noise signal $(d, i) = (5, i)$, which will act, if the critical emergence values match the observed situation with the constraint $((e_x \geq t_x) \text{ AND } (e_y \geq 0.1)) \text{ OR } (e_h \geq 0.3)$ varying $t_x \in \{0.1, \ldots, 0.6\}$ and $i \in \{0, 10, 20, \ldots, 50\}$.

In total, 648 parameter combinations ($\#t_x \times \#t_y \times \#t_h \times \#d \times \#i = 6 \times 6 \times 1 \times 3 \times 6 = 648$) were tested. These parameter combinations have been varied, each combination has been simulated for 10 000 ticks with 20 different seed values (to get a statistically valid result), and the average number of killed chickens $\#kc$ has been computed for

149

Table 8.2: *Combinations of fixed single rules controller parameters*

t_x	t_y	t_h	d	i	Figure
0.1, 0.2, ..., 0.6	0.1	0.3	5	0, 10, 20, ..., 50	8.2(a)
0.1, 0.2, ..., 0.6	0.2	0.3	5	0, 10, 20, ..., 50	8.3(a)
0.1, 0.2, ..., 0.6	0.3	0.3	5	0, 10, 20, ..., 50	8.4(a)
0.1, 0.2, ..., 0.6	0.4	0.3	5	0, 10, 20, ..., 50	8.5(a)
0.1, 0.2, ..., 0.6	0.5	0.3	5	0, 10, 20, ..., 50	8.6(a)
0.1, 0.2, ..., 0.6	0.6	0.3	5	0, 10, 20, ..., 50	8.7(a)
0.1, 0.2, ..., 0.6	0.1	0.3	10	0, 10, 20, ..., 50	8.2(b)
0.1, 0.2, ..., 0.6	0.2	0.3	10	0, 10, 20, ..., 50	8.3(b)
0.1, 0.2, ..., 0.6	0.3	0.3	10	0, 10, 20, ..., 50	8.4(b)
0.1, 0.2, ..., 0.6	0.4	0.3	10	0, 10, 20, ..., 50	8.5(b)
0.1, 0.2, ..., 0.6	0.5	0.3	10	0, 10, 20, ..., 50	8.6(b)
0.1, 0.2, ..., 0.6	0.6	0.3	10	0, 10, 20, ..., 50	8.7(b)
0.1, 0.2, ..., 0.6	0.1	0.3	15	0, 10, 20, ..., 50	8.2(c)
0.1, 0.2, ..., 0.6	0.2	0.3	15	0, 10, 20, ..., 50	8.3(c)
0.1, 0.2, ..., 0.6	0.3	0.3	15	0, 10, 20, ..., 50	8.4(c)
0.1, 0.2, ..., 0.6	0.4	0.3	15	0, 10, 20, ..., 50	8.5(c)
0.1, 0.2, ..., 0.6	0.5	0.3	15	0, 10, 20, ..., 50	8.6(c)
0.1, 0.2, ..., 0.6	0.6	0.3	15	0, 10, 20, ..., 50	8.7(c)

each parameter combination. An excerpt of these experiments is shown in Figures 8.2, 8.3, 8.4, 8.5, 8.6, and 8.7. Every figure corresponds to one line of Table 8.2. E. g., the group of 36 experiments, denoted in line 2, corresponds to the values of Figure 8.3(a). The absolute values of killed chickens, as shown in Figure 8.3(a), are also given in Table 8.3.

In other words, Figures 8.2, 8.3, 8.4, 8.5, 8.6, and 8.7 provide a special (but limited) view on the whole search space. To find a global optimum of these fixed single rules controllers, every figure has to be searched for a minimum. The minimum of all numbers of killed chickens indicates the best found parameter combination.

Alternatively, ranking the results of the *reduced and simplified* search space from the best to the lowest average number of killed chickens $\#kc$ shows that the best solution (approximately 91 killed chickens) is found for one specific mapping of critical thresholds t_x, t_y, t_h and corresponding values of duration d and intensity i. Finally, this ranking is shown in Table 8.4 (only an extract of the results is presented here). The best found single fixed rules controller corresponds to the rule: If the condition $((e_x \geq 0.2)$ AND $(e_y \geq 0.2))$ OR $(e_h \geq 0.3)$ is true, then the controller will intervene with noise having the parameters $d = 5$ and $i = 50$.

In the following sections, this single fixed rules controller is used to evaluate the quality of the learning process of the investigated adaptive controllers. Furthermore,

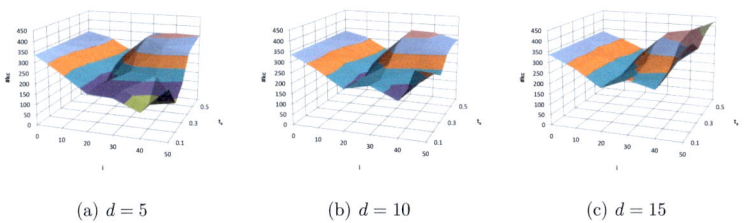

(a) $d = 5$ (b) $d = 10$ (c) $d = 15$

Figure 8.2: *Chicken simulation with single fixed rules controller, $t_y = 0.1$, $t_h = 0.3$, $i \in \{0, 10, 20, \ldots, 50\}$, and $t_x \in \{0.1, 0.2, \ldots, 0.6\}$*

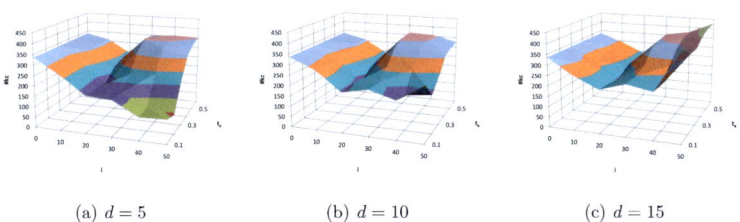

(a) $d = 5$ (b) $d = 10$ (c) $d = 15$

Figure 8.3: *Chicken simulation with single fixed rules controller, $t_y = 0.2$, $t_h = 0.3$, $i \in \{0, 10, 20, \ldots, 50\}$, and $t_x \in \{0.1, 0.2, \ldots, 0.6\}$*

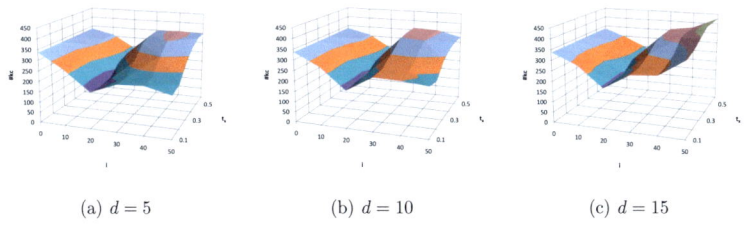

(a) $d = 5$ (b) $d = 10$ (c) $d = 15$

Figure 8.4: *Chicken simulation with single fixed rules controller, $t_y = 0.3$, $t_h = 0.3$, $i \in \{0, 10, 20, \ldots, 50\}$, and $t_x \in \{0.1, 0.2, \ldots, 0.6\}$*

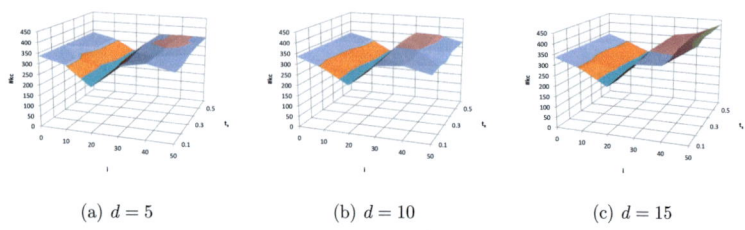

(a) $d = 5$ (b) $d = 10$ (c) $d = 15$

Figure 8.5: *Chicken simulation with single fixed rules controller, $t_y = 0.4$, $t_h = 0.3$, $i \in \{0, 10, 20, \ldots, 50\}$, and $t_x \in \{0.1, 0.2, \ldots, 0.6\}$*

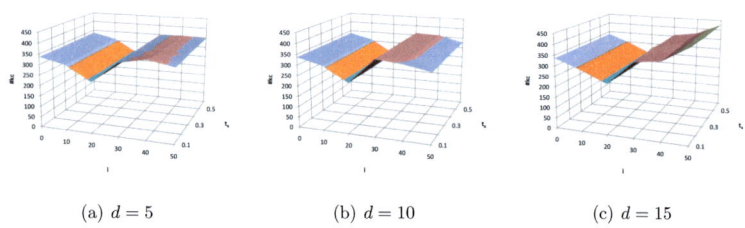

(a) $d = 5$ (b) $d = 10$ (c) $d = 15$

Figure 8.6: *Chicken simulation with single fixed rules controller, $t_y = 0.5$, $t_h = 0.3$, $i \in \{0, 10, 20, \ldots, 50\}$, and $t_x \in \{0.1, 0.2, \ldots, 0.6\}$*

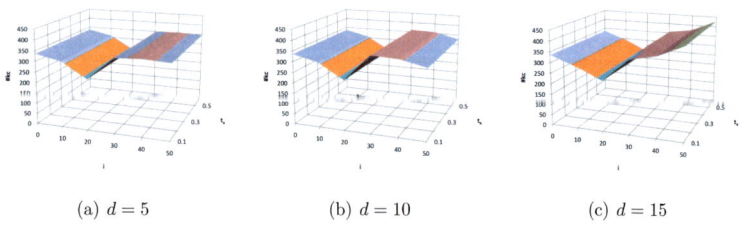

(a) $d = 5$ (b) $d = 10$ (c) $d = 15$

Figure 8.7: *Chicken simulation with single fixed rules controller, $t_y = 0.6$, $t_h = 0.3$, $i \in \{0, 10, 20, \ldots, 50\}$, and $t_x \in \{0.1, 0.2, \ldots, 0.6\}$*

Table 8.3: Results of the fixed single rule controller experiments over 10 000 ticks with the parameter combination $d = 5$, $t_y = 0.2$, and $t_h = 0.3$

t_x	i					
	0	10	20	30	40	50
0.1	336.00	265.65	179.30	173.35	108.40	113.80
0.2	336.00	263.65	176.65	168.70	116.65	91.00
0.3	336.00	266.60	169.30	228.90	240.20	214.95
0.4	336.00	299.45	223.25	315.80	332.95	311.50
0.5	336.00	309.90	240.95	353.80	351.85	340.75
0.6	336.00	309.90	240.95	346.30	355.35	351.30

it concretises the challenge an XCS has to learn. This single fixed rules controller will help to evaluate, if an XCS is able to find (at least) similar solutions within the same simulation time (10 000 ticks) or if other (better) values are found. Not all possible values of t_x, t_y, t_h and combinations of these three critical emergence thresholds (i. e., AND, OR, XOR, etc.) have been investigated, when the real-valued search space is searched step by step in discrete distances. The best found single fixed rules controller provides an optimum in the case of the investigated parameter studies, but it does not claim to be the best solution of this chicken scenario.

Table 8.4: Results of the single fixed rules experiments over 10 000 ticks sorted for the average #kc

t_x, t_y, t_h	d, i	Average $\#kc$	Standard deviation	Standard error
0.2, 0.2, 0.3	5, 50	91.00	11.03	2.47
0.1, 0.2, 0.3	5, 40	108.40	10.52	2.35
0.1, 0.2, 0.3	5, 50	113.80	15.01	3.36
0.2, 0.1, 0.3	5, 40	115.65	15.60	3.49
0.2, 0.2, 0.3	5, 40	116.65	11.83	2.65
0.1, 0.1, 0.3	5, 40	119.05	12.29	2.75
0.2, 0.1, 0.3	5, 50	138.20	11.89	2.66
0.2, 0.3, 0.3	5, 20	166.40	0.99	0.22
0.2, 0.2, 0.3	5, 30	168.70	9.10	2.03
0.3, 0.2, 0.3	5, 20	169.30	4.21	0.94
...	...	...	...	...

To summarise, these parameter studies provide an overview of the programmed simulation. They produce experience about the behaviour of the chicken simulation at all and give answers to questions like: How do the chickens react to a special noise signal? Which is a good combination of critical emergence values and corresponding noise parameters that shows a minimal number of killed chickens? Which are the critical parameters with the highest impact on the results? With respect to the constraint of searching the real-valued search space in discrete distances, these parameter studies find an optimal solution. However, this found single fixed rules controller will not stringently be an optimal solution, as shown in Section 8.2.6. The single fixed rules controller similarly acts as an LCS, which only uses one single classifier matching all possible situations and intervening with one specific noise signal. But, using different classifiers with respect to different situations and noise signals will obtain a better control strategy.

Furthermore, the experiments argue for the general need of adaptive and continuously learning approaches. OC systems are faced with real world problems, which continuously act in dynamically changing environments, where time is a crucial factor and no time exists to perform *a priori* time consuming parameter studies. Decisions have to be taken on-line – as soon as possible, as optimal as possible. Thus, learning is a major capability of OC systems, which is specially focussed on in the following sections.

8.2 Learning to Control

Parameter studies using fixed single rules controller have been presented in the last section. Fixed control has been defined such that in predefined critical emergent situations the chickens are always frightened with a fixed noise signal. This noise signal is static, duration and intensity are predefined, before the simulation is started. For each parameter combination a set of simulations has been performed and the average number of killed chickens $\#kc$ has been computed for each combination. The goal of these studies has been to search the search space step by step for a possibly existent global optimum. The results are used to compare the quality of the XCS investigations.

In this section, on-line learning is investigated using an XCS: As shown in Chapter 5, the idea of XCS fits well to the organic observer/controller architecture. The *XCSJava1.0* reference implementation [But00] is adopted to the chicken scenario, as described in Section 6.2. An XCS should learn to minimise the chicken death rate. Thus, the following investigations focus on level 1 of the two-level learning architecture. The full two-level approach, as mentioned in Section 1.3, is a possible combination of searching on-line the condition-action-mapping by using off-line generated knowledge. It is investigated in Section 8.4.

In general, learning the best action for changing situations in the context of the chicken scenario means the following: At every simulation tick the global behaviour of the 40 agents characterised by three emergence values, e_x for the x-coordinates, e_y for the y-coordinates, and e_h for the heading of all chicken, is evaluated. Based on this system fingerprint, an XCS will be used to learn, if and which noise signal (in terms of duration d and intensity i) is applied to the chicken cage.

154

e_x	e_y	e_h	d	i	p	ϵ	F
(44, 54)	(30, 40)	(58, 68)	07	10	40	4.80	0.34
(44, 54)	(30, 40)	(58, 68)	08	00	40	7.50	0.17
(25, 35)	(48, 58)	(10, 20)	09	10	40	15.00	0.25
(28, 38)	(37, 47)	(89, 99)	05	00	40	10.00	0.15
(28, 38)	(28, 38)	(77, 87)	05	00	40	1.97	0.70
(28, 38)	(28, 38)	(77, 87)	05	20	40	3.07	0.79
(28, 38)	(28, 38)	(77, 87)	07	20	40	3.07	0.20
(28, 38)	(28, 38)	(77, 87)	08	20	40	15.00	0.17
(44, 54)	(06, 16)	(31, 41)	08	00	40	15.00	0.17
(09, 19)	(44, 54)	(09, 19)	08	00	40	3.07	0.17

Figure 8.8: *Excerpt of a typical XCS's population*

The XCS reference implementation works with binary encoded classifiers. This encoding has been changed to work with real-valued and accordingly integer-valued condition values. The three emergence values coming from the observer are real-values limited to $[0.0, 1.0]$. Each emergence value is mapped to an encoded interval using lower and upper boundaries. Thus, a classifier's condition consists of six values, where the first two values characterise the interval for the e_x-emergence value, the third and fourth value match the e_y-value, and the fifth and sixth value cover the e_h-value. In a first implementation the six condition values have been implemented and stored as double-coded values. To simplify the XCS' internal structure (i.e., functionalities as subsumption, etc.) this encoding has been changed. Now, the six condition values are integer values limited to $[0, 99]$. Thus, each emergence value is multiplied with hundred and all decimal places are deleted. Figure 8.8 shows a typical excerpt from a population. Moreover, the encoded action consists of two integer-encoded parameters, duration and intensity, respectively.

Controlling the chicken scenario has been implemented as a single-step learning problem, since the scenario allows for an immediate reward calculation. The XCS does not have to wait, until the impact of the action becomes visible or a special event is reached. If a chicken is killed, the chosen action will be punished. If no chicken is killed, the chosen action will positively be rewarded, respectively, because the selected noise signal has correctly been applied to the observed situation.

Thus, two implementations of a single-step learning cycle have been investigated, which correspond to the two adaptive controllers, as introduced in Figures 6.18 and 6.19. To adopt the single-step XCS implementation, two main questions must be addressed: *What* is learned and *how* is the reward computed and subsequently distributed among the involved classifiers?

In Figure 8.9 a learning cycle is depicted, which works without predefining critical thresholds. I.e., this XCS autonomously learns classifiers for *all possible* situations.

155

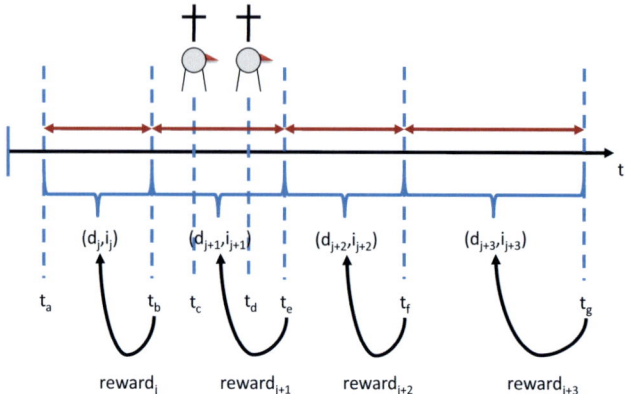

Figure 8.9: Learning condition-action-mappings for all situations

Therefore, this XCS has to learn whether noise is applied or the situation is not characterised as critical and thus, no noise should be applied. As introduced in Section 6.2.4, this decision is encoded into the noise parameter intensity. Actions with an intensity value of zero are defined as special control actions of making no noise. All other values define different noise signals.

Furthermore, if no other action is active, a new XCS learning cycle will be triggered and a new action will be applied. No pauses between two following actions exist. Additionally, when a new action is applied, an old action is evaluated. E. g., as depicted in Figure 8.9, at time t_b the $reward_j$ is computed to evaluate the action $A_j = (d_j, i_j)$. Moreover, a decision is made, which action A_{j+1} is applied until t_e is reached. The impact of possible payoff functions on learning is discussed in Section 8.2.4.

In Figure 8.10 another approach is depicted, which only learns condition-action-mappings in the case of situations that have been predefined as *critical*. Thus, the designer has to define a rule consisting of critical thresholds for all emergence indicators. The designer can use *a priori* knowledge of the learning problem to *delegate* the XCS to a reduced search space, which only contains critical situations. If this rule is satisfied, the XCS learning cycle will be triggered to search in its population for those classifiers, which match the current situation. The best classifiers are selected according to the XCS algorithm and the best action is applied. If the rule is not satisfied, no learning cycle will be started.

As depicted in Figure 8.10, a special reward function – to compute the classifier's fitness – is defined, which measures the time $\Delta t = t_d - (t_a + d_j)$ between two sequent

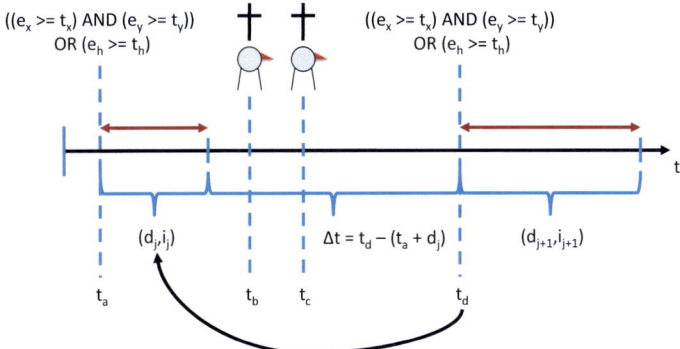

reward = Δt – #kc × discount factor

Figure 8.10: *Learning condition-action-mappings for* critical *situations only*

actions $A_j = (d_j, i_j)$ and $A_{j+1} = (d_{j+1}, i_{j+1})$. This period of time will be used to evaluate, if the mapping of situation $S_i = (e_x^j, e_y^j, e_h^j)$ and action A_j has successfully been applied. Additionally, the number of killed chickens $\#kc$ is observed, which counts chickens that have been killed during and after an action A_j takes place and before the next action A_{j+1} occurs (which again will depend on the decision, if predefined critical situations are satisfied or not). This number of killed chickens $\#kc$ discounts the period of time with $\Delta t - \#kC \times discount factor$[1]. Therefore, the XCS maximises the period of time and minimises the number of killed chickens at the same time. Results of this XCS, which only learns actions for *critical* situations, are presented in Section 8.2.7.

8.2.1 Effect of Varying the Search Space

First investigations with an XCS, which learns condition-action-mappings for *all possible* situations, have been made with an action space spanned by the duration $d \in \{1, 2, \ldots, 15\}$ and an intensity $i \in \{0, 10, 20, \ldots, 50\}$ (which results in $\#d \times \#i = 15 \times 6 = 90$ possible actions). However, using the standard XCS configuration, see [BW00, BW02], the XCS did not converge in the given time. Figures 8.11(a) and 8.12(a) show these investigations of varying the search space with respect to two population sizes with maximal 2 500 and 5 000 classifiers. Moreover, Table 8.5 lists the investigated search spaces concerning subsets of duration and intensity.

---

[1]This *discount factor* is predefined and has been set to 5.

157

Table 8.5: *Varying values of duration and intensity*

$\#d \times \#i$	d	i
15	5, 6, 7, 8, 9	0, 10, 20
18	4, 5, 6, 7, 8, 9	0, 10, 20
21	4, 5, 6, 7, 8, 9, 10	0, 10, 20
24	3, 4, 5, 6, 7, 8, 9, 10	0, 10, 20
27	3, 4, 5, 6, 7, 8, 9, 10, 11	0, 10, 20
30	2, 3, 4, 5, 6, 7, 8, 9, 10, 11	0, 10, 20
33	2, 3, 4, 5, 6, 7, 8, 9, 10, 11, 12	0, 10, 20
36	1, 2, 3, 4, 5, 6, 7, 8, 9, 10, 11, 12	0, 10, 20
39	1, 2, 3, 4, 5, 6, 7, 8, 9, 10, 11, 12, 13	0, 10, 20
45	3, 4, 5, 6, 7, 8, 9, 10, 11	0, 10, 20, 30, 40
50	2, 3, 4, 5, 6, 7, 8, 9, 10, 11	0, 10, 20, 30, 40
55	2, 3, 4, 5, 6, 7, 8, 9, 10, 11, 12	0, 10, 20, 30, 40
60	1, 2, 3, 4, 5, 6, 7, 8, 9, 10, 11, 12	0, 10, 20, 30, 40
90	1, 2, 3, 4, 5, 6, 7, 8, 9, 10, 11, 12, 13, 14, 15	0, 10, 20, 30, 40, 50

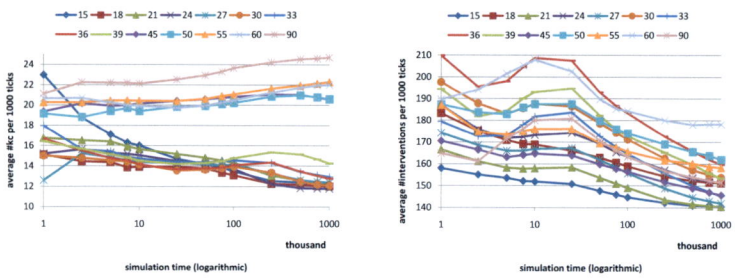

(a) Average number of killed chickens $\#kc$ per 1 000 ticks

(b) Average number of interventions per 1 000 ticks

Figure 8.11: *Learning over time in scenarios with different search spaces, varying parameters of duration and intensity, as shown in Table 8.5, and having a population of maximal 2 500 classifiers*

Thus, experiments have been performed with 15 up to 90 different noise signals. The results show that scenarios with up to 39 different noise signals provide decreasing average numbers of killed chickens $\#kc$ over time. Scenarios with greater search spaces do not converge in the investigated maximal time of 1 000 000 ticks. As depicted in Figures 8.11(a) and 8.12(a), scenarios with more than 39 different noise signals only provide constant average numbers of killed chickens $\#kc$ per 1 000 ticks.

Furthermore, some curves show an increasing behaviour over time. This is a strong indicator that the investigated search space cannot be learned with respect to a population size of maximal 2 500 and 5 000 classifiers, respectively.

To make the XCS converge, the following experiments have been limited to 15 different noise signals $(A_j = (d_j, i_j)$ with $d_j \in \{5, \ldots, 9\}$ and $i_j \in \{0, 10, 20\})$, which have provided the best learning results, as shown in Figures 8.11(a) and 8.12(a). In this scenario of 15 different noise signals, the average number of killed chickens $\#kc$ per 1 000 ticks has been decreased from 23 killed chickens at the beginning to 12 at the end after simulating 1 000 000 ticks. This is an reduction around 50% per 1 000 ticks in the given time.

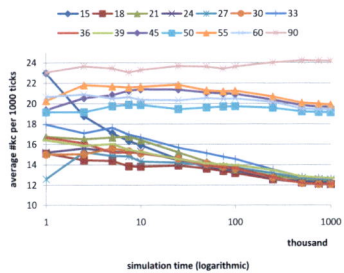
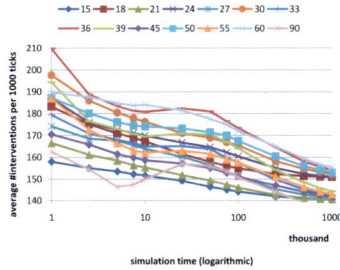

(a) Average number of killed chickens $\#kc$ per 1 000 ticks

(b) Average number of interventions per 1 000 ticks

Figure 8.12: *Learning over time in scenarios with different search spaces, varying parameters of duration and intensity, as shown in Table 8.5, and having a population of maximal 5 000 classifiers*

8.2.2 Effect of Simulation Time

As shown in Figures 8.11(a) and 8.12(a), simulation time has a positive impact on the achieved simulation results. If the simulation runs longer, more evaluations will be learned and the average number of killed chickens $\#kc$ per 1 000 ticks will continuously decrease. Simulation runs of the scenario with 15 different noise signals, which stop after 1 000 000 ticks, have generally performed 142 857 learning cycles, since the average duration of a noise signal is seven ticks. Keep in mind that the parameter duration has been limited to values from the set $\{5, 6, 7, 8, 9\}$.

Additionally, the number of interventions per 1 000 ticks decreases. This correlation is depicted in Figures 8.11(b) and 8.12(b). In a scenario of 15 different noise signals, the average number of interventions per 1 000 ticks has been decreased from 158 interventions at the beginning to 140 at the end after 1 000 000 ticks. However, the performed experiments have been very time consuming. Several runs needed more than a day to determine using *JoSchKa* [Bon08][2]. Thus, no general experiments have been done with a simulation time greater than 1 000 000 ticks.

8.2.3 Effect of Varying Maximal Population Sizes

Additionally, varying the search space (i. e., varying ranges of duration d and intensity i) also means that the value of the maximal population size (the maximal number of classifiers) has to be changed. If the value is too small, covering will not sensibly occur, since classifiers are always deleted to integrate new classifiers into the population, see [BW02]. Starting from an empty population, the population size should be large enough so that covering only occurs at the beginning of the learning process. Thus, experiments have been performed, which investigate the effect of varying the maximal population size on the ability to converge.

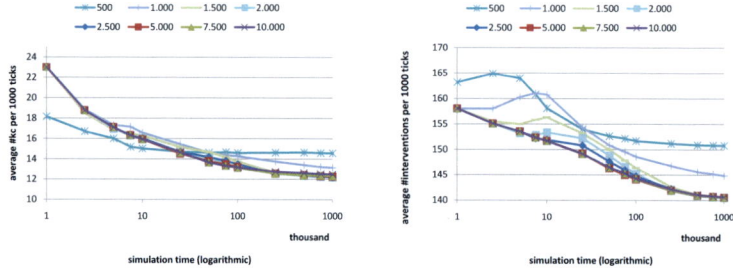

(a) Average number of killed chickens $\#kc$ per 1 000 ticks

(b) Average number of interventions per 1 000 ticks

Figure 8.13: *Effect of varying the maximal population size in a scenario with 15 different actions*

A theoretical consideration shows that in the case of a scenario with 15 different noise signals $10 \times 10 \times 10 \times 15 = 15\,000$ classifiers are needed to cover the whole search space into a non-overlapping condition-action-mapping. This discussion is based on an assumption, which excludes (important) XCS' mechanisms like *subsumption* or *don't care symbols*. Every possible situation is only covered by one classifier. Conditions of different classifiers do not overlap. If the three emergence values e_x, e_y, e_h are limited to values of $\{0.0, 1.0\}$ or $\{0, 99\}$ respectively, then 10 equally spaced and non-overlapping intervals similar to $[0, 9], [10, 19], [20, 29], [30, 39], [40, 49],$

---

[2]A typical computer, which has been used for job scheduling, is characterised by an Intel Core TM2 Duo E2180 CPU (2.0GHz/1MB level cache), it has 2GB DDR II RAM (800Mhz, 3 000MB/s), and it has an SATA storage with a capacity of 250GB.

$[50, 59]$, $[60, 69]$, $[70, 79]$, $[80, 89]$, and $[90, 99]$ will be needed to cover all possible situations. Certainly, more fine-granular or coarsely structured intervals are possible, but the investigated XCS works as follows: If a new situation is observed, which is unknown to the classifiers that have been learned so far, a new classifier will be generated using covering. Each emergence indicator is represented by an interval. Lower and upper boundaries lie around the observed emergence indicator having a predefined distance and taking the emergence value in the middle. This distance value has been set to 0.5 or five in all experiments.

In Figure 8.13, experiments are depicted with different values of the maximal population size. All other values are constant and have not been varied in these experiments. The results show that 2 500 classifiers are sufficient. Thus, in further experiments of this scenario the population size has been set to maximal 2 500 classifiers.

8.2.4 Effect of Reward Functions

Different parametrised reward functions have been evaluated. Since the observation range of the observer is limited, as explained in Section 6.2.3, only few parameters can be used as input variables for a reward function. Thus, experiments have been performed with several functions, which are always maximised by the XCS algorithm. Some *selected* reward functions are given and explained in the following. Some more functions have been evaluated, but the best results have been found with these four mentioned functions.

- Reward function 3:

$$reward = \begin{cases} 0.0 & : \quad \#kc > 0 \\ \Delta e_x + \Delta e_y & : \quad \#kc = 0 \end{cases} \quad (8.1)$$

I. e., if a chicken has been killed during an intervention, the reward, which is given to the applied classifiers, will be zero. If no chicken is killed, the sum of $\Delta e_x + \Delta e_y$ will be computed, where Δe_x and Δe_y are the differences between the emergence indicators before and after the intervention takes place.

- Reward function 4:

$$reward = \max(0.0, (\#c - \#kc \times 10)) \quad (8.2)$$

I. e., the reward is always equal to the total number of chickens $\#c$, which is degraded by every killed chicken. When simulations are performed with a total number of 40 chickens and 4 chickens are killed during an intervention, then the given reward will be zero, since every killed chicken is multiplied by ten.

- Reward function 5:

$$reward = \max(0.0, (d - \#kc \times d/2)) \tag{8.3}$$

I. e., the given reward is equal to the duration d of an intervention. It is argued that an intervention, which takes place for a longer duration, has a higher risk that a chicken is killed during this control action is active. The payoff will be better rewarded, if no chicken is killed. Thus, every killed chicken decreases the duration by the half of the duration. If more than two chickens are killed, the given reward will be zero.

- Reward function 6:

$$reward = \left\{ \begin{array}{ccc} 0.0 & : & \#kc > 0 \\ d & : & \#kc = 0 \end{array} \right. \tag{8.4}$$

I. e., if no chicken is killed, the payoff will be equal to the duration d of the intervention. The payoff will be zero, if a chicken has been killed.

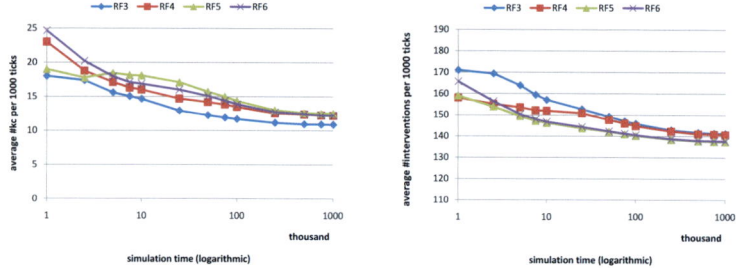

(a) Average number of killed chickens $\#kc$ per 1 000 ticks

(b) Average number of interventions per 1 000 ticks

Figure 8.14: *Effect of varying the reward function in a scenario with 15 different actions*

Results of varying the reward function are presented in Figure 8.14. The differences seem to be small. Moreover, the investigated functions explicitly differ at the beginning in the case of the average number of killed chickens $\#kc$ per 1 000 ticks, as depicted in Figure 8.14(a). These differences specially depend on the badly selected default initialisation of a new classifier's prediction value with $p_I = 10.0$, taken from the reference implementation [BW00]. In general, an initial prediction value of classifiers, which have not been applied in any action set $[A]$, should be parametrised defensively. E. g., reward function 5 has a maximal payoff of nine in a scenario with possible durations $d \in \{5, 6, 7, 8, 9\}$. It is obvious that a default initialisation with $p_I = 10.0$ suggests faulty predictions in the case of reward function 5, which particularly manipulate the experimental results at the beginning and are eliminated during simulation time. However, to compare the impact of the different reward functions on the learning process, it has been argued that the default initialisation of the prediction value should be equal in all experiments.

However, in scenarios with greater search spaces (not presented here to keep clarity of the discussed experiments) the reward function 4 performs best. Thus, reward function 4 has been used as the default reward function in the following experiments.

8.2.5 Effect of Other Parameters as Known from Literature

The XCS is a learning heuristic with many parameters that could be varied and customised concerning the special learning scenario, see [BW00, BW02, But06]. The impact on the learning behaviour varying

1. the search space,

2. the simulation time,

3. the maximal population size, or

4. the reward function

have been introduced before. Several other parameters are note presented here in detail. Thus, these aspects are only summarised in short, as known from literature.

- A population of classifiers could be initialised with predefined classifiers. These could be randomly initialised or set up with learned knowledge from previous runs. The presented experiments are always starting from scratch and leave the population empty. Populations are not initialised with randomly covered classifiers or with learned knowledge from previous experiments. To start with an empty population or a randomly initialised population seems to have no deeper impact on the learning behaviour, as explained in [BW02]. Initialising with *a priori* knowledge may speed up the learning process.

- New classifiers arise through covering or evolution using genetic operators. Evolution can be turned on and off. The presented results are all performed with genetic operators, which have been customised to fit into the selected scenario. A two-point crossover is used instead of a one-point crossover. Similar to the one-point crossover, the two-point crossover only affects the conditions. Mutation takes place in both, the condition and the action. A mutation in the condition modifies the encoded boundaries. Mutation in the action changes the values of duration and intensity to other values of duration and intensity.

Mutation is similarly applied as done in the XCS reference implementation. However, the final sub-procedure, which runs the genetic operators, has not been changed: Firstly, the action set $[A]$ will be checked to see, if the genetic operators should be applied at all. In order to apply genetic operators the average time period since the last application of genetic operators in the set must be greater than the predefined threshold Θ_{GA}. Secondly, two classifiers are selected as parents by roulette wheel selection based on the classifier's fitness and the offspring are created. The offspring are possibly crossed and mutated. If the offspring are crossed, their prediction, prediction error, and fitness values are set to the average of the parents' values. Finally, the offspring are inserted in the population. If the maximal population size is reached, deletion of other classifiers will follow. Further investigations on these mechanisms could perform better learning results, but are not part of this thesis. Modifications concerning covering are introduced in Section 8.4.

- The standard single-step XCS implementation continuously switches between *exploitation* and *exploration* phases, which addresses the question, use what you know or learn something new? *Exploitation* of acquired knowledge means that those classifiers with highest fitness values in the prediction array are always used. This provides a deterministic behaviour, evaluation of (few) classifiers becomes more reliable, and no improvements of knowledge occur. *Exploration* of new possibilities means that new classifiers are generated using evolution, and classifiers are randomly chosen in the prediction array. Thus, the goal is to enhance knowledge about the problem. The learning performance is decreased for the benefit of finding an optimum. This mechanism of continuous changing between exploitation and exploration phases over the whole simulation time has not been changed within this work. Further investigations may be useful.

8.2.6 Pure On-Line Learning

Summarising the achieved experience, as presented in the last sections, experiments with an pure on-line controller have been performed, which bases on the XCSJava1.0 reference implementation [But00] that has been modified to work with real- and integer-valued input. In general, the main experiments have been performed with parameter values, as characterised in the following.

- The search space of possible noise signals has been limited to $d \in \{5, 6, 7, 8, 9\} \times i \in \{0, 10, 20\}$.

- The population size is set to a maximum of $2\,500$ classifiers.

- The XCS starts with an empty population. Decreasing the number of killed chickens $\#kc$ is learned from scratch.

- Full covering takes place.

- Genetic operators are turned on.

- Reward function 4 is used.

- The simulation is performed over $1\,000\,000$ ticks.

- The XCS continuously changes between exploitation and exploration phases over the whole simulation time.

- Simulation runs are repeated with 20 different seed values. Presented results are always averaged over these repeated runs.

Table 8.6 shows the averaged number of killed chickens $\#kc$ of simulation runs with overall $1\,000\,000$ ticks. The attained average of 160.05 after $10\,000$ ticks is very close to the best result of the parameter study (approximately 166.40), which is a very promising result. Since the XCS only uses noise signals, which have been limited to $d \in \{5, 6, 7, 8, 9\} \times i \in \{0, 10, 20\}$, the comparison between the XCS and the best founded single fixed rules controller is limited to those controllers, which correspond to the restricted search space. Thus, the best single fixed rules controller is found in line eight of Table 8.4.

Table 8.6: *Results of the XCS vs. the best single fixed rules controller with $(t_x, t_y, t_h, d, i) = (0.2, 0.3, 0.3, 5, 20)$ established in parameter studies with varying the simulation time*

	XCS		Best single fixed rules controller	
Simulated ticks	Average $\#kc$	Standard error	Average $\#kc$	Standard error
$1\,000$	23.00	0.00	17.00	0.00
$2\,500$	46.90	0.35	40.20	0.20
$5\,000$	85.50	0.98	83.25	0.25
$7\,500$	122.20	1.33	128.20	0.20
$10\,000$	160.05	2.02	166.40	0.22
$25\,000$	367.30	6.46	425.35	1.54
$50\,000$	708.80	9.22	867.00	2.79
$75\,000$	$1\,036.50$	11.19	$1\,311.45$	2.97
$100\,000$	$1\,347.55$	14.84	$1\,754.70$	2.97
$250\,000$	$3\,133.20$	26.77	$4\,411.35$	7.92
$500\,000$	$6\,189.40$	26.69	$8\,831.00$	12.02
$750\,000$	$9\,187.35$	32.71	$13\,256.25$	12.13
$1\,000\,000$	$12\,210.15$	44.02	$17\,676.20$	15.43

Furthermore, Table 8.6 verifies that an XCS converges with more simulation time to a better optimum. The same results are also shown in Figure 8.15. The XCS is able to converge to a steady result.

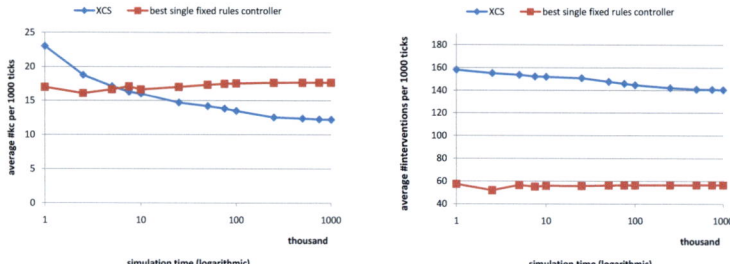

(a) Average number of killed chickens $\#kc$ per 1 000 ticks, see Table 8.6

(b) Average number of interventions per 1 000 ticks

Figure 8.15: *Learning over time using an XCS vs. the best found single fixed rules controller*

Figure 8.15 depicts the learning behaviour over time of the XCS in comparison to the best single fixed rule controller found through the parameter studies. It plots the average number of killed chickens $\#kc$ per 1 000 ticks with increasing simulation time and each plotted value is the average over 20 runs. As expected, the best found single fixed rules controller shows a constant progression. In comparison the XCS controller begins with a greater number of lost chickens, which decreases in the course of time until becoming constant.

Furthermore as shown in Figure 8.15(b), the average number of interventions per 1 000 ticks is decreased from 158 at the beginning to 140 interventions at the end. This is a reduction of 11.39%. However, compared to the best found single fixed rules controller the XCS needs more than twice as much interventions.

8.2.7 Learning over Thresholds

As illustrated in Figures 8.9 and 8.10, the single-step implementation causes two slightly different approaches. In this section, the results of the adaptive controller are presented, where the XCS is only triggered, when predefined *critical* thresholds of emergence values are exceeded. This corresponds to the rule, as introduced in Section 8.1.2. If the condition $((e_x \geq t_x) \text{ AND } (e_y \geq t_y)) \text{ OR } (e_h \geq t_h)$ with $t = (t_x, t_y, t_h)$ being the critical emergence thresholds is true, then the observed emergence values will be given to the XCS, which hereupon decides, which parameters of noise will be chosen.

Table 8.7: *Average number of killed chickens #kc after 10 000 simulated ticks in ascending order using an XCS, which is triggered when predefined thresholds are exceeded*

e_x, e_y, e_h	Average $\#kc$	Standard deviation	Standard error
0.1, 0.1, 0.3	80.80	9.32	2.08
0.1, 0.2, 0.3	93.55	13.57	3.04
0.2, 0.1, 0.3	103.40	10.32	2.31
0.2, 0.2, 0.3	100.55	9.00	2.01
0.3, 0.2, 0.3	131.45	5.93	1.33
0.1, 0.3, 0.3	132.85	5.83	1.30
0.3, 0.1, 0.3	133.25	7.50	1.68
0.2, 0.3, 0.3	135.15	7.50	1.68
0.3, 0.3, 0.3	139.60	3.95	0.88
0.2, 0.4, 0.3	167.55	3.76	0.84
...	...	...	...

Thus, the XCS just learns the best mapping of situations and actions in cases that have been classified as critical by the developer. This XCS implementation uses knowledge that is given by the user to optimise the learning behaviour. As shown in Table 8.7, the results of these modifications are remarkable. Using predefined thresholds improves searching the condition-action-mappings and drastically decreases the average number of killed chickens $\#kc$. The presented results are an excerpt of the obtained results. The values of t_x and t_y are varied from $\{0.1, 0.2, \ldots, 0.6\}$ and $t_h = 0.3$ has been constant. The implemented reward function maximises the time between two periods of time, as depicted in Figure 8.10. It should be mentioned that this is a special reward function, which bases on the constraints made within this implementation. This reward function cannot be used within the XCS, as presented in the section before, where the XCS is used to learn the condition-action-mappings for the whole search space.

Figure 8.16 presents results, which compare learning over time between the best XCS using predefined critical thresholds $(t_x, t_y, t_h) = (0.1, 0.1, 0.3)$ and the XCS, which learns condition-action-mappings for all situations. The results draw the conclusion that better results in terms of the average number of killed chickens $\#kc$ are obtained when the process of controlling is not completely learned by an XCS and the controller is equipped with *a priori* knowledge. Thus, the correlation between an increasing learning performance and *a priori* knowledge seems obvious.

8.2.8 Summary

In OC scenarios, there is often no time for time consuming parameter studies and *a priori* knowledge is also unknown. Therefore, on-line learning techniques are needed

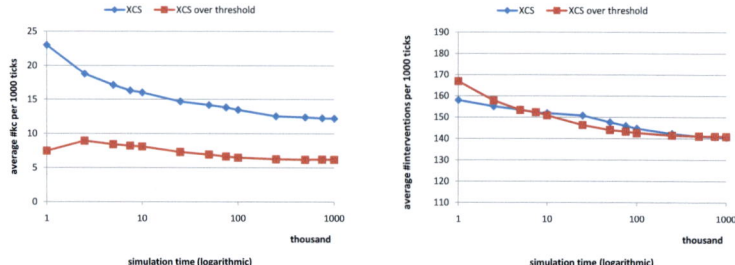

(a) Average number of killed chickens $\#kc$ per 1 000 ticks

(b) Average number of interventions per 1 000 ticks

Figure 8.16: *XCS over threshold with* $(t_x, t_y, t_h) = (0.1, 0.1, 0.3)$ *vs. XCS*

that adapt as soon as possible to changing environments. However, observing and controlling technical systems means that decisions have to be taken with respect to hard time constraints and systems cannot only learn through making (bad) experiences in the real world. Thus, learning techniques, which combine off-line generated knowledge, e. g., by time consuming and thus low efficient parameter studies, and on-line adaptation capabilities, seem to be an adequate approach. This idea is investigated in more detail in Section 8.4.

The results have shown that an XCS is able to learn the best parameters of making noise in the chicken scenario, and thus to decrease the number of killed chickens. But, the XCS needs a lot of time to converge to steady results. Furthermore, when the search space of possible actions increases, the XCS does not converge – in the course of the simulated period of time as investigated here.

To make use of LCSs as a fast on-line learning mechanism that can be integrated into the general observer/controller architecture, improvements are necessary. An LCS architecture is needed that

1. needs less reinforcement learning loops to learn while

2. exhibiting the same or better learning results compared to existing LCSs.

Solutions to this challenge might include the following mechanisms.

- Parallel or distributed learning architectures: By dividing the problem into sub-problems and allowing various LCSs to work together and run in parallel, the complete learning task is decomposed and improvements in learning speed should be possible.

- Algorithmic advancements: Covering techniques and genetic operators like crossover and mutation could be varied and improved.

- More training phases before acting on real world problems: In the case of OC systems that should continuously adapt in dynamic environments more training phases do not seem to be an adequate strategy (in all scenarios), because changes occur on-line and adaptation has to cope with these changes.

The following results will firstly concentrate on improvements through parallelism and distribution in the next section. Then, the two-levelled learning approach is investigated in Section 8.4.

8.3 Parallel XCS Architectures

A promising way to deal with complex problems should be to divide them into sub-problems and assign each sub-problem to a single LCS instance – if possible. Not every learning task can be decomposed. In this way, each single LCS learns to solve a specific subtask and the subtask results can be combined resulting in a parallel learning system that performs as well as or hopefully better than a single LCS.

The design approach of task decomposition (as presented in the following) is not provided in an automated way. Depending on the problem, a decomposition might be difficult or even impossible due to strong interdependencies of the subtasks. The system designer needs to identify independent and basic subtasks that could be assigned to different LCS instances.

8.3.1 2PXCS

As depicted in Figure 8.17(b), the single XCS, see Figure 8.17(a), is replaced by two completely separated parallel learning loops – one responsible for mapping the three emergence values to the duration d of the noise intervention, the other one responsible for finding the best intensity i of the intervention. Thus, decomposition takes place along the two parameters of the action space. This approach will investigate, if the two parameters duration d and intensity i, which characterise the noise signal, are independent and can be learned in parallel.

The two parallel LCSs use the same standard parameters, as given in [But00], get the same reward, as mentioned in Section 8.2.6, and both have a four-dimensional search space. This scenario is called 2PXCS for two XCSs, which learn in parallel. Referring to Figure 8.17(b), XCS_1 maps the emergence values e_x, e_y, and e_h to the duration d, XCS_2 does the same with the intensity i. The experiments are again performed in a scenario with 15 different noise signals ($d \in \{5, 6, \ldots, 9\} \times i \in \{0, 10, 20\}$). Figure 8.18 compares the obtained results of 2PXCS with the results of the corresponding single XCS.

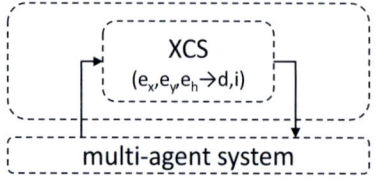 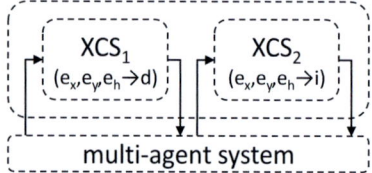

(a) A single XCS learns the best mapping of three integer-valued condition values (e_x, e_y, e_h) and two action parameters (d, i)

(b) Decomposition into two sub-problems, two separated XCS instances learn to solve each sub-problem

Figure 8.17: *XCS vs. 2PXCS*

Figure 8.18(a) depicts the average number of killed chickens $\#kc$ per 1 000 simulation ticks over 20 runs. Figure 8.18(b) depicts the average number of interventions per 1 000 simulation ticks over 20 runs. It is shown that both, the single XCS and the 2PXCS implementation, improve their condition-action-mappings over time and finally converge to a steady result. Comparing XCS and 2PXCS, it is noted that the XCS specially outperforms the 2PXCS at the beginning. At the end both curves converge to the same values.

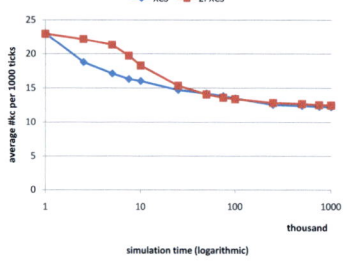 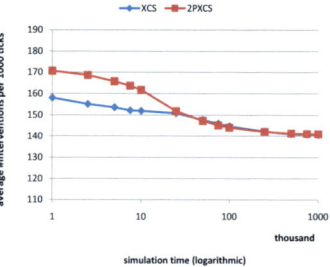

(a) Average number of killed chickens $\#kc$ per 1 000 ticks

(b) Average number of interventions per 1 000 ticks

Figure 8.18: *Learning over time: XCS vs. 2PXCS, averaged values over 20 runs, 15 possible actions, $d \in \{5, \dots, 9\} \times i \in \{0, 10, 20\}$*

In the 2PXCS variant, XCS_1 and XCS_2 have to learn a four-dimensional condition-action-mapping, i.e., that is their condition-action-mapping is reduced by one dimension compared to the single XCS implementation. Moreover, the reduction of one dimension (from a five-dimensional to a four-dimensional condition-action-mapping) seems not sufficient to speed up the learning process, as from theoretically considerations expected. However, the results show that the parameters duration d and intensity i are not sufficiently independent to be learned by two separated XCS instances. Thus, another – more reasonable – parallel learning architecture has been tried, as described in the following.

8.3.2 3PXCS

As depicted in Figure 8.19(a), the single XCS, see Figure 8.17(a), is decomposed into three separated parallel learning loops – every LCS is responsible for mapping one of the three emergence values to the duration d and the intensity i of the noise intervention, i.e., every XCS has to learn a three-dimensional condition-action-mapping. This approach takes the results of 2PXCS into account that duration d and intensity i cannot independently learned in parallel LCSs. This scenario is called 3PXCS because of the three parallel XCS instances.

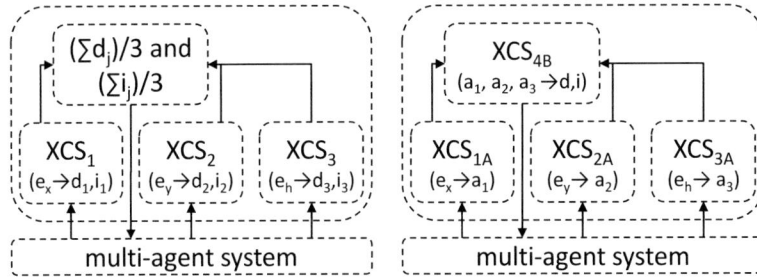

(a) Decomposition into three sub-problems and three separated instances learn to solve each sub-problem

(b) Decomposition into three sub-problems on level A with $a_j \in \{0,1\}$ and $j \in \{1,2,3\}$ and one XCS learns the aggregated results on level B

Figure 8.19: 3PXCS vs. HXCS

The LCSs again use the same standard parameters, as proposed in [But00], and get the same reward as mentioned in Section 8.2.6. Every XCS_j with $j \in \{1,2,3\}$ determines in every reinforcement learning loop one specific noise signal (d_j, i_j), based on which the average proposed duration $\bar{d}$ with $\bar{d} = \frac{1}{3} \cdot \sum_{j=1}^{3} d_j$ and the average intensity $\bar{i}$ with $\bar{i} = \frac{1}{3} \cdot \sum_{j=1}^{3} i_j$ are computed. The triggered noise signal is the average $(\bar{d}, \bar{i})$ of all three decisions and the reward every XCS_j receives is the reward received under the control action $(\bar{d}, \bar{i})$.

Figure 8.20(a) depicts the average number of killed chickens $\#kc$ per 1 000 simulation ticks over 20 runs. Figure 8.20(b) depicts the average number of interventions per 1 000 simulation ticks over 20 runs. It is shown that the 3PXCS implementation

171

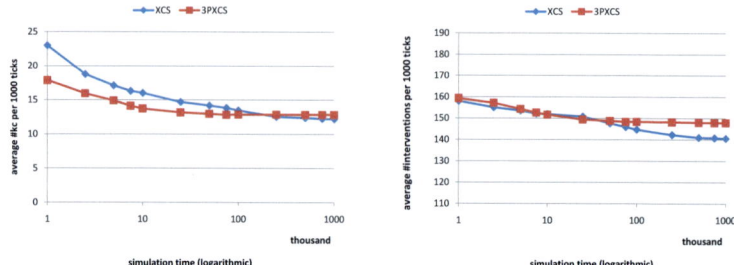

(a) Average number of killed chickens $\#kc$ per 1 000 ticks

(b) Average number of interventions per 1 000 ticks

Figure 8.20: *Learning over time: XCS vs. 3PXCS, averaged values over 20 runs, 15 possible actions, $d \in \{5, \ldots, 9\} \times i \in \{0, 10, 20\}$*

improves the condition-action-mappings over time and finally converges to a steady result. Comparing XCS and 2PXCS in the case of the average number of killed chickens $\#kc$ per 1 000 ticks, it is noted that 3PXCS outperforms the single XCS variant from the beginning. At the end both curves nearly converge to the same values. Taking the average number of interventions per 1 000 ticks into account, it is shown that the number also decreases in the case of the 3PXCS, but not as explicit as in the case of the single XCS. Moreover, 3PXCS achieves better results than the single XCS – with nearly the same amount of control.

Thus, the new design decision to learn both parameters of a noise signal in one single LCS and to simplify the condition part of a classifier seems to be the better design decision in the case of controlling the chickens. The results outperform the results achieved with 2PXCS and with the single XCS, respectively.

8.3.3 HXCS

Based on the results, which have been obtained for 2PXCS and 3PXCS, a third implementation has been tested, which decomposes the learning problem within hierarchically organised LCSs, as depicted in Figure 8.19(b). This type of architecture is called HXCS for the hierarchically organised XCS instances.

On level A three LCSs are implemented that work in parallel on different sub-problems. XCS_{1A} will only map the emergence value e_x to the decision/action $a_1 \in \{0, 1\}$, if a noise intervention is preferred or not. XCS_{2A} and XCS_{3A} do the same with e_y and e_h, respectively. The three LCSs on level A have to learn a binary coded decision, where *zero* means no noise signal should be applied and *one* represents a noise intervention.

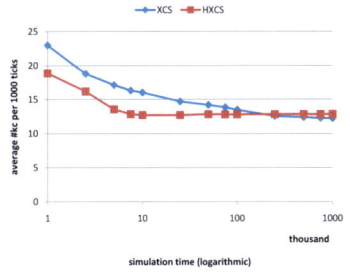 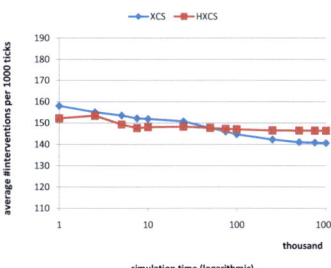

(a) Average number of killed chickens $\#kc$ per 1 000 ticks

(b) Average number of interventions per 1 000 ticks

Figure 8.21: *Learning over time: XCS vs. HXCS, averaged values over 20 runs, 15 possible actions, $d \in \{5, \ldots, 9\} \times i \in \{0, 10, 20\}$*

A fourth LCS, XCS_{4B}, collects the decisions of XCS_{1A}, XCS_{2A}, and XCS_{3A} and maps this input data to a noise signal that is again characterised by a duration d and an intensity i – while an action (d, i) with $d \in \{5, \ldots, 9\}$ and $i = 0$ is explicitly possible on level B. As mentioned before, this special type of actions is equal to the effect of intervening the chickens without any noise.

XCS_{1A}, XCS_{2A}, and XCS_{3A} have to solve a sub-problem with a two-dimensional condition-action-mapping, XCS_{4B} has to solve a five-dimensional problem where the situation is characterised as a three bit binary vector – an thus, the new condition is very simplified in comparison to the real- or integer-coded condition of the single XCS implementation, see Section 8.2.6.

As done before, the hierarchically organised HXCS implementation is compared to the single XCS in the case of a scenario with 15 different noise signals. The results are presented in Figure 8.21. The HXCS implementation improves its condition-action-mappings over time and finally converges to a steady result. However, HXCS demonstrates significant advantages of this new LCS arrangement. HXCS shows improvements in learning speed and quality of the results. Even if the condensed situation information available to XCS_{4B} is heavily simplified, HXCS is able to learn the best condition-action-mappings.

8.3.4 Limitations of the Single-Agent Learning Approach

Aiming at enhancing the learning speed of LCSs, Section 8.3 has especially focused on the XCS implementation provided in [But00], which has been modified to work with real- and integer-valued parameters. Caused by drawbacks LCSs have in learning speed, the provided experimental results validate the idea of distributed LCSs that solve smaller sub-problems of a larger problem in parallel. Significant improvements in the performance and learning speed could specially be shown for the 3PXCS and HXCS implementation. The 2PXCS architecture started with a promising idea, but exhibited no convincing results in the investigated scenario.

To conclude, improvements in learning speed could be achieved by dividing a problem into sub-problems that are solved in parallel. Identifying appropriate sub-problems is a difficult task that (depending on the problem) might even be impossible. The developer of a learning mechanism needs a lot of information about the investigated problem to divide the learning task into separately solvable sub-problems. The design decision, how to decompose a problem, should be plausible. In some cases, parameters are correlated and cannot separately learned with different XCS instances, see Section 8.3.1.

Thus, the investigated single-agent learning approach has also limitations. In general, the decomposition of a learning task into simpler subtasks and allocating it to distinct LCSs has four limitations, as proposed by the single-agent learning approach, see Section 5.5.1.

1. Parallelism is limited by the size of the problem. Generally, decomposing a general task into a number of subtasks is limited by the dependencies of the involved parameters of the learning problem.

2. The task of decomposing a task into subtasks is static and predefined. How to decompose the task and into how many subtasks a task is decomposed is decided *a priori*. These decisions are connected to the relative difficulties of subtasks, which are not known in advance.

3. Furthermore, it will often be not known, if the new decomposed learning problem is equal to the old learning problem. As explained and shown in Section 8.3.1, parameters, which are correlated, could not be learned in parallel and have to be learned together in one learning instance.

4. Any single-agent solution presents a bottleneck, which is caused by the interaction with the environment. Even though its internal structure is parallel, the agent has to interact with the environment in a serial way. When different subtasks faced by distinct LCSs regard unrelated actions, distinct LCSs of the agent may interface distinct effectors, which is investigated in [BFS95], where four different legs of a robot are controlled by four different modules. However, the number of actions an agent is simultaneously allowed to perform cannot be very large. Furthermore, the global experience of the complete agent is still sequential. Thus, a multi-agent learning approach has theoretically been introduced in Section 5.5.2 to overcome the limitations of the single-agent learning approach.

However, the decomposition of complex learning tasks is a promising approach for learning difficult problems. Some techniques have recently been proposed, some others are addressed in this thesis.

8.4 Using Level 2 Learning

As depicted in Figure 6.20, a further controller type has been investigated, which learns on-line using an XCS that simulates possible new classifier on level 2 using a simulation model. Therefore, the covering operator of the original XCS implementation has been modified.

The *minimal number of different actions* that must be present in a match set $[M]$ is specified by Θ_{mna}. If there are less than Θ_{mna} classifiers in a match set $[M]$, covering will occur. To cause covering to provide classifiers for every possible action, the standard XCS implementation sets Θ_{mna} equal to the number of available actions. In the investigated scenario with duration $d \in \{5, 6, 7, 8, 9\}$ and $i \in \{0, 10, 20\}$ the parameter Θ_{mna} is set to $\#d \times \#i = 5 \times 3 = 15$. Thus, if a new situation is observed, which is unknown to the existing condition-action-mapping, 15 new classifiers will be generated using covering.

The single XCS implementation, as investigated in Section 8.2.6, initialises these 15 new classifiers with predefined values p_I, ϵ_I, and F_I, which denote the initial prediction, prediction error, and fitness values and which are initialised with very small values. As described in [But00], the default values in the experiments have equally been chosen and set to $(p_I, \epsilon_I, F_I) = (10.0, 0.0, 0.01)$.

In the case of unknown situations, the modified covering mechanism starts for every possible action a single simulation run on level 2, where the action is applied to a situation that is equal to the one observed in the real system. Since in this simulated chicken environment every design decision seems possible, the real simulation used on level 1 is completely cloned to be used on level 2. Thus, level 2 is no abstracted copy of the real world and no simplifications are done according to the used simulation model on level 2. Certainly, this may be artificial assumptions, which are not reasonable in real world scenarios, but it is tried to investigate, what is possible in the best case using this two-level learning approach.

Furthermore, the controller of this level 2 simulation counts the number of killed chickens during the time the selected action is applied to the simulated model on level 2. Subsequently, level 2 reports the information of killed chickens to level 1. There, this information is used to initialise the new classifier with another – hopefully better – prediction value p_I. Depending on the used reward function (see reward function 4 in Section 8.2.4), the prediction value will be set to the given reward. In other words, the initialisation of the prediction value is always equal to the total number of chickens $\#c$, which is degraded by every killed chicken on level 2. When simulations on level 2 are performed with a total number of 40 chickens and four chickens are killed during an intervention, then the given prediction value will be zero, since every killed chicken is multiplied by ten. Results, which have been achieved with a controller that combines on-line learning with off-line planning capabilities on level 2, as proposed in Section 4.3, are presented in Figure 8.22.

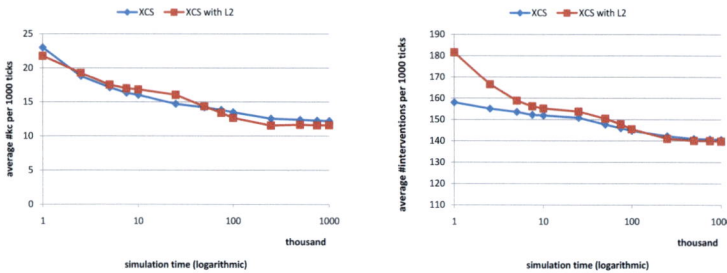

(a) Average number of killed chickens $\#kc$ per 1 000 ticks

(b) Average number of interventions per 1 000 ticks

Figure 8.22: *Learning over time: XCS vs. XCS with level 2, averaged values over 20 runs, 15 possible actions, $d \in \{5, \ldots, 9\} \times i \in \{0, 10, 20\}$*

The achieved results are surprising, since the difference between the original and the modified covering mechanism are marginal in the case of the average number of killed chickens $\#kc$ per 1 000 ticks, as depicted in Figure 8.22(a). Interpreting the results positively, modified covering outperforms the original variant a little bit at the beginning and at the end, but the difference between the two depicted curves totally belongs to one or two killed chickens per 1 000 ticks. Furthermore, the average number of interventions per 1 000 ticks, as shown in Figure 8.22(b), clearly demonstrates that the two-level learning approach cannot outperform the original mechanism, if the number of interventions is solely used as benchmark criterion. In other words, the two-level learning approach does not perform as well as expected – with respect to this investigated variant of implementation and this selected test scenario.

The question, which automatically arises, is why this two-level learning approach does not work as expected? One single simulation run of each unknown condition-action-mapping on level 2 seems to be not sufficient. The results obtained by level 2 may serve as a good initialisation (since they are based on experience), but their prediction and information content are limited caused by several reasons.

1. In this investigated scenario, the classifier's condition encodes a set of possible emergence situations, which are merged into a single situation, see Section 8.2. The three emergence indicators e_x, e_y, e_h are aggregated values and serve as a

clustering indicator. From the controller's viewpoint, they hide the different energy values of the chickens. Thus, the effectiveness of a possible control intervention could not be shown and evaluated in a single simulation run on level 2. E.g., in a first case, the three emergence values indicate a clustering situation, where all chickens are very healthy. In another situation, the same emergence values will indicate a similar clustering situation, but all chickens are wounded a little bit. The same noise signal will have a different impact on the chickens. This problem is not only limited to this two-level learning approach. The same problem also appears without having planning capabilities on level 2. However, it clarifies that a single evaluation of a new condition-action-mapping cannot be sufficient with respect to this scenario.

2. Furthermore, LCSs learn over time using reinforcement learning. It is in the nature of things that the initialisation of the prediction value is a vanish value. Combining on-line learning and off-line planning may outperform an LCS, which only learns on-line on level 1, at the beginning, but it cannot continuously outperform it. The impact of the initialisation value on the whole learning process is low.

3. Another reason is the detrimental correlation between using a full covering mechanism and the investigated reward function (see reward function 4 in Section 8.2.4). Here, when an observed situation is unknown, 15 new classifiers are tested on level 2. Possible results of these simulation runs on level 2 will initialise the prediction value with $p_I \in \{0, 10, 20, 30, 40\}$. If 15 classifiers force 15 different initialisations, it will be easier to decide, which classifier should be chosen. But, if 15 classifiers are rewarded with more or less similar results on level 2, the experience of level 2 will not support the decision, which has to be taken on level 1. Since no sufficient experience is provided, it becomes – taken the worst case – a random decision, which classifier of the match set will form an action set.

To conclude, combining on-line learning and planning capabilities theoretically seems to be a powerful mechanism to overcome drawbacks of pure on-line learning. However, this hypothesis could not be verified in the investigated chicken scenario. Further investigations in scenarios, where pure on-line learning is not applicable, are necessary, see [PRT+08, TPR+08].

8.5 Using Another Metric on the Observer's Side

As argued in Section 6.2.5, a controller's decision is mainly based on the intelligence and logic of the observer. If the used metrics on the observer's side do not give a precise characterisation of the system behaviour, the controller will not correctly act. Moreover, learning cannot optimally be performed.

The investigated chicken scenario is observed and characterised by three emergence indicators, which are computed according to an entropy-based metric, as summarised in Section 4.1.5. Furthermore, critical remarks have been made on this metric and its proposed general significance to quantify emergent behaviour. To investigate, that this selected metric performs a well defined job in the chicken scenario, another metric has been developed, which is specially based on this scenario, as outlined in Section 6.2.5.

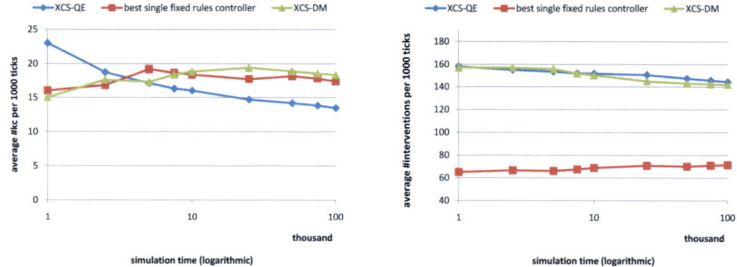

(a) Average number of killed chickens $\#kc$ per 1 000 ticks

(b) Average number of interventions per 1 000 ticks

Figure 8.23: *Comparing learning over time, which is based on different metrics on the observer's side, averaged values over 20 runs, 15 possible actions, $d \in \{5, \ldots, 9\} \times i \in \{0, 10, 20\}$*

This *density metric* computes the density of chickens in each smaller grid of the two-dimensional grid and passes the information about the grid with the highest density to the controller. Then, the noise intervention takes place in the centroid of the chicken cluster that relies on the most densely packed (smaller) grid.

Again as successfully elaborated on quantitative emergence, parameter studies with this special density metric have been performed, an XCS is compared to the best found single fixed rules controller, and then the results are compared to the results obtained with an XCS using quantitative emergence on the observer's side. Figure 8.23 summarises the results obtained with these experiments. It is shown that the controller, which is based on the density metric (XCS-DM), will converge to results as found in the parameter studies, if the view is limited to the average number of killed chickens $\#kc$ per 1 000 ticks. In comparison to the controller, which is based on quantitative emergence (XCS-QE), it is shown that XCS-QE achieves in summary better results than XCS-DM. This might not be true at the beginning of learning, but until the end this is obvious. Comparing the number of interventions, both approaches will show similar performances, even if the low number of interventions per 1 000 ticks of the best found single fixed rules controller seems unreachable. The static controller is very efficient in controlling the clustering behaviour.

Thus, the critical remarks on quantitative emergence may only be justifiable from a theoretical point of view. However, the investigations achieved so far do not claim that another metric is needed to measure clustering in the chicken scenario. These conclusions are mainly based on the specific behaviour of the chickens. They do not behave as shown in the particular cases, mentioned in Section 6.2.5.

8.6 Concluding Remarks on the Experiments

Within this chapter, several experiments have been performed and gained cognisance of the influencing factors on the effectiveness of the observer/controller architecture. In the following, a concise outline of the main insights is given.

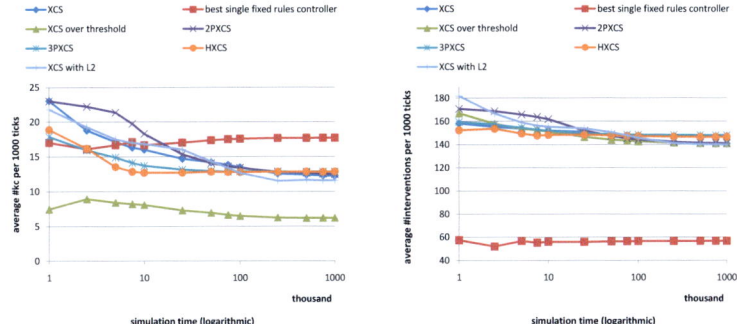

(a) Average number of killed chickens $\#kc$ per 1 000 ticks

(b) Average number of interventions per 1 000 ticks

Figure 8.24: *Learning over time: All investigated approaches, averaged values over 20 runs, 15 possible actions, $d \in \{5, \ldots, 9\} \times i \in \{0, 10, 20\}$*

Based on three emergence indicators different types of control strategies ranging from static to adaptive ones have been investigated in the context of a nature-inspired chicken scenario. The results, as summarised in Figure 8.24, have shown that the controller, which uses an XCS to learn the whole condition-action-mapping, is able to converge to the results, which have been found in preliminary parameter studies. Moreover, the controller type, which *only* starts learning in the case of *critical* situations, outperforms the results achieved with the XCS, which learns condition-action-mappings for *all possible* situations. This result is not surprising, since using *a priori* knowledge to distinguish between critical and non-critical situations should

179

always provide a better learning performance than starting from scratch. However, searching for *a priori* knowledge is a time consuming and exhausting process, as explained in Section 8.1.2. Such preliminary investigations are often not suitable – specially in the case of OC scenarios. Thus, comparing the controller type, which *only* starts learning in the case of *critical* situations, to the controller, which learns the mapping of *all possible* situations, seems not fair and realistic. Finally, all investigations have suggested that LCSs need many reinforcement cycles to converge to steady results and to learn an optimal condition-action-mapping. Thus, techniques have been investigated that speed up this learning process.

Especially, parallel implementations have been investigated to decrease the number of learning cycles. These investigations have shown that the learning process is significantly speeded up at the beginning in the case of 3PXCS and HXCS. It could be shown that decomposition of a learning problem into several sub-problems, which could be solved in parallel, provides a successful technique. Furthermore, the two-level learning approach has been applied and the covering mechanism has been modified. However, the results of these modifications are not satisfying (with respect to the assumptions of the investigated scenario) and further investigations on this approach are necessary, as outlined in Section 9.3.

Chapter 9

Conclusion and Outlook

People do not like to think. If one thinks, one must reach a conclusion. Conclusions are not always pleasant. (Helen Keller)

Motivated by the challenges of OC, the goal of this thesis has been to design, develop, and investigate an observer/controller architecture, which establishes controlled self-organisation in technical, real-time, noisy, collaborative, and competitive environments. This chapter summarises the main contributions. Section 9.1 describes the results achieved within this thesis. In Section 9.2, some conclusions are outlined in the light of the objectives made in Section 1.2. Furthermore, Section 9.3 discusses and outlines possible challenges to extend this work. Final remarks complete this thesis in Section 9.4.

9.1 Summary

To get closer to the overarching vision of OC has just started. OC systems will involve an evolution of innovation in systems and software engineering as well as collaboration with many other diverse scientific fields. Since OC focusses on the challenge of increasing complexity in technical systems, this thesis introduces a regulatory feedback mechanism, the generic observer/controller architecture, to establish controlled self-organisation.

To cope with unwanted (emerging) global behaviour as a result of bestowing upon the systems some life-like characteristics, the idea of an observer/controller architecture has been introduced and refined. This architecture allows organising several aspects of the system behaviour in an autonomous way, independent from an explicit external interference that keeps a system alive and running. Thus, the SuOC adapts to changes in its environment and is controlled by an observer/controller in order to acquire robustness and the ability to overcome breakdowns. It has been shown, how observer and controller are designed, which functions should be implemented, and how the main loop consisting of the SuOC, an observer (observing the behaviour of the SuOC in terms of well defined system parameters), and a controller (selecting adequate actions to optimise system behaviour with respect to certain global objectives) may work together.

The defined components of the OC architecture strongly rely on other established scientific areas like data mining, time series analysis, machine learning, or control theory. Results and methods from these areas have been used to extend the proposed toolbox and to test the developed metrics and adaptive control strategies with different test scenarios. In doing so, the focus has been set on the controller – and specially on learning capabilities using LCSs.

The proposed concepts have been tested with respect to some multi-agent scenarios (e. g., a group of self-organising lifts, different simulated environments from the area of mobile robotics, or a nature-inspired scenario of a collection of freely moving simple agents (chickens) showing some undesired emerging effects). All scenarios could be seen as instances of the generic predator/prey example, which is frequently used in the multi-agent community and which has successfully been studied in a wide variety of instantiations. Moreover, the predator/prey example has demonstrated its generality to many real world applications, and thus, it has served as well as test scenario for OC research to evaluate the ideas proposed in this thesis.

Especially, the generic approach of the *centralised* observer/controller architecture has been applied to a nature-inspired predator/prey scenario of a swarm of chickens. Each chicken has been implemented as a simple agent, which presents in cooperation with the other agents a macroscopic behaviour that only depends on local rules. The investigated chicken simulation shows clustering from a global point of view as an unwanted (emergent) behaviour of local interaction.

If chickens perceive a wounded chicken, they chase and pick on it. This leads to the emergent building of chicken swarms (or clusters). A swarm disperses, when the wounded chicken is killed or the chickens are frightened by noise. The emergent behaviour in this scenario is spatial, but swarms move over time. To summarise the idea of this scenario, clustering is characterised as a case of negative, i. e., unwanted (emergent) behaviour, since the global goal should be to reduce chicken death rate.

In other words: Providing feedback and decision capabilities to this nature-inspired scenario, it has been shown that the unwanted (emergent) behaviour, clustering of agents around wounded agents, can automatically be observed and prevented with respect to a global objective function.

The observer reports a quantified context of the underlying system to the controller. The controller evaluates the situation and reacts with adequate control actions to disperse swarms or to prevent their formation.

An entropy-based measurement method has been used to observe the described order pattern. For controlling the robots, different methods have been implemented ranging from static to adaptive controllers, which learn on-line and off-line the best condition-action mapping, i. e., the best mapping between clustering behaviour and noise. All investigated controllers change the environment, and thus, indirectly affect the local behaviour of the agents.

The presented simulation results validate the idea of the proposed generic observer/controller architecture and have shown advantages and potentials of controlled self-organisation in technical scenarios. Without control actions the chickens will show clustering behaviour, hinder or attack each other, and the system might break down. The controller extends the life of the chickens and keeps on running the whole system.

Furthermore, endowing the controller with adaptation capabilities has shown that the controller is able to evaluate the success of its interventions and to adapt the fitness and the parameters of the used rules depending on the global objective function. This suggests the ability of (on-line) learning. Moreover, the controller is also able to generate new rules with adequate parameters. Adaptation over time optimises the controller's behaviour and guides the process of controlled self-organisation. Therefore, a two-level learning architecture as part of the controller has been defined, which combines on-line learning and off-line planning capabilities. It combines the advantage of on-line adaptation and prevents the disadvantage of testing bad solutions in the real world by using a reality model for validation of promising new rules.

As a machine learning technique, LCSs have specially been investigated, because they fit well to the observer/controller framework and are in the focus of other OC projects. LCSs aim at the autonomous production of potentially human-readable results, which seem to be beneficial in the context of designing self-organising technical systems. If a system designer can understand, what a system has autonomously learnt, this will provide trust to OC systems and their reliable performance.

In the investigated chicken scenario, an LCS is used to learn the best control intervention on-line on level 1 of the two-level learning controller. The experimental results have been compared with results drawn from fixed rules parameter studies. On-line learning leads to significant improvements in the performance of the global system behaviour. However, since LCSs are a reinforcement learning technique, which require a substantial amount of computation time to even improve in simple learning tasks, several ideas have been investigated to speed up this learning process. The presented work has focussed on parallelism and decomposing a problem into a set of sub-problems, which could be solved in parallel.

Furthermore, the two-level learning approach is adopted to an XCS, which learns on-line about the real system and which covers new classifiers testing and evaluating their condition-action-mapping off-line by a simulation model. Although first experiments of this new architecture are promising, further investigations are needed to show the (complete) advances of level 2 in combination with level 1.

9.2 Conclusion

To conclude, interesting insights depending on the chicken scenario allow several implications. Summarising the main contributions of this thesis a number of questions is emphasized, this thesis has tried to answer.

- Are LCSs a viable approach to learn condition-action-mappings on-line on level 1 of the observer/controller architecture?

- Are parallel/distributed LCSs a viable approach to improve learning? In other words, do they outperform the sequential/monolithic XCS in terms of learning cycles required to solve a problem?

- How do design choices affect the learning speed up?

- Is the organic approach of combining on-line learning and off-line planning capabilities a viable approach?

- It is possible to generalise the results presented in this thesis?

9.2.1 LCSs as Part of the On-Line Learning Level

LCSs have been investigated in manifold domains. In [BLG02], the two most current versions of the LCS formalism (GALE [Llo02] and XCS [Wil95]) have been investigated on data mining tasks and have been compared to a number of other machine learning techniques. The results have shown that LCSs are extremely competitive and, in particular, XCS has demonstrated excellent performance, since XCS builds a *complete map* of the given problem surface. This corresponds to the characteristic that XCS has the ability to create maximally general rules that map the search space in the production system format using the most efficient rule set possible.

An XCS has been investigated to learn condition-action-mappings in a nature-inspired chicken scenario. Results have shown that a monolithic XCS implementation is able to find solutions that are equal to solutions, which have been found in parameter studies. The investigated scenario has also demonstrated that an LCS is a complex heuristic consisting of many parameters, which needs expensive parametrisation according to a scenario. Moreover, learning accurate classifiers is a (very) time consuming process and when the search space increases, this learning process increases accordingly. In addition, parameter combinations have been covered, which could not be solved in the investigated limit of simulation time.

Thus, the conclusion is drawn based on experimental results that LCSs do not seem applicable to OC systems in their original form, since OC systems should quickly adapt to dynamically changing environments. Furthermore, several modifications have been introduced and investigated to speed up the learning process.

9.2.2 Speeding up the Learning Process by Parallelism

The learning process is time consuming, a major drawback of applying LCSs to real world scenarios. As the complexity of the task – the dimension of the condition-action-mapping – increases, the demand of computational time to solve a problem becomes critical. Theoretically, every possible condition is mapped to each possible action. The mapping is applied to the environment. The utility of the mapping is tested, rewarded, and evaluated in the course of time. In other words, the number of learning cycles increases dramatically, when the learning task increases.

A single-agent learning approach has been proposed to design parallel LCSs, which is based on the higher level idea of decomposing a problem into several modules/sub-problems, which can be solved independently. Difficult learning tasks are tackled in a modular or hierarchical way and the performance is speeded up by decreasing the number of learning iterations.

Significant improvements in the performance and learning speed could specially be shown in the case of two implementations (3PXCS and HXCS). The third investigated architecture (2PXCS) started with a promising idea, but exhibited no convincing results in the investigated scenario.

However, the developer of a learning mechanism needs a lot of information about the learning task so that he can adequately divide it into separate solvable sub-problems. How to decompose a problem into sub-problems, is based on a plausible design decision. In some cases, parameters depend on each other and cannot separately be learned in different XCS instances.

Thus, applying the single-agent learning approach has led to the conclusion that it generally speeds up the learning process and an XCS converges in less reinforcement cycles. However, the single-agent learning approach is based on predefined design decisions, which also provide limitations, as discussed in Section 8.3.4.

9.2.3 Combining On-Line Learning and Off-Line Planning

Since speeding up the learning behaviour of LCSs has been in the focus of this thesis, another approach has been introduced, which is based on the two-level learning architecture as part of the generic controller.

Two discovery mechanisms coexist in an LCS to explore new classifiers. The genetic operators are inspired by evolution. Covering is the second mechanism, which is not inspired by evolution. This mechanism provides classifiers for every possible action, whose condition matches the detected situation and the action is chosen randomly. Newly covered classifiers are often badly initialised and many reinforcement learning cycles have to be taken to adapt these predefined default values. The inherent problem is that nothing is known about new classifiers. The original LCS randomly covers missing condition-action-mappings and evaluates this relationship by trial and error on the real problem.

Thus, the default covering operator has been extended and some kind of off-line planning capability has been added to the covering mechanism. Always, when covering occurs, new classifiers are evaluated by simulation on level 2. Then, new classifiers are initialised by this simulated experience instead of worse default initialisations.

Even if this approach seems (very) plausible from the viewpoint of designing and engineering OC systems, the performed experiments provide no convincing results. The tendency to converge is similar to the learning behaviour without learning on level 2. The parallel approach considerably outperforms the organic two-level learning approach – in the investigated chicken scenario. Possible explanations have been discussed in Section 8.4.

9.2.4 Generality of the Experimental Results

The chicken simulation has no obvious technical motivation by its own. However, it can be used to study general multi-agent systems bearing obvious similarities to technical systems. In the simulation, a chicken is directed by predefined rules, and will be influenced by the behaviour of other chickens in its local neighbourhood or by the environment, e. g., by noise that frightens it. Therefore, chickens can be considered as autonomous robots or agents with simple rules and local goals. There are many analogous technical scenarios with a similar structure such as cleaning robots, weeding robots, collaborating agent swarms, and others.

Moreover, it has been argued that the chicken simulation could be seen as an instance of the homogeneous and communicating predator/prey scenario. Results achieved within this scenario should be assignable to other instances of this category of predator/prey examples.

Furthermore, methods have been investigated to cope with unwanted (emergent) behaviour. A generic observer/controller framework has been refined to establish controlled self-organisation and to design OC systems. This generic architecture is applicable to other scenarios. Similarly, the ideas of speeding up learning are generic approaches, which do not depend on this single (chicken) scenario.

9.3 Outlook

According to the OC vision, an organic computer system should be aware of its own capabilities, the requirements of the environment, and it should be equipped with a number of so-called self-x-properties. These self-x-properties provide the anticipated adaptiveness and allow to reduce the complexity of system management. To name a few characteristics, organic systems can self-organise, self-adapt, self-configure, self-optimise, self-heal, self-protect, or self-explain. To achieve these ambitious goals of designing and controlling complex systems, adequate methods, techniques, and system architectures have to be developed, while no general approach exists to build complex systems.

Adaptation and learning capabilities play a major role in the context of OC systems. As outlined in this thesis, it is complicated to endow systems with appropriate learning capabilities and to customise well known machine learning techniques to show great performance in investigated scenarios. Moreover, the presented results propose cognisance that LCSs fit well to the observer/controller paradigm, although disadvantages in terms of learning time are obvious. Even if approaches are successfully applied to overcome these drawbacks, the question is still unanswered, whether LCSs are the best known technique for learning as stated in the context of OC systems. Further investigations on other learning techniques are needed that could be applied to the two-level learning approach, as partially investigated in [Pat08].

The power of learning is based on the expectation that technical systems behave in a more robust and flexible way in situations, which they have not been programmed for explicitly. In the case of the investigated chicken scenario this would mean that the observer/controller architecture always learns robust condition-action-mappings, even if the applied noise emitter has broken down, e.g., the controller thinks that a noise signal with $(d_j, i_j) = (7, 20)$ is applied, but in fact the emitter makes noise equal to $(d_j, i_j) = (2, 10)$. If the controller is able to overcome such disturbances, learning will provide robust and flexible system behaviour.

Furthermore, a short summary of other topics is given that provide great research questions for future work.

9.3.1 Outlook from the Viewpoint of the Investigated Scenario

The aspect of food is left out in the chicken scenario. Agents run over the two-dimensional grid, search for wounded chickens, get wounded by picking, are frightened by noise, and heal over time. To make the scenario or the agent's behaviour more complex, chickens could be extended with an ability of searching food. Moreover, the investigated chicken behaves according to predefined static rules. Applying some more degrees of freedom, a chicken could be equipped with its own LCS to learn its single behaviour, as outlined in [Lod09]. To make the scenario more complex and to enhance the task of the observer/controller architecture, the integration of distributed and collective (collaborative) learning seems to be interesting for future work. Agents with local adaptation will show a more complex – and thus challenging – system behaviour.

Furthermore, the chicken simulation could be endowed with other control possibilities. Currently, the controller only has the possibility to control the agents with noise. However, other control actions are possible, e.g., the controller can spread some food around the cluster to attract the chickens into another direction. Further control strategies have already been discussed in Section 6.2.4.

9.3.2 Outlook from the Viewpoint of the OC Community

An observer/controller architecture has been introduced to design OC systems. However, this architecture has not completely been investigated within the presented thesis, since learning has been in the focus. The impact of changing the model of observation or using prediction methods on the controlling behaviour has not been addressed.

Secondly, the two-level learning architecture uses a simulation model on level 2. This off-line planning instance allows to find appropriate actions without the need to test different alternatives in the real world. This is beneficial, since testing potentially bad strategies in the real world can cause the system's permanent failure. But, model-based planning, as provided on level 2, is always limited by the necessary simplifications made in the model or by incomplete model calibration due to the fact that the modelled environment changes dynamically/continuously. Thus, the best action with respect to the model is not necessarily the best action with respect to the real world. If the simulation model and the reality differ too much, the used simulation model will need modifications. The aspect of (autonomous) model calibration has currently been excluded from OC research and the generic observer/controller architecture, but asks for further investigations.

The centralised observer/controller framework has intensively been investigated in the context of the nature-inspired chicken scenario. This chicken scenario could be seen as an instance of the homogeneous and communicating predator/prey example. However, multi-agent scenarios could be divided into several categories ranging from homogeneous and non-communicating up to heterogeneous and communicating scenarios with collaborative and competitve goals on the agent's level. Furthermore, several variants of the generic observer/controller architecture have been discussed in Section 4.4. To achieve deeper and more generic results about this regulatory feedback mechanism, further investigations are needed, which apply the manifold variants of the observer/controller architecture to different multi-agent scenarios. Investigations could start with a scenario of homogeneous and non-communicating agents, then tackling the full range of possible multi-agent systems, up to highly heterogeneous and communicating agents.

9.3.3 Outlook from the Viewpoint of the LCSs Community

LCSs are widespread in research and have not only been investigated in the OC community. In this thesis, the aspect of speeding up the learning process of LCSs has especially been investigated, when learning starts from scratch. OC proposes the idea of two-level learning as a more intelligent covering mechanism. The presented work has also focussed on parallelism and problem decomposition to achieve better learning performance. Moreover, a LCS is a complex learning heuristic, which requires intelligent customising to the investigated scenarios. Further work could also focus on intelligent covering mechanisms or better genetic operators to make evolution a more powerful mechanism, which speeds up the learning process accordingly.

Since OC systems are composed of many components, which interact with each other, a multi-agent learning approach has theoretically been discussed in Section 5.5.2. But, this idea has not practically been investigated within the presented results. The idea of multi-agent learning arises further challenges, since the Markov property is not fulfilled. To overcome this problem step by step, more research is needed on problems that do not fulfil the Markov property. Then, it might be shown that LCSs have the following potential: Generality to show a good performance on more real world problems, scalability to maintain the same level of performance in large-scale problems, and high performance, which corresponds to better results than could be achieved with single-agent learning approaches.

9.4 Final Remarks

Within the limits of this thesis several questions could be answered and many new ones have arisen worthwhile to be addressed by further research. The bottom line has been a successful application of the observer/controller architecture within the nature-inspired predator/prey scenario. Controlled self-organisation using LCSs has shown to be a promising concept although limited by the basic implementation of the current scenario.

It is believed that the observer/controller framework will be applied to technical scenarios more and more frequently in the near future. Hopefully, the contributions of this thesis will prove useful in addressing the problems that arise in these domains. Ultimately, the understanding is improved of what it is needed to design and build complete, organic systems.

References

[ACE+03] R. Allrutz, C. Cap, S. Eilers, D. Fey, H. Haase, C. Hochberger, W. Karl, B. Kolpatzik, J. Krebs, F. Langhammer, P. Lukowicz, E. Maehle, J. Maas, C. Müller-Schloer, R. Riedl, B. Schallenberger, V. Schanz, H. Schmeck, D. Schmid, W. Schröder-Preikschat, T. Ungerer, H.-O. Veiser, and L. Wolf. VDE/ITG/GI–Positionspapier Organic Computing: Computer- und Systemarchitektur im Jahr 2010, 2003.

[ACE06] ACE Auto Club Europa. Schwache Batterie Pannenursache Nummer 1. `http://www.ace-online.de/cps/rde/xchg/ace_internet_new/hs.xsl/21_1640_DEU_xHTML.htm`, April 2006.

[Ant07] C. Antoniou. *On-line calibration for dynamic traffic assignment models: Theory, methods, and application.* Vdm Verlag Dr. Müller, 2007.

[Art94] W. Arthur. Complexity in economic theory: Inductive reasoning and bounded rationality. *The American Economic Review*, 84(2):406–411, May 1994.

[AS93] L. R. Al-Sharif. Bunching in lift systems. In *Proceedings of the International Conference on Elevator Technology (ELEVCON 1993)*, November 1993.

[AS96] L. R. Al-Sharif. Bunching in lifts...: Why does bunching in lifts increase waiting time? *Elevator World*, 11:75–77, 1996.

[ASB92a] L. R. Al-Sharif and G. C. Barney. Bunching factors in lift systems (1). Control Systems Centre Report 749, University of Manchester Institute of Science and Technology (UMIST), Manchester, United Kingdom, February 1992.

[ASB92b] L. R. Al-Sharif and G. C. Barney. Bunching factors in lift systems (2). Control Systems Centre Report 754, University of Manchester Institute of Science and Technology (UMIST), Manchester, United Kingdom, June 1992.

[Ash47]   W. R. Ashby. Principles of the self-organising dynamic system. *Journal of General Psychology*, 37:125–128, 1947.

[Ash62]   W. R. Ashby. Principles of the self-organising system. In H. von Foerster and G. W. Zopf, Jr., editors, *Principles of Self-Organisation: Transactions of the University of Illinois Symposium*, pages 255–278. Pergamon Press, 1962.

[ÅW08]   K. J. Åström and B. Wittenmark. *Adaptive control.* Dover Publications Incorporation, 2nd edition, 2008.

[BA84]   H. J. Blokhuis and J. G. Arkes. Some observations on the development of feather-pecking in poultry. *Applied Animal Behaviour Science*, 12(1–2):145–157, March 1984.

[Bar96]   A. Barry. Hierarchy formation within classifier systems: A review. In *Proceedings of the 1st International Conference on Evolutionary Algorithms an their Applications (EVCA 1996)*, pages 195–211, 1996.

[Bar03]   G. C. Barney. *Elevator traffic handbook: Theory and practice.* Spon Press, 2003.

[BB05]   T. Bartz-Beielstein. *New experimentalism applied to evolutionary computation.* PhD thesis, Universität Dortmund, Fachbereich Informatik, Dortmund, Germany, 2005.

[BCD+06]   O. Babaoglu, G. Canright, A. Deutsch, G. A. Di Caro, F. Ducatelle, L. M. Gambardella, N. Ganguly, M. Jelasity, R. Montemanni, A. Montresor, and T. Urnes. Design patterns from biology for distributed computing. *ACM Transactions on Autonomous and Adaptive Systems (TAAS)*, 1(1):26–66, September 2006.

[BDHZ06]   S. A. Brueckner, G. Di Marzo Serugendo, D. Hales, and F. Zambonelli, editors. *Engineering self-organising systems*, volume 3910 of *LNAI*. Springer, 2006.

[BDKN05]   S. A. Brueckner, G. Di Marzo Serugendo, A. Karageorgos, and R. Nagpal, editors. *Engineering self-organising systems: Methodologies and applications*, volume 3464 of *LNAI*. Springer, 2005.

[BDT99]   E. Bonabeau, M. Dorigo, and G. Theraulaz. *Swarm intelligence: From natural to artificial systems.* Oxford University Press, 1999.

192

[Bea03] P. Beart. Emergent behaviour. `http://www.beart.org.uk/emergent`, 2003.

[Bee66] S. Beer. *Decision and control: The meaning of operational research and management cybernetics.* John Wiley & Sons, 1966.

[Bee72] S. Beer. *Brain of the firm.* Allen Lane, 1972.

[Bel57] R. E. Bellman. A Markovian decision process. *Journal of Mathematics and Mechanics*, 6:679–684, 1957.

[Ber06] P. Berkhin. A survey of clustering data mining techniques. In J. Kogan, C. Nicholas, and M. Teboulle, editors, *Grouping multi-dimensional data: Recent advanes in clustering*, pages 25–71. Springer, 2006.

[BFR08] A. Bernauer, D. Fritz, and W. Rosenstiel. Evaluation of the learning classifier system XCS for system on chip runtime control. In H.-G. Hegering, A. Lehmann, H. J. Ohlbach, and C. Scheideler, editors, *INFORMATIK 2008, Beherrschbare Systeme – dank Informatik*, volume 134 of *LNI*, pages 763–770. GI, 2008.

[BFS95] L. Bull, T. C. Fogarty, and M. Snaith. Evolution in multi-agent systems: Evolving communicating classifier systems for gait in a quadrupedal robot. In L. J. Eshelman, editor, *Proceedings of the 6th International Conference on Genetic Algorithms and Their Applications (GECCO 1995)*, pages 382–388. Morgan Kaufmann, 1995.

[BGL05] M. V. Butz, D. E. Goldberg, and P. L. Lanzi. Gradient descent methods in learning classifier systems: Improving XCS performance in multi-step problems. *IEEE Transactions on Evolutionary Computation*, 9(5):452–473, October 2005.

[BGM+08] S. Burmester, H. Giese, E. Münch, O. Oberschelp, F. Klein, and P. Scheideler. Tool support for the design of self-optimising mechatronic multi-agent systems. *International Journal on Software Tools for Technology Transfer*, 10(3):207–222, June 2008.

[BHJY07] S. A. Brueckner, S. Hassas, M. Jelasity, and D. Yamins, editors. *Engineering self-organising systems*, volume 4335 of *LNAI*. Springer, 2007.

[BJD86] M. Benda, V. Jagannathan, and R. Dodhiawala. An optimal cooperation of knowledge sources: An empirical investigation. Technical Report BCS-G2010-28, Boeing Advanced Technology Center, Boeing Computing Services, Seattle, United States of America, July 1986.

[BKLW04] M. V. Butz, T. Kovacs, P. L. Lanzi, and S. W. Wilson. Toward a theory of generalisation and learning in XCS. *IEEE Transactions on Evolutionary Computation*, 8(1):28–46, February 2004.

[BLG02] E. Bernadó, X. Llorà, and J. M. Garrell. XCS and GALE: A comparative study of two learning classifier systems on data mining. In P. L. Lanzi, W. Stolzmann, and S. W. Wilson, editors, *Proceedings of the 4th International Workshop on Learning Classifier Systems (IWLCS 2001)*, volume 2321 of *LNAI*, pages 115–132. Springer, 2002.

[BMMS+06] J. Branke, M. Mnif, C. Müller-Schloer, H. Prothmann, U. Richter, F. Rochner, and H. Schmeck. Organic computing: Addressing complexity by controlled self-organisation. In T. Margaria, A. Philippou, and B. Steffen, editors, *Post-Conference Proceedings of the 2nd International Symposium on Leveraging Applications of Formal Methods, Verification, and Validation (ISoLA 2006)*, IEEE-ISoLA, pages 185–191. IEEE, November 2006.

[BN06] T. Benouhiba and J.-M. Nigro. An evidential cooperative multi-agent system. *Expert Systems with Applications*, 30(2):255–264, February 2006.

[Bon98] A. Bonarini. Reinforcement distribution for fuzzy classifiers: A methodology to extend crisp algorithms. In *Proceedings of the 1998 IEEE International Conference on Evolutionary Computation (CEC 1998)*, pages 699–704. IEEE, 1998.

[Bon00] A. Bonarini. An introduction to learning fuzzy classifier systems. In P. L. Lanzi, W. Stolzmann, and S. W. Wilson, editors, *Learning classifier systems: From foundations to applications*, volume 1813 of *LNAI*, pages 83–104. Springer, 2000.

[Bon08] M. Bonn. *JoSchKa: Jobverteilung in heterogenen und unzuverlässigen Umgebungen*. PhD thesis, Institut für Angewandte Informatik und Formale Beschreibungsverfahren, Universität Karlsruhe (TH), Karlsruhe, Germany, 2008.

[Bro86] R. A. Brooks. A robust layered control system for a mobile robot. *IEEE Journal of Robotics and Automation*, 2(1):14–23, March 1986.

[Bro91] W. L. Brogan. *Modern control theory*. Prentice Hall, 3rd edition, 1991.

[BSBW05] L. Bull, M. Studley, A. Bagnall, and I. Whittley. On the use of rule-sharing in learning classifier system ensembles. In *Proceedings of the 2005 IEEE Congress on Evolutionary Computation (CEC 2005)*, volume 1, pages 612–617, September 2005.

[BSBW07] L. Bull, M. Studley, A. Bagnall, and I. Whittley. Learning classifier system ensembles with rule-sharing. *IEEE Transactions on Evolutionary Computation*, 11(4):496–502, August 2007.

[BSH+07] J. Bacardit, M. Stout, J. D. Hirst, K. Sastry, X. Llorà, and N. Krasnogor. Automated alphabet reduction method with evolutionary algorithms for protein structure prediction. In D. Thierens, H.-G. Beyer, M. Birattari, J. Bongard, J. Branke, J. A. Clark, D. Cliff, C. B. Congdon, K. Deb, B. Doerr, T. Kovacs, S. Kumar, J. F. Miller, J. Moore, F. Neumann, M. Pelikan, R. Poli, K. Sastry, K. O. Stanley, T. Stützle, R. A. Watson, and I. Wegener, editors, *Proceedings of the 9th Annual Conference on Genetic and Evolutionary Computation (GECCO 2007)*, pages 346–353. ACM, 2007.

[BST07] S. M. Baneamoon, R. A. Salam, and A. Z. H. Talib. Learning process enhancement for robot behaviours. *International Journal of Intelligent Technology*, 2(3):172–177, 2007.

[Bul05] L. Bull. Two simple learning classifier systems. In L. Bull and T. Kovacs, editors, *Foundations of Learning Classifier Systems*, volume 183 of *Studies in Fuzziness and Soft Computing*, pages 63–89. Springer, 2005.

[But00] M. V. Butz. XCSJava 1.0: An implementation of the XCS classifier system in Java. Technical Report 2000027, Illinois Genetic Algorithms Laboratory, Urbana, United States of America, 2000.

[But06] M. V. Butz. *Rule-based evolutionary online learning systems: A principled approach to LCS analysis and design*. Studies in Fuzziness and Soft Computing. Springer, 2006.

[BW00] M. V. Butz and S. W. Wilson. An algorithmic description of XCS. In P. L. Lanzi, W. Stolzmann, and S. W. Wilson, editors, *Proceedings of the International Workshop on Learning Classifier Systems (IWLCS 2000)*, volume 1996 of *LNAI*, pages 253–272, 2000.

[BW02] M. V. Butz and S. W. Wilson. An algorithmic description of XCS. *Soft Computing*, 6(3–4):144–153, June 2002.

[BZ91] C. Brezinski and M. R. Zaglia. *Extrapolation methods: Theory and practice*. North-Holland Publishing Co, 1991.

[BZ05]   A. J. Bagnall and Z. V. Zatuchna. On the classification of Maze problems. In L. Bull and T. Kovacs, editors, *Foundations of Learning Classifier Systems*, volume 183 of *Studies in Fuzziness and Soft Computing*, pages 305–316. Springer, 2005.

[BZL06]   J. Bongard, V. Zykov, and H. Lipson. Resilient machines through continuous self-modelling. *Science*, 314(5802):1118–1121, November 2006.

[BZS+06]   A. Bouajila, J. Zeppenfeld, W. Stechele, A. Herkersdorf, A. Bernauer, O. Bringmann, and W. Rosenstiel. Organic computing at the system on chip level. In *2006 IFIP International Conference on Very Large Scale Integration*, pages 338–341, October 2006.

[CB98]   R. H. Crites and A. G. Barto. Elevator group control using multiple reinforcement learning agents. *Machine Learning*, 33:235–262, 1998.

[CB04]   E. F. Camacho and C. Bordons. *Model predictive control*. Springer, 2004.

[CDF+03]   S. Camazine, J.-L. Deneubourg, N. R. Franks, J. Sneyd, G. Theraulaz, and E. Bonabeau. *Self-organisation in biological systems*. Princeton Studies in Complexity. Princeton University Press, 2003.

[CFM96]   B. Carse, T. C. Fogarty, and A. Munro. Evolving fuzzy rule-based controllers using genetic algorithms. *Fuzzy Sets and Systems*, 80(3):273–293, June 1996.

[CGJ96]   D. A. Cohn, Z. Ghahramani, and M. I. Jordan. Active learning with statistical models. *Journal of Artificial Intelligence Research*, 4:129–145, 1996.

[CGL08]   V. Crespi, A. Galstyan, and K. Lerman. Top-down vs. bottom-up methodologies in multi-agent system design. *Autonomous Robots*, 24(3):303–313, April 2008.

[CHMR87]   J. P. Cohoon, S. U. Hegde, W. N. Martin, and D. S. Richards. Punctuated equilibria: A parallel genetic algorithm. In J. J. Grefenstette, editor, *Proceedings of the 2nd International Conference on Genetic Algorithms and their Application*, pages 148–154. L. Erlbaum Associates Incorporation, 1987.

[ÇHMS08a] E. Çakar, J. Hähner, and C. Müller-Schloer. Creating collaboration patterns in multi-agent systems with generic observer/controller architectures. In *Proceedings of the 2nd International ACM Conference on Autonomic Computing and Communication Systems (Autonomics 2008)*. ICST (Institute for Computer Sciences, Social-Informatics, and Telecommunications Engineering), 2008.

[ÇHMS08b] E. Çakar, J. Hähner, and C. Müller-Schloer. Investigation of generic observer/controller architectures in a traffic scenario. In H.-G. Hegering, A. Lehmann, H. J. Ohlbach, and C. Scheideler, editors, *INFORMATIK 2008, Beherrschbare Systeme – dank Informatik*, volume 134 of *LNI*, pages 733–738. GI, 2008.

[ÇMMS+07] E. Çakar, M. Mnif, C. Müller-Schloer, U. Richter, and H. Schmeck. Towards a quantitative notion of self-organisation. In *Proceedings of the 2007 IEEE Congress on Evolutionary Computation (CEC 2007)*, pages 4222–4229. IEEE, 2007.

[CNSW00] D. S. Callaway, M. E. J. Newman, S. H. Strogatz, and D. J. Watts. Network robustness and fragility: Percolation on random graphs. *Physical Review Letters*, 85(25):5468–5471, 2000.

[CP00] E. Cantú-Paz. *Efficient and accurate parallel genetic algorithms*. Kluwer Academic Publishers, 2000.

[Cri02] M. Crichton. *Prey*. HarperCollins Publishers Incorporation, 1st edition, 2002.

[DAL05a] H. H. Dam, H. A. Abbass, and C. Lokan. Be real! XCS with continuous-valued inputs. In F. Rothlauf, M. Blowers, J. Branke, S. Cagnoni, I. I. Garibay, O. Garibay, J. Grahl, G. Hornby, E. D. de Jong, T. Kovacs, S. Kumar, C. F. Lima, X. Llorà, F. Lobo, L. D. Merkle, J. Miller, J. H. Moore, M. O'Neill, M. Pelikan, T. P. Riopka, M. D. Ritchie, K. Sastry, S. L. Smith, H. Stringer, K. Takadama, M. Toussaint, S. C. Upton, and A. H. Wright., editors, *Proceedings of the Genetic and Evolutionary Computation Conference (GECCO 2005)*, pages 85–87. ACM, 2005.

[DAL05b] H. H. Dam, H. A. Abbass, and C. Lokan. DXCS: An XCS system for distributed data mining. In H.-G. Beyer, U.-M. O'Reilly, D. V. Arnold, W. Banzhaf, C. Blum, E. W. Bonabeau, E. Cantu-Paz, D. Dasgupta, K. Deb, J. A. Foster, E. D. de Jong, H. Lipson, X. Llorà, S. Mancoridis, M. Pelikan, G. R. Raidl, T. Soule, A. M. Tyrrell, J.-P. Watson, and E. Zitzler, editors, *Proceedings of the Genetic and Evolutionary Computation Conference (GECCO 2005)*, pages 1883–1890. ACM, 2005.

[DB94] M. Dorigo and H. Bersini. A comparison of Q-learning and classifier systems. In *Proceedings of the 3rd International Conference on Simu-*

lation of Adaptive Behaviour: From Animals to Animats (SAB 1994), pages 248–255. MIT Press, 1994.

[DBS+02] M. Diehl, H. G. Bock, J. P. Schlöder, R. Findeisen, Z. Nagy, and F. Allgöwer. Real-time optimisation and nonlinear model predictive control of processes governed by differential-algebraic equations. *Journal of Process Control*, 12(4):577–585, June 2002.

[de 88] K. A. de Jong. Learning with genetic algorithms: An overview. *Machine Learning*, 3(2–3):121–138, October 1988.

[de 99] B. de Boer. *Self-organisation in vowel systems*. PhD thesis, Faculteit Wetenschappen, Laboratorium voor Artificiële Intelligentie, Vrije Universiteit Brussel, Brussels, Belgium, 1999.

[Dec87] K. S. Decker. Distributed problem solving: A survey. *IEEE Transactions on Systems, Man, and Cybernetics*, 17(5):729–740, 1987.

[DF98] V. Decugis and J. Ferber. Action selection in an autonomous agent with a hierarchical distributed reactive planning architecture. In K. P. Sycara and M. Wooldridge, editors, *Proceedings of the 2nd International Conference on Autonomous Agents (AGENTS 1998)*, pages 354–361. ACM, 1998.

[DFH+04] G. Di Marzo Serugendo, N. Foukia, S. Hassas, A. Karageorgos, S. Kouadri Mostéfaoui, O. F. Rana, M. Ulieru, P. Valckenaers, and C. Van Aart. Self-organisation: Paradigms and applications. In G. Di Marzo Serugendo, A. Karageorgos, O. F. Rana, and F. Zambonelli, editors, *Engineering self-organising systems*, volume 2977 of *LNAI*, pages 1–19. Springer, 2004.

[DGK04] G. Di Marzo Serugendo, M.-P. Gleizes, and A. Karageorgos. Agentlink first technical forum group self-organisation in multi-agent systems. http://www.agentlink.org/newsletter/16/AL-16h.pdf, December 2004.

[DGK06] G. Di Marzo Serugendo, M.-P. Gleizes, and A. Karageorgos. Self-organisation and emergence in multi-agent systems: An overview. *Informatica*, 30(1):45–54, 2006.

[DKRZ04] G. Di Marzo Serugendo, A. Karageorgos, O. F. Rana, and F. Zambonelli, editors. *Engineering self-organising systems: Nature-inspired approaches to software engineering*, volume 2977 of *LNAI*. Springer, 2004.

[DM93] R. Davidson and J. G. MacKinnon. *Estimation and inference in econometrics.* Oxford University Press, 1993.

[Dor95] M. Dorigo. ALECSYS and the AutonoMouse: Learning to control a real robot by distributed classifier systems. *Machine Learning*, 19(3):209–240, June 1995.

[DP04] R. Dittmar and B.-M. Pfeiffer. *Modellbasierte prädiktive Regelung: Eine Einführung für Ingenieure.* Oldenbourg, 2004.

[DS93] M. Dorigo and U. Schnepf. Genetics-based machine learning and behaviour-based robotics: A new synthesis. *IEEE Transactions on Systems, Man, and Cybernetics*, 23(1):141–154, 1993.

[DS98] N. R. Draper and H. Smith. *Applied regression analysis.* John Wiley & Sons, 1998.

[DS04] M. Dorigo and T. Stützle. *Ant colony optimisation.* MIT Press, 2004.

[Ed08] W. Elmenreich and H. de Meer. Self-organising networked systems for technical applications: A discussion on open issues. In K. A. Hummel and J. P. G. Sterbenz, editors, *Proceedings of the 3rd International Workshop on Self-Organising Systems (IWSOS 2008)*, volume 5343 of *LNCS*, pages 1–9. Springer, December 2008.

[EE99] G. Énée and C. Escazut. Classifier systems: Evolving multi-agent system with distributed elitism. In *Proceedings of the 1999 Congress on Evolutionary Computation (CEC 1999)*, volume 3, pages 1740–1746. IEEE, 1999.

[Ele07] G. Elert. The chaos hypertextbook: Mathematics in the age of the computer. http://hypertextbook.com/chaos, 2007.

[ELM08] A. El Sayed Auf, M. Litza, and E. Maehle. Distributed fault-tolerant robot control architecture based on organic computing principles. In *Biologically-Inspired Collaborative Computing*, volume 268 of *IFIP International Federation for Information Processing*, pages 115–124. Springer, 2008.

[Eng02] A. P. Engelbrecht. *Computational intelligence: An introduction.* John Wiley & Sons, 2002.

[EP08] G. Énée and M. Peroumalnaïk. Adapted Pittsburgh classifier system: Building accurate strategies in non-Markovian environments. In M. Keijzer, G. Antoniol, C. B. Congdon, K. Deb, B. Doerr, N. Hansen, J. H.

Holmes, G. S. Hornby, D. Howard, J. Kennedy, S. Kumar, J. F. Miller, J. Moore, F. Neumann, M. Pelikan, J. Pollack, K. Sastry, K. Stanley, A. Stoica, E.-G. Talbi, and I. Wegener, editors, *Proceedings of the Conference Companion on Genetic and Evolutionary Computation (GECCO 2008)*, pages 2001–2008. ACM, 2008.

[FB95]   T. C. Fogarty and L. Bull. Optimising individual control rules and multiple communicating rule-based control systems with parallel distributed genetic algorithms. *IEE Proceedings of Control Theory and Applications*, 142(3):211–215, May 1995.

[FCG06]   B. Feltz, M. Crommelinck, and P. Goujon, editors. *Self-organisation and emergence in life sciences*, volume 331 of *Synthese Library*. Springer, 2006.

[Fer92]   I. A. Ferguson. Touringmachines: Autonomous agents with attitudes. *IEEE Computer*, 25(5):51–55, 1992.

[Fif79]   P. C. Fife. *Mathematical aspects of reacting and diffusing systems*, volume 28 of *LNB*. Springer, 1979.

[Fir89]   R. J. Firby. *Adaptive execution in complex dynamic worlds*. PhD thesis, Yale University, New Haven, United States of America, 1989.

[Fly72]   M. J. Flynn. Some computer organisations and their effectiveness. *IEEE Transactions on Computers*, 21(9):948–960, September 1972.

[FOW66]   L. J. Fogel, A. J. Owens, and M. J. Walsh. *Artificial intelligence through simulated evolution*. John Wiley & Sons, 1966.

[FPS00]   G. Folino, C. Pizzuti, and G. Spezzano. Genetic programming and simulated annealing: A hybrid method to evolve decision trees. In R. Poli, W. Banzhaf, W. B. Langdon, J. F. Miller, P. Nordin, and T. C. Fogarty, editors, *Proceedings of the 3dr European Conference on Genetic Programming (EuroGP 2000)*, volume 1802 of *LNCS*, pages 294–303. Springer, 2000.

[Fre83]   J. M. Freeman. *Relevance trees by empirical method*. UMIST, Department of Management Sciences, 1983.

[Fri09]   A. Fritz. Using XCS for self-organising cleaning robots. Bachelor's thesis, Institute of Applied Informatics and Formal Description Methods, Universität Karlsruhe (TH), 2009.

[Fro04]   J. Fromm. *The emergence of complexity*. Kassel University Press, 2004.

[Fro05]   J. Fromm. Ten questions about emergence. `http://arxiv.org/abs/nlin/0509049v1`, September 2005.

[Ful87]   W. A. Fuller. *Measurement error models*. John Wiley & Sons, 1987.

[Gat98]   E. Gat. On three-layer architectures. In D. Kortenkamp, R. P. Bonnasso, and R. Murphy, editors, *Artificial Intelligence and Mobile Robots*, pages 195–210. AAAI Press, 1998.

[Ger07]   C. Gershenson. *Design and control of self-organising systems*. PhD thesis, Faculteit Wetenschappen, Center Leo Apostel for Interdisciplinary Studies, Vrije Universiteit Brussel, Brussels, Belgium, March 2007.

[GH06]   P. I. Good and J. W. Hardin. *Common errors in statistics (and how to avoid them)*. Wiley & Sons, 2006.

[Gia97]   A. Giani. Parallel cooperative classifier systems: A proposal for a unifying framework, January 1997.

[GMM+06]   H. Giese, N. Montealegre, T. Müller, S. Oberthür, and B. Schulz. Acute stress response for self-optimising mechatronic systems. In Y. Pan, F. J. Rammig, H. Schmeck, and M. Solar, editors, *Proceedings of the 1st IFIP Conference on Biologically Inspired Cooperative Computing (BICC 2006)*, volume 216 of *IFIP International Federation for Information Processing*, pages 157–167. Springer, August 2006.

[Gol89]   D. E. Goldberg. *Genetic algorithms in search, optimisation, and machine learning*. Addison-Wesley Longman, 1989.

[GP71]   P. Glansdorff and I. Prigogine. *Thermodynamic study of structure, stability, and fluctuations*. John Wiley & Sons, 1971.

[GPM89]   C. E. Garciaa, D. M. Prett, and M. Morari. Model predictive control: Theory and practice – A survey. *Automatica*, 25(3):335–348, May 1989.

[GR92]   J. J. Grefenstette and C. L. Ramsey. An approach to anytime learning. In *Proceedings of the 9th International Workshop on Machine Learning*, pages 189–195. Morgan Kaufmann, 1992.

[Gra59]   P.-P. Grassé. La reconstruction du nid et les interactions interindividuelles chez les bellicositermes natalenis et cubitermes sp. la théorie de la stigmergie: Essai d'interprétation des termites constructeurs. *Insectes Sociaux*, 6:41–83, 1959.

[Gra91]   C. Granger. *Modelling economic series: Readings in econometric methodology*. Oxford University Press, 1991.

[GS02]   D. Garlan and B. Schmerl. Model-based adaptation for self-healing systems. In *Proceedings of the 1st Workshop on Self-healing Systems (WOSS 2002)*, pages 27–32. ACM, 2002.

[GS07]   M. Gershoff and S. Schulenburg. Collective behaviour based hierarchical XCS. In *Proceedings of the 2007 Genetic And Evolutionary Computation Conference (GECCO 2007)*, pages 2695–2700. ACM, July 2007.

[Gui08]   E. Guizzo. Three engineers, hundreds of robots, one warehouse. http://spectrum.ieee.org/jul08/6380, July 2008.

[GWTS05] A. Gloye, F. Wiesel, O. Tenchio, and M. Simon. Reinforcing the driving quality of soccer playing robots by anticipation. *it – Information Technology*, 47(5):250–257, 2005.

[Hak81]   H. Haken. Synergetics and the problem of self-organisation. In G. Roth and H. Schwegler, editors, *Self-Organising Systems: An Interdisciplinary Approach*, pages 9–13. Campus Verlag, 1981.

[HBC+00] J. H. Holland, L. B. Booker, M. Colombetti, M. Dorigo, D. E. Goldberg, S. Forrest, R. L. Riolo, R. E. Smith, P. L. Lanzi, W. Stolzmann, and S. W. Wilson. What is a learning classifier system? In P. L. Lanzi, W. Stolzmann, and S. W. Wilson, editors, *Learning classifier systems: From foundations to applications*, volume 1813 of *LNAI*, pages 3–32. Springer, 2000.

[HBN01]   T. Hestermeyer, M. Becker, and N. Neuendorf. Nichtlineare ABC-Regelungen mit Operator-Controller-Struktur, abgestimmt auf Führung und Störung der Straße. Technical report, Haus der Technik, Driveability, Essen, Germany, 2001.

[HF02a]   L. M. Hercog and T. C. Fogarty. Co-evolutionary classifier systems for multi-agent simulation. In *Proceedings of the 2002 Congress on Evolutionary Computation (CEC 2002)*, volume 2, pages 1798–1803. IEEE, 2002.

[HF02b]   L. M. Hercog and T. C. Fogarty. Social simulation using a multi-agent model based on classifier systems: The emergence of vacillating behaviour in "el farol" bar problem. In P. L. Lanzi, W. Stolzmann, and S. W. Wilson, editors, *Proceedings of the 4th International Workshop on Learning Classifier Systems (IWLCS 2001)*, volume 2321 of *LNAI*, pages 88–111. Springer, 2002.

[HG03]   F. Heylighen and C. Gershenson. The meaning of self-organisation in computing. *IEEE Intelligent Systems*, 18(4):72–75, July/August 2003.

[Hil85] W. Hillis. *The connection machine.* Series in Artificial Intelligence. MIT Press, 1985.

[HMT83] D. C. Hoaglin, F. Mosteller, and J. W. Tukey. *Understanding robust and exploratory data analysis.* John Wiley & Sons, 1983.

[HO03] T. Hestermeyer and O. Oberschelp. Selbstoptimierende Fahrzeugregelung – Verhaltensbasierte Adaption. In *Proceedings of the 1st Paderborner Workshop on Intelligent Mechatronic Systems.* HNI, 2003.

[HOG04] T. Hestermeyer, O. Oberschelp, and H. Giese. Structured information processing for self-optimising mechatronic systems. In H. Araújo, A. Vieira, J. Braz, B. Encarnação, and M. Carvalho, editors, *Proceedings of the 1st International Conference on Informatics in Control, Automation, and Robotics (ICINCO 2004)*, pages 230–237. IEEE, August 2004.

[Hol75] J. H. Holland. *Adaptation in natural and artificial systems.* University of Michigan Press, 1975.

[Hol76] J. H. Holland. Adaptation. In R. Rosen and F. M. Snell, editors, *Progress in Theoretical Biology*, volume 4, pages 263–293. Academic Press, 1976.

[Hol86] J. H. Holland. Escaping brittleness: The possibilities of general-purpose learning algorithms applied to parallel rule-based systems. In R. S. Michalski, J. G. Carbonell, and T. M. Mitchell, editors, *Machine learning: An artificial intelligence approach*, volume 2, pages 593–623. Morgan Kaufmann, 1986.

[Hol98] J. H. Holland. *Emergence from chaos to order.* Oxford University Press, 1998.

[How60] R. A. Howard. *Dynamic programming and Markov processes.* MIT Press, 1960.

[HP91] R. Hartley and F. Pipitone. Experiments with the subsumption architecture. In *Proceedings of the 1991 IEEE International Conference on Robotics and Automatian*, pages 1652–1658. IEEE, 1991.

[HR78] J. H. Holland and J. S. Reitman. Cognitive systems based on adaptive algorithms. In D. A. Waterman and F. Hayes-Roth, editors, *Pattern-Directed Inference Systems*, pages 313–329. Academic Press, 1978.

[HR05] H. Henri and L. Risto. Calculation of elevator round-trip time for the collective control algorithm in general traffic situations. TUCS

Technical Report 671, Turku Centre for Computer Science, Turku, Finland, March 2005.

[HTP+05] P. J. Hoen, K. Tuyls, L. Panait, S. Luke, and J. A. L. Poutré. An overview of cooperative and competitive multi-agent learning. In *Proceedings of the 1st International Workshop on Learning and Adaption in Multi-Agent Systems (LAMAS 2005)*, volume 3898 of *LNAI*, pages 1–46. Springer, 2005.

[HTTS02] J. He, A.-H. Tan, C.-L. Tan, and S.-Y. Sung. On quantitative evaluation of clustering systems. In W. Wu and H. Xiong, editors, *Information Retrieval and Clustering*. Kluwer Academic Publishers, 2002.

[HU97] T. Hikihara and S. Ueshima. Emergent synchronisation in multi-elevator system and dispatching-control. *IEICE Transactions on Fundamentals of Electronics, Communications, and Computer Sciences*, 80(9):1548–1553, September 1997.

[IBM06] IBM Corporation. An architectural blueprint for autonomic computing. http://www-01.ibm.com/software/tivoli/autonomic/pdfs/AC_Blueprint_White_Paper_4th.pdf, June 2006.

[IK98] T. Ibaraki and N. Katoh. *Resource allocation problems: Algorithmic approaches*. MIT Press, 1998.

[ITS05] H. Inoue, K. Takadama, and K. Shimohara. Exploring XCS in multi-agent environments. In *Proceedings of the 2005 Workshops on Genetic and Evolutionary Computation Conference (GECCO 2005)*, pages 109–111. ACM, 2005.

[Jal94] P. Jalote. *Fault tolerance in distributed systems*. Prentice Hall, 1994.

[Jet89] G. Jetschke. *Mathematik der Selbstorganisation – Qualitative Theorie nichtlinearer dynamischer Systeme und gleichgewichtsferner Strukturen in Physik, Chemie und Biologie*. Deutscher Verlag der Wissenschaften, 1989.

[JMF99] A. Jain, M. Murty, and P. Flynn. Data clustering: A review. *ACM Computing Surveys*, 31(3):264–323, 1999.

[Joh01] S. Johnson. *Emergence: The connected lives of ants, brains, cities, and software*. Scribner Book Company, 2001.

[Jol02] I. T. Jolliffe. *Principal component analysis*. SSS. Springer, 2nd edition, 2002.

[JPF06] A. B. Jensen, R. Palme, and B. Forkman. Effect of brooders on feather pecking and cannibalism in domestic fowl (Gallus gallus domesticus). *Applied Animal Behaviour Science*, 99(3–4):287–300, September 2006.

[Kál60] R. E. Kálmán. A new approach to linear filtering and prediction problems. *Journal of Basic Engineering*, 82(1):35–45, 1960.

[Kau93] S. Kauffman. *The origins of order: Self-organisation and selection in evolution.* Oxford University Press, 1993.

[KC03] J. O. Kephart and D. M. Chess. The vision of autonomic computing. *IEEE Computer*, 36(1):41–50, January 2003.

[KL00] T. Kovacs and P. L. Lanzi. A bigger learning classifier systems bibliography. In P. L. Lanzi, W. Stolzmann, and S. W. Wilson, editors, *Proceedings of the International Workshop on Learning Classifier Systems (IWLCS 2000)*, volume 1996 of *LNAI*, pages 213–249. Springer, 2000.

[KLST06] D. H. Krantz, R. D. Luce, P. Suppes, and A. Tversky. *Foundations of measurement: Additive and polynomial representations*, volume 1. Dover Pubn Incorporation, 2006.

[KM07] J. Kramer and J. Magee. Self-managed systems: An architectural challenge. In *Proceedings of the International Conference the Future of Software Engineering (FOSE 2007)*, pages 259–268. IEEE, 2007.

[KM09] J. Kramer and J. Magee. A rigorous architectural approach to adaptive software engineering. *Journal of Computer Science and Technology*, 24(2):183–188, March 2009.

[Kös90] A. Kösztler. *The ghost in the machine.* Penguin Group, 1990.

[Kov97] T. Kovacs. XCS classifier system reliably evolves accurate, complete, and minimal representations for boolean functions. In P. K. Chawdhry, R. Roy, and R. K. Pant, editors, *Soft Computing in Engineering Design and Manufacturing*, pages 59–68. Springer, August 1997.

[Kov02] T. Kovacs. Learning classifier systems resources. *Soft Computing*, 6(3–4):240–243, June 2002.

[Kub03] A. Kubík. Toward a formalisation of emergence. *Artificial Life*, 9(1):41–65, 2003.

[Lan98]   P. L. Lanzi. Adding memory to XCS. In *Proceedings of the IEEE International Conference on Evolutionary Computation (CEC 1998)*, pages 609–614. IEEE, 1998.

[Lan08]   P. L. Lanzi. Learning classifier systems: Then and now. *Evolutionary Intelligence*, 1(1):63–82, March 2008.

[Leh88]   J.-M. Lehn. Supramolecular chemistry – Scope and perspectives molecules, supermolecules, and molecular devices (Nobel lecture). *Angewandte Chemie International Edition in English*, 27(1):89–112, 1988.

[Leh90]   J.-M. Lehn. Perspectives in supramolecular chemistry – From molecular recognition towards molecular information processing and self-organisation. *Angewandte Chemie International Edition in English*, 29(11):1304–1319, 1990.

[Len64]   G. G. Lendaris. On the definition of self-organising systems. *Proceedings of the IEEE*, 52(3):324–325, March 1964.

[Les95]   V. R. Lesser. Multi-agent systems: An emerging subdiscipline of artificial intelligence. *ACM Computing Surveys*, 27(3):340–342, 1995.

[Lew75]   G. H. Lewes. *Problems of life and mind*, volume 2. Kegan Paul, Trench, Turbner & Co, 1875.

[LKST06]   R. D. Luce, D. H. Krantz, P. Suppes, and A. Tversky. *Foundations of measurement: Representation, axiomatisation, and invariance*, volume 3. Dover Pubn Incorporation, 2006.

[Llo23]   C. Lloyd Morgan. Emergent evolution. In Williams and N. Ltd., editors, *The Gifford Lectures*. Delivered in the University of St. Andrews in the Year 1922, 1923.

[Llo02]   X. Llorà. *Genetic based machine learning using fine-grained parallelism for data mining*. PhD thesis, Enginyeria i Arquitectura La Salle, Ramon Llull University, Barcelona, Spain, February 2002.

[Lod09]   C. Lode. XCS in dynamischen Multiagenten-Überwachungsszenarien. Diploma thesis, Institut für Angewandte Informatik und Formale Beschreibungsverfahren, Universität Karlsruhe (TH), March 2009.

[LRBB04]   T. Lange, V. Roth, M. L. Braun, and J. M. Buhmann. Stability-based validation of clustering solutions. *Neural Computation*, 16(6):1299–1323, 2004.

[LRMB07] X. Llorà, R. Reddy, B. Matesic, and R. Bhargava. Towards better than human capability in diagnosing prostate cancer using infrared spectroscopic imaging. In D. Thierens, H.-G. Beyer, M. Birattari, J. Bongard, J. Branke, J. A. Clark, D. Cliff, C. B. Congdon, K. Deb, B. Doerr, T. Kovacs, S. Kumar, J. F. Miller, J. Moore, F. Neumann, M. Pelikan, R. Poli, K. Sastry, K. O. Stanley, T. Stützle, R. A. Watson, and I. Wegener, editors, *Proceedings of the 9th Annual Conference on Genetic and Evolutionary Computation (GECCO 2007)*, pages 2098–2105. ACM, 2007.

[LS06] L. Liu and H. Schmeck. A roadmap towards autonomic service-oriented architectures. *International Transactions on Systems Science and Applications*, 2(3):245–255, 2006.

[LSW00] P. L. Lanzi, W. Stolzmann, and S. W. Wilson, editors. *Learning classifier systems: From foundations to applications*, volume 1813 of *LNAI*. Springer, 2000.

[LT75] H. A. Linstone and M. Turoff. *Delphi method: Techniques and applications.* Addison-Wesley Educational Publishers Incorporation, 1975.

[LTS08] L. Liu, S. Thanheiser, and H. Schmeck. A reference architecture for self-organising service-oriented computing. In U. Brinkschulte, T. Ungerer, C. Hochberger, and R. G. Spallek, editors, *Proceedings of the 21th International Conference on Architecture of Computing Systems (ARCS 2008)*, volume 4934 of *LNCS*, pages 205–219. Springer, February 2008.

[LTSK06] Y. I. Leon Suematsu, K. Takadama, K. Shimohara, and O. Katai. Towards collective learning for MAS. http://www.ai.soc.i.kyoto-u.ac.jp/iswa2006/Yutaka%20I.%20Leon%20Suematsu.pdf, May 2006.

[LW00] P. L. Lanzi and S. W. Wilson. Toward optimal classifier system performance in non-Markov environments. *Evolutionary Computation*, 8(4):393–418, December 2000.

[LW05] S. Lorkowski and P. Wagner. Parameter calibration of traffic models in microscopic on-line simulations. In *Proceedings of the 84th Transportation Research Board Annual Meeting (TRB 2005)*, 2005.

[Mac00] S. MacDonald. *Rolling the iron dice: Historical analogies and decisions to use military force in regional contingencies.* Greenwood Press, 2000.

[Mar54] A. A. Markov. *Theory of algorithms.* Academy of Sciences of the USSR, 1954.

[MB06]   S. H. Mahdavi and P. J. Bentley. Innately adaptive robotics through embodied evolution. *Autonomous Robots*, 20(2):149–163, 2006.

[MCD96]   M. Mitchell, J. P. Crutchfield, , and R. Das. Evolving cellular automata with genetic algorithms: A review of recent work. In *Proceedings of the First International Conference on Evolutionary Computation and its Applications (EvCA 1996)*, pages 1–14, 1996.

[MH06]   M. Meyer and K. Hufschlag. A generic approach to an object-oriented learning classifier system library. *Journal of Artificial Societies and Social Simulation (JASSS)*, 9(3), June 2006.

[Mil43]   J. S. Mill. *A system of logic: Ratiocinative and inductive*, volume VII and VIII. University of Toronto Press, Routledge and Kegan Paul, 1974 edition, 1843.

[Mit97]   T. M. Mitchell. *Machine learning*. WCB/McGraw-Hill, 1997.

[MKKBB06]   S. Markon, H. Kita, H. Kise, and T. Bartz-Beielstein. *Control of traffic systems in buildings*. Advances in Industrial Control. Springer, 2006.

[MMB02]   A. Montresor, H. Meling, and Ö. Babaoğlu. Messor: Load-balancing through a swarm of autonomous agents. In G. Moro and M. Koubarakis, editors, *Proceedings of the 1st International Workshop on Agents and P2P Computing (AP2PC 2002)*, volume 2530 of *LNAI*, pages 125–137. Springer, 2002.

[MMS06]   M. Mnif and C. Müller-Schloer. Quantitative emergence. In *Proceedings of the 2006 IEEE Mountain Workshop on Adaptive and Learning Systems (IEEE SMCals 2006)*, pages 78–84. IEEE, July 2006.

[MMTZ06]   M. Mamei, R. Menezes, R. Tolksdorf, and F. Zambonelli. Case studies for self-organisation in computer science. *Journal of Systems Architecture*, 52(8–9):443–460, August–September 2006.

[Mni09]   M. Mnif. *Quantitative Emergenz: Eine Quantifizierunqsmethodik für die Entstehung von Ordnung in selbstorganisierenden technischen Systemen*. PhD thesis, Institut für Systems Engineering, Leibniz Universität Hannover, Hannover, Germany, 2009. To be published.

[Mon05]   D. C. Montgomery. *Design and analysis of experiments*. John Wiley & Sons, 6th edition, 2005.

[MRB+07]   M. Mnif, U. Richter, J. Branke, H. Schmeck, and C. Müller-Schloer. Measurement and control of self-organised behaviour in robot swarms.

In P. Lukowicz, L. Thiele, and G. Tröster, editors, *Proceedings of the 20th International Conference on Architecture of Computing Systems (ARCS 2007)*, volume 4415 of *LNCS*, pages 209–223. Springer, March 2007.

[MRRS00] D. Q. Mayne, J. B. Rawlings, C. V. Rao, and P. O. M. Scokaert. Constrained model predictive control: Stability and optimality. *Automatica*, 36(6):789–814, June 2000.

[MS89] B. Manderick and P. Spiessens. Fine-grained parallel genetic algorithms. In J. Schaffer, editor, *Proceedings of the 3rd International Conference on Genetic Algorithms*, pages 428–433. Morgan Kaufmann, 1989.

[MS04] C. Müller-Schloer. Organic computing: On the feasibility of controlled emergence. In *Proceedings of the 2nd IEEE/ACM/IFIP International Conference on Hardware/Software Codesign and System Synthesis (CODES + ISSS 2004)*, pages 2–5. ACM, 2004.

[MSS06] C. Müller-Schloer and B. Sick. Emergence in organic computing systems: Discussion of a controversial concept. In L. T.Yang, H. Jin, J. Ma, and T. Ungerer, editors, *Proceedings of the 3rd International Conference on Autonomic and Trusted Computing (ATC 2006)*, volume 4158 of *LNCS*, pages 1–16. Springer, 2006.

[MV91] H. Maturana and F. J. Varela. *Autopoiesis and cognition: The realisation of the living (Boston studies in the philosophy of science)*. Springer, 1991.

[NCV06] M. J. North, N. T. Collier, and J. R. Vos. Experiences creating three implementations of the repast agent modelling toolkit. *ACM Transactions on Modelling and Computer Simulation (TOMACS)*, 16(1):1–25, 2006.

[New94] A. Newell. *Unified theories of cognition*. Harvard University Press, 1st edition, 1994.

[NG95] F. Neri and A. Giordana. A parallel genetic algorithm for concept learning. In L. J. Eshelman, editor, *Proceedings of the 6th International Conference on Genetic Algorithms*, pages 436–443. Morgan Kaufmann, 1995.

[Nil86] N. J. Nilsson. *Principles of artificial intelligence*. Morgan Kaufmann, 1986.

[NP77]   G. Nicolis and I. Prigogine. *Self-organisation in nonequilibrium system: From dissipative structures to order through fluctuations.* John Wiley & Sons, 1977.

[OGT+99]   P. Oreizy, M. M. Gorlick, R. N. Taylor, D. Heimbigner, G. Johnson, N. Medvidovic, A. Quilici, D. S. Rosenblum, and A. L. Wolf. An architecture-based approach to self-adaptive software. *IEEE Intelligent Systems*, 14(3):54–62, 1999.

[OHKK02]   O. Oberschelp, T. Hestermeyer, B. Kleinjohann, and L. Kleinjohann. Design of self-optimising agent-based controllers. In C. Urban, editor, *Proceedings of the 3rd International Workshop on Agent Based Simulation*. SCS European Publishing House, April 2002.

[Ost04]   M. Ostrowski. Simulation von Gruppenverhalten bei Hühnern. Research paper, Institute of Systems Engineering, Leibniz Universität Hannover, July 2004.

[Par96]   H. V. D. Parunak. Applications of distributed artificial intelligence in industry. In *Foundations of distributed artificial intelligence*, pages 139–164. John Wiley & Sons, 1996.

[Par98]   H. V. D. Parunak. What can agents do in industry, and why? An overview of industrially-oriented R&D at CEC. In *Proceedings of the 2nd International Workshop on Cooperative Information Agents II, Learning, Mobility, and Electronic Commerce for Information Discovery on the Internet (CIA 1998)*, pages 1–18. Springer, 1998.

[Pat08]   D. Pathmaperuma. Lernende und selbstorganisierende Putzroboter. Diploma thesis, Institut für Angewandte Informatik und Formale Beschreibungsverfahren, Universität Karlsruhe (TH), April 2008.

[Pic06]   C. Pickardt. Implementierung unterschiedlicher Steuerungsstrategien für eine Fahrstuhlgruppe zur Untersuchung des Zusammenhangs von Bunching-Effekt und Leistungsfähigkeit. Research paper, Institut für Angewandte Informatik und Formale Beschreibungsverfahren, Universität Karlsruhe (TH), September 2006.

[PMG98]   D. Poole, A. Mackworth, and R. Goebel. *Computational intelligence: A logical approach.* Oxford University Press, 1998.

[Pol03]   D. Polani. Measuring self-organisation via observers. In W. Banzhaf, T. Christaller, P. Dittrich, J. T. Kim, and J. Ziegler, editors, *Proceedings of the 7th European Conference on Advances in Artificial Life (ECAL 2003)*, volume 2801 of *LNCS*, pages 667–675. Springer, September 2003.

[Pow95]   B. A. Powell. Measurement and reduction of bunching in elevator dispatching with multiple term objection function (usp 5447212), September 1995.

[PRT+08]   H. Prothmann, F. Rochner, S. Tomforde, J. Branke, C. Müller-Schloer, and H. Schmeck. Organic control of traffic lights. In C. Rong, M. G. Jaatun, F. E. Sandnes, L. T. Yang, and J. Ma, editors, *Proceedings of the 5th International Conference on Autonomic and Trusted Computing (ATC 2008)*, volume 5060 of *LNCS*, pages 219–233. Springer, 2008.

[PS90]   I. Prigogine and I. Stengers. *Dialog mit der Natur: Neue Wege naturwissenschaftlichen Denkens.* Piper, 6th edition, 1990.

[PU99]   A. Pagan and A. Ullah. *Nonparametric econometrics.* Cambridge University Press, 1999.

[Put05]   M. L. Puterman. *Markov decision processes: Discrete stochastic dynamic programming.* Wiley Series in Probability and Statistics. John Wiley & Sons, 2nd edition, 2005.

[Ray92]   T. S. Ray. An approach to the synthesis of life. In C. G. Langton, C. Taylor, D. J. Farmer, and S. Rasmussen, editors, *Proceedings of Artificial Life II*, pages 371–408. Addison Wesley, 1992.

[Ray94]   T. S. Ray. Evolution, complexity, entropy, and artificial reality. *Physica D*, 75(1–3):239–263, August 1994.

[RG94]   C. L. Ramsey and J. J. Grefenstette. Case-based anytime learning. In *Case-Based Reasoning: Papers from the 1994 Workshop*, 1994.

[RGH+06]   M. A. Riedmiller, T. Gabel, R. Hafner, S. Lange, and M. Lauer. Die Brainstormers: Entwurfsprinzipien lernfähiger autonomer Roboter. *Informatik Spektrum*, 29(3):175–190, June 2006.

[Rib07]   O. Ribock. Using organic computing to control bunching effects. Diploma thesis, Institute of Applied Informatics and Formal Description Methods, Universität Karlsruhe (TH), October 2007.

[Rin06]   G. Ringland. *Scenario planning: Managing for the future.* John Wiley & Sons, 2006.

[Rio88]   R. L. Riolo. *Empirical studies of default hierarchies and sequences of rules in learning classifier systems.* PhD thesis, University of Michigan, Ann Arbor, United States of America, 1988.

[RKE+08]   T. Rodenburg, H. Komen, E. D. Ellen, K. A. Uitdehaag, and J. A. M. van Arendonk. Selection method and early-life history affect behavioural development, feather pecking, and cannibalism in laying hens: A review. *Applied Animal Behaviour Science*, 110(3–4):217–228, April 2008.

[RM01]   N. Roy and A. McCallum. Towards optimal active learning through sampling estimation of error reduction. In C. E. Brodley and A. P. Danyluk, editors, *Proceedings of the 18th International Conference on Machine Learning (ICML 2001)*, pages 441–448. Morgan Kaufmann, 2001.

[RM08]   U. Richter and M. Mnif. Learning to control the emergent behaviour of a multi-agent system. In F. Klügl, K. Tuyls, and S. Sen, editors, *Proceedings of the 2008 Workshop on Adaptive Learning Agents and Multi-Agent Systems at AAMAS 2008 (ALAMAS+ALAg 2008)*, pages 33–40, May 2008.

[RMB+06]   U. Richter, M. Mnif, J. Branke, C. Müller-Schloer, and H. Schmeck. Towards a generic observer/controller architecture for organic computing. In C. Hochberger and R. Liskowsky, editors, *INFORMATIK 2006 – Informatik für Menschen!*, volume P-93 of *LNI*, pages 112–119. Bonner Köllen Verlag, October 2006.

[RN02]   S. J. Russell and P. Norvig. *Artificial intelligence: A modern approach.* Prentice Hall, 2002.

[Rob87]   G. G. Robertson. Parallel implementation of genetic algorithms in a classifier system. In J. J. Grefenstette, editor, *Proceedings of the 2nd International Conference on Genetic Algorithms (ICGA 1987)*, pages 140–147. Lawrence Erlbaum Associates Incorporation, 1987.

[Rot05]   G. Roth. Selbstorganisationseffekte und Prinzipien der Informationsverarbeitung im Gehirn. *Information Technology*, 47(4):182–187, 2005.

[RPB+06]   F. Rochner, H. Prothmann, J. Branke, C. Müller-Schloer, and H. Schmeck. An organic architecture for traffic light controllers. In C. Hochberger and R. Liskowsky, editors, *INFORMATIK 2006 – Informatik für Menschen!*, volume P-93 of *LNI*, pages 120–127. Köllen Verlag, October 2006.

[RPS08]   U. Richter, H. Prothmann, and H. Schmeck. Improving XCS performance by distribution. In X. Li, M. Kirley, M. Zhang, D. Green, V. Ciesielski, H. Abbass, Z. Michalewicz, T. Hendtlass, K. Deb, K. C. Tan, J. Branke, and Y. Shi, editors, *Proceedings of the 7th International*

Conference on Simulated Evolution And Learning (SEAL 2008), volume 5361 of *LNCS*, pages 111–120. Springer, 2008.

[RRS08]   O. Ribock, U. Richter, and H. Schmeck. Using organic computing to control bunching effects. In U. Brinkschulte, T. Ungerer, C. Hochberger, and R. G. Spallek, editors, *Proceedings of the 21th International Conference on Architecture of Computing Systems (ARCS 2008)*, volume 4934 of *LNCS*, pages 232–244. Springer, February 2008.

[RvB+04]   T. Rodenburg, Y. M. van Hierden, A. J. Buitenhuis, B. Riedstra, P. Koene, S. M. Korte, J. J. van der Poel, T. G. G. Groothuis, and H. J. Blokhuis. Feather pecking in laying hens: New insights and directions for research? *Applied Animal Behaviour Science*, 86(3–4):291–298, June 2004.

[SB98]   R. S. Sutton and A. G. Barto. *Reinforcement learning: An introduction.* MIT Press, 1998.

[SB03]   C. Stone and L. Bull. For real! XCS with continuous-valued inputs. *Evolutionary Computation*, 11(3):299–336, 2003.

[Sch96]   P. Schwartz. *Art of the long view: Planning for the future in an uncertain world.* Bantam Dell, 1996.

[Sch01]   A. Scholl. *Robuste Planung und Optimierung – Grundlagen, Konzepte und Methoden, Experimentelle Untersuchungen.* Physica-Verlag, 2001.

[Sch03]   F. Schweitzer, editor. *Self-organisation of complex structures: From individual to collective dynamics.* Gordon and Breach Science Publishers, 2003.

[Sch05a]   H. Schmeck. Organic Computing. *Künstliche Intelligenz*, 3:68–69, 2005.

[Sch05b]   H. Schmeck. Organic computing: A new vision for distributed embedded systems. In *Proceedings of the 8th IEEE International Symposium on Object-Oriented Real-Time Distributed Computing (ISORC 2005)*, pages 201–203. IEEE, May 2005.

[Sch07]   M. C. Schut. Scientific handbook for simulation of collective intelligence. http://sci.collectivae.net, February 2007.

[SCK95]   F. Seredyński, P. Cichosz, and G. P. Klebus. Learning classifier systems in multi-agent environments. In *Proceedings of the 1st International Conference on Genetic Algorithms in Engineering Systems: Innovations and Applications (GALESIA 1995)*, pages 287–292, September 1995.

[SFKS02]   A. Seznec, S. Felix, V. Krishnan, and Y. Sazeides. Design tradeoffs for the alpha EV8 conditional branch predictor. In *Proceedings of the 29th Annual International Symposium on Computer Architecture*, pages 295–306. IEEE, 2002.

[SG94]   A. C. Schultz and J. J. Grefenstette. Evolving robot behaviours. Technical report, Navy Center for Applied Research in Artificial Intelligence, Naval Research Laboratory, Washington, United States of America, 1994.

[Sha48a]   C. E. Shannon. A mathematical theory of communication. *Bell System Technical Journal*, 27:379–423, July 1948.

[Sha48b]   C. E. Shannon. A mathematical theory of communication. *Bell System Technical Journal*, 27:623–656, October 1948.

[Sha01]   C. R. Shalizi. *Causal architecture, complexity and self-organisation in time series and cellular automata*. PhD thesis, University of Wisconsin, Madison, Physics Department, Madison, United States of America, 2001.

[She94]   W.-M. Shen. *Autonomous learning from the environment*. W. H. Freeman & Co., March 1994.

[Sii93]   M.-L. Siikonen. Elevator traffic simulation. *Simulation*, 61(4):257–267, October 1993.

[Sii97a]   M.-L. Siikonen. Elevator group control with artificial intelligence. Technical report, Helsinki Universtity of Technology, Systems Analysis Laboratory, Helsinki, Finland, 1997.

[Sii97b]   M.-L. Siikonen. *Planning and control models for elevators in high-rise buildings*. PhD thesis, Helsinki Universtity of Technology, Systems Analysis Laboratory, Helsinki, Finland, October 1997.

[Sim98]   J. S. Simonoff. *Smoothing methods in statistics*. Springer, 1998.

[SKLT06]   P. Suppes, D. H. Krantz, R. D. Luce, and A. Tversky. *Foundations of measurement: Geometrical, threshold, and probabilistic representations*, volume 2. Dover Pubn Incorporation, 2006.

[SL90]   J.-J. E. Slotine and W. Li. *Applied nonlinear control*. Prentice Hall, 1990.

[SM06]   D. A. Samuelson and C. M. Macal. Agent-based simulation comes of age: Software opens up many new areas of application. *OR/MS Today*, 33(4):34–38, August 2006.

[Smi80]   S. F. Smith. *A learning system based on genetic adaptive algorithms*. Phd thesis, University of Pittsburgh, Pittsburgh, United States of America, 1980.

[Smi82]   J. M. Smith. *Evolution and the theory of games*. Cambridge University Press, 1982.

[Smi83]   S. F. Smith. Flexible learning of problem solving heuristics through adaptive search. In *Proceedings of the 8th International Joint Conference on Artificial Intelligence*, 1983.

[SMR+04] C. Safarowsky, L. Merz, A. Rang, P. Broekmann, B. A. Hermann, and C. A. Schalley. Template zweiter Ordnung: Geordnete Schichten aus supramolekularen Quadraten auf einer Chlorid-bedeckten Cu(100)-Oberfläche. *Angewandte Chemie*, 116(10):1311–1314, February 2004.

[SMS05]   T. Schöler and C. Müller-Schloer. An observer/controller architecture for adaptive reconfigurable stacks. In M. Beigl and P. Lukowicz, editors, *Proceedings of the 18th International Conference on Architecture of Computing Systems (ARCS 2005)*, volume 3432 of *LNCS*, pages 139–153. Springer, March 2005.

[SMS08]   H. Schmeck and C. Müller-Schloer. A characterisation of key properties of environment-mediated multi-agent systems. In D. Weyns, S. A. Brueckner, and Y. Demazeau, editors, *Proceedings of the International Workshop Engineering Environment-Mediated Multi-Agent Systems (EEMMAS 2007)*, volume 5049 of *LNAI*, pages 17–38. Springer, 2008.

[SMSÇ+07] H. Schmeck, C. Müller-Schloer, E. Çakar, M. Mnif, and U. Richter. Adaptivity and self-organisation in organic computing systems. Submitted to ACM Transactions on Autonomous and Adaptive Systems (TAAS), June 2007.

[SQN06]   M. F. Santos, H. Quintela, and J. Neves. Agent-based learning classifier systems for grid data mining. In *Proceedings of the International Workshop on Learning Classifier Systems (IWLCS 2006) at Genetic and Evolutionary Computation Conference (GECCO 2006)*. ACM, 2006.

[SSE03]   J. Sorsa, M.-L. Siikonen, and H. Ehtamo. Optimal control of double-deck elevator group using genetic algorithm. *International Transactions in Operational Research*, 10(2):103–114, 2003.

[Ste05]   R. Sterritt. Autonomic computing. *Innovations in systems and software engineering*, 1(1):79–88, March 2005.

[Str67]   G. R. Strakosch. *Vertical transportation: Elevators and escalators*. John Wiley & Sons, 1967.

[Str98]   G. R. Strakosch, editor. *The vertical transportation handbook*. John Wiley & Sons, 3rd edition, 1998.

[Sut88]   R. S. Sutton. Learning to predict by the methods of temporal differences. *Machine Learning*, 3(1):9–44, August 1988.

[SV00]   P. Stone and M. Veloso. Multi-agent systems: A survey from a machine learning perspective. *Autonomous Robots*, 8(3):345–383, June 2000.

[SWd05]   N. P. Sood, A. G. Williams, and K. A. de Jong. Evaluating the XCS learning classifier system in competitive simultaneous learning environments. In *Proceedings of the 2005 Workshops on Genetic and Evolutionary Computation Conference (GECCO 2005)*, pages 112–118. ACM, 2005.

[Tag92]   G. Taguchi. *Taguchi on robust technology development: Bringing quality engineering upstream*. ASME Press, 1992.

[TGD04]   M. Tomassini, M. Giacobini, and C. Darabos. Evolution of small-world networks of automata for computation. In XinYao, E. Burke, J. A. Lozano, J. Smith, J. J. Merelo-Guervós, J. A. Bullinaria, J. Rowe, P. Tiňo, A. Kabán, and H.-P. Schwefel, editors, *Proceedings of the 8th International Conference on Parallel Problem Solving from Nature (PPSN VIII)*, volume 3242 of *LNCS*, pages 672–681. Springer, 2004.

[TK01]   S. Tong and D. Koller. Support vector machine active learning with applications to text classification. *Journal of Machine Learning Research*, 2:45–66, 2001.

[TLS07]   S. Thanheiser, L. Liu, and H. Schmeck. Towards collaborative coping with IT complexity by combining SOA and organic computing. *System and Information Sciences Notes*, 2(1):82–87, 2007.

[TNS02]   K. Takadama, S. Nakasuka, and K. Shimohara. Robustness in organisational-learning oriented classifier system. *Soft Computing*, 6(3–4):229–239, June 2002.

[TPR+08]   S. Tomforde, H. Prothmann, F. Rochner, J. Branke, J. Hähner, C. Müller-Schloer, and H. Schmeck. Decentralised progressive signal systems for organic traffic control. In S. Brueckner, P. Robertson, and U. Bellur, editors, *Proceedings of the 2nd IEEE International Conference on Self-Adaption and Self-Organisation (SASO 2008)*, pages 413–422. IEEE, 2008.

[Tri06]   V. Trianni. *On the evolution of self-organising behaviours in a swarm of autonomous robots.* PhD thesis, Faculty of Applied Sciences of the Université Libre de Bruxelles, Brussels, Belgium, 2006.

[TTS01]   K. Takadama, T. Terano, and K. Shimohara. Learning classifier systems meet multi-agent environments. In P. L. Lanzi, W. Stolzmann, and S. W. Wilson, editors, *Advances in Learning Classifier Systems*, volume 1996 of *LNAI*, pages 192–212. Springer, 2001.

[Twi92]   B. C. Twiss. *Forecasting for technologists and engineers: A practical guide for better decisions.* Institution of Engineering and Technology, 1992.

[Var79]   F. J. Varela. *Principles of biological autonomy.* North Holland, 1979.

[von60]   H. von Foerster. On self-organising systems and their environments. In M. C. Yovitts and S. Cameron, editors, *Self-Organising Systems*, pages 31–50. Pergamon Press, 1960.

[von05]   I. von Richthofen. Simulation von adaptivem Verhalten bei Hühnern in Käfighaltung. Bachelor's thesis, Institute of Systems Engineering, Leibniz Universität Hannover, September 2005.

[Wat89]   C. J. C. H. Watkins. *Learning from delayed rewards.* PhD thesis, University of Cambridge, Cambridge, United Kingdom, May 1989.

[WD92]   C. J. C. H. Watkins and P. Dayan. Technical note: Q-learning. *Machine Learning*, 8(3–4):279–292, May 1992.

[Wei91]   M. Weiser. The computer for the twenty-first century. *Scientific American*, 265(3):94–104, 1991.

[WHRL03]   A. Webb, E. Hart, P. Ross, and A. Lawson. Controlling a simulated Khepera with an XCS classifier system with memory. In W. Banzhaf, T. Christaller, P. Dittrich, J. T. Kim, and J. Ziegler, editors, *Proceedings of the 7th European Conference on Artificial Life (ECAL 2003)*, volume 2801 of *LNAI*, pages 885–892. Springer, September 2003.

[Wil94]   S. W. Wilson. ZCS: A zeroth level classifier system. *Evolutionary Computation*, 2(1):1–18, 1994.

[Wil95]   S. W. Wilson. Classifier fitness based on accuracy. *Evolutionary Computation*, 3(2):149–175, 1995.

[Wil98]   S. W. Wilson. Generalisation in the XCS classifier system. In J. R. Koza, W. Banzhaf, K. Chellapilla, K. Deb, M. Dorigo, D. B. Fogel, M. H.Garzon, D. E. Goldberg, and a. R. R. Hitoshi Iba, editors, *Proceedings of the 3rd Annual Conference on Genetic Programming*, pages 665–674. Morgan Kaufmann, 1998.

[Wil00a]   S. W. Wilson. Get real! XCS with continuous-valued inputs. In P. L. Lanzi, W. Stolzmann, and S. W. Wilson, editors, *Learning classifier systems: From foundations to applications*, volume 1813 of *LNAI*, pages 209–219. Springer, 2000.

[Wil00b]   S. W. Wilson. Mining oblique data with XCS. In P. L. Lanzi, W. Stolzmann, and S. W. Wilson, editors, *Proceedings of the 3rd International Workshop on Advances in Learning Classifier Systems (IWLCS 2000)*, volume 1996 of *LNCS*, pages 158–174. Springer, 2000.

[Woo02]   M. J. Wooldridge. *An introduction to multi-agent systems*. John Wiley & Sons, 1st edition, 2002.

[YGWY88]   F. E. Yates, A. Garfinkel, D. O. Walter, and G. B. Yates. *Self-organising systems: The emergence of order*. Springer, 1988.

[ZBSH08]   J. Zeppenfeld, A. Bouajila, W. Stechele, and A. Herkersdorf. Learning classifier tables for autonomic systems on chip. In H.-G. Hegering, A. Lehmann, H. J. Ohlbach, and C. Scheideler, editors, *INFORMATIK 2008, Beherrschbare Systeme – dank Informatik*, volume 134 of *LNI*, pages 771–778. GI, 2008.

[ZE04]   P. Zikopoulos and J. Escott. DB2 UDB Version 8.2 and autonomic computing. http://www-106.ibm.com/developerworks/db2/library/techarticle/dm-0406zikopoulos/index.html, June 2004.